Michael Jacobs

Michael Jacobs was born in Italy and studied art history at the Courtauld Institute of Art, from which he has a doctorate. Spain has obsessed him since childhood and his numerous books include *Andalucía, Between Hopes and Memories: A Spanish Journey, Alhambra* and *In the Glow of the Phantom Palace: Travels Between Granada and Timbuktu*. He has also translated a number of Spanish and Latin American plays. He is a member of the Andalucían Academy of Gastronomy and in 2002 was made the first foreign knight of 'The Very Noble and Illustrious Order of the Wooden Spoon'.

THE FACTORY
OF LIGHT

Tales from My Andalucían Village

Michael Jacobs

JOHN MURRAY

*For my guardian angels in Frailes, and in particular
'El Sereno', Merce, 'Caño', Lolo, Alejandro, Paqui
and Juan Matías*

© Michael Jacobs 2003

First published in 2003 by John Murray (Publishers)
A division of Hodder Headline

Paperback edition 2004

4

The moral right of the author has been asserted

A CIP catalogue record for this title is available from the British Library

ISBN 0-7195-6173 6

Typeset in Monotype Bembo by Servis Filmsetting Ltd, Manchester

Printed and bound in Great Britain by Clays Ltd, St Ives plc

John Murray (Publishers)
338 Euston Road
London
NW1 3BH

Contents

Foreword

The Journey to the Sierra Sur

ABOVE A VILLAGE in southern Spain, in between olive trees and virgin sierra, a giant star is shining. Its light is guiding me to a house higher than all the others, isolated, half-hidden behind an almond tree, mysteriously pale in the winter night. Dogs are barking below, and a distant chime, like that of a musical box, is sounding from the town hall's toy-like clock. The street turns into a rough track, at the top of which a donkey stares in silence behind an open door. I am at the threshold of what will one day be my home. The incandescent star is now revealed as an illuminated Christmas decoration attached by scaffolding to the steep rocky slope above. The donkey is old and diseased, and a pungent smell of goat hangs in the air. Yet reality does not diminish the sensation I have so often felt since coming to this obscure corner of Andalucía. I feel as if my every step is being directed by a supernatural force.

I sometimes think I have been travelling to this place since childhood. While still at school I became obsessed by Spain, and first set off there convinced I had embarked upon an epic quest. Wandering around on my own, overwhelmed by the emptiness of the landscape, I had a premonition of a life spent journeying towards a distant horizon of olive trees. I went back to Spain after Franco's death, and later drifted into travel writing. I started staying in Spain for ever longer periods, until eventually I was making a living largely from my Spanish travels and researches. But my existence there seemed destined to be a rootless one, moving from region to region, and from one group of friends to another. Then something changed. Trying now to explain these past few years, I keep on looking back to that autumn's day in 1997, when I first became aware of the village of Frailes, and of the strange spirit who is its guardian.

It was my birthday, October 15, but everything appeared to be conspiring against me. I was on a train from Prague to Budapest. The train was late, and new visa regulations, unknown to me, had come into force a few minutes before our belated arrival at the Slovakian frontier. I ended up in a Slovakian police station, together with an elderly and irate Australian couple. The certainty now of missing out on a birthday party in Budapest that evening soon came to seem only a minor irritation. Far worse was the prospect of having to spend several hours listening to the religious views of these Australians. They were, they shamelessly explained, 'millenarians', and their detention in Slovakia meant they would probably lose their places on a special cruise whose passengers all shared the belief that 'the Lord was about to reveal Himself in a way that would make us all reflect on our lives.' Our guards, as indifferent to our personal dilemmas as they were to the fate of the universe, soon left the room, leaving me to face on my own the Australians' tales of collapsing skyscrapers and other imminent catastrophes. But then, for reasons not immediately apparent, the subject of the conversation turned to Spain.

Had I heard, they asked, of the region of Andalucía? I nodded yes, and waited for the usual gushing words of praise about the magical Alhambra, the colour and passion of flamenco, the sensuality of streets fragrant with jasmine and orange blossom. But instead they began talking about an Andalucían province far removed from all these stereotypical images. They began talking about Jaén.

Jaén was the part of Andalucía I knew least well. Living as I had once done in distant Seville, I had scarcely thought of it as Andalucía at all, but rather as a transitional zone between central and southern Spain. I retained conflicting images of vast expanses of olive trees, dramatic, pine-forested peaks of almost Alpine character, and a handful of stone-walled towns evocative of the scorched austerity of Castile. As with the Moors, who referred to this whole area as the '*Jeen*' or the 'caravan route', I had perceived Jaén essentially as somewhere you passed through on your way to and from the true south.

'We'll never forget our stay in Jaén,' the husband continued. I wondered if they had visited the Renaissance towns of Baeza and Úbeda, or had gone hiking in the shady mountains of the Sierras de Segura and Cazorla, or even had spent time in the eagle's nest castle-hotel where General de Gaulle had written part of his memoirs. Once again, however, I had completely misjudged them. They had, it turned out, been to none of the few places where tourism was con-centrated in Jaén. 'We had no time for sight-seeing,' the wife butted in.

'Our son was ill, you see. He was born with this strange, degenera-tive disease, we thought he would die, there was no real cure for what he had.'

'It was then', the husband added, 'that we became interested in faith healing. We had never really believed in conventional medicine. We put our trust instead in the Lord. And the Lord came to our help. He introduced us to this Spanish woman who had been brought up in an isolated farm in Jaén. Then her parents had emigrated to Germany, and she had ended up marrying an Australian tourist, and living in Sydney. She never stopped talking about Spain. In the mountainous district where she was born, she used to tell us, there were no doctors to be found. Whenever anyone fell ill, the only solu-tion was to go to a faith healer. She remembered how they used to scribble on a sheet of cigarette paper and then place this in the sick person's palm, as if it were a prescription. Most of these healers were probably charlatans. But once every decade or so there came along someone so special, so sought after, that this person was known by everyone as a "saint".'

At this point the husband interrupted his speech to take out a wallet that was tightly tucked into his trouser pocket. He struggled for a few moments as I waited to see what sorcery he was about to perform. But all he did was show me a hand-tinted and heavily lined passport-size photo of a decidedly sinister-looking man. The man had broad features, a savagely cropped fringe, and deep-set eyes staring intensely from beneath thick eyebrows that appeared to be stuck on like those of a pantomime disguise. Were it not for this slight touch of absurdity, he could have been described as a cross between an American gangster and the leader of a right-wing sect that advo-cated the return of the Tridentine mass.

'The Santo Custodio,' the husband announced in a tone of rever-ential awe, 'He was the greatest healer of them all. He's been dead now for nearly forty years, but I've always kept his image in every wallet I've ever possessed.'

'As soon as our Spanish neighbour showed us his photo,' the wife said, taking over the story, 'we knew that he was the man who would cure our son. We had little money at the time, so we had to save up for a while. Then we flew to Britain. That was in 1958, it took about three days to get there. And then we went to Madrid by train, and I thought, once we'd crossed the Spanish border, "Oh Lord what are we doing here?" It was like going back to the Middle Ages. And that was before we got to Jaén, where we had to finish our journey by donkey. Can you imagine?'

'But then when we got to this tiny mountain hamlet where the Santo Custodio lived,' said the husband, 'we had this extraordinary sensation of peace, as if we were returning to a place we already knew intimately. Nothing seemed more normal than turning up here on a donkey. Nor did the Santo Custodio seem in the slightest bit put out when we told him through an interpreter that we'd come all the way from Australia. And do you know what? We didn't have to say a word to him about our son's medical condition. He just saw the poor boy sitting on the saddle behind his mother and barely able to move, and he said with total assurance: "You can get down now, you'll be able to walk." And the boy did, and he was cured.'

'That's amazing,' I politely commented, while wondering to myself how much more of their lunatic ramblings I was going to have to put up with. 'And what part of Jaén was this?' I asked without any real interest in the answer.

'The far south,' the husband replied, 'near the border with Granada. We didn't really see much of the area, we spent all our time in a farm next to the Santo Custodio's. But we went a couple of times to the local village, it had a funny name, something like Frailes, which means "Monks". I don't remember much about it, except that it had a cinema. I thought how odd it was to have a cinema in such an out-of-the-way place . . .'

I was hardly registering now what he and his wife were saying, I had had enough, I wanted to be in Budapest. When the border guards finally came back into the room to tell us that we were free, and that the next train was due shortly, this seemed to me at the time like a miracle greater than any performed by the Santo Custodio, whose name, like that of Frailes, soon slipped into the back of my consciousness.

Nearly two years later, when I was next to hear of Frailes, I was sitting in the Seville office of the Andalucían rural accommodation agency. I was desperately looking, at the last minute, for somewhere to rent with friends for the month of August. I was happy to accept anywhere in Andalucía, but the secretary kept on shaking her head. Every suitable property had been taken. But as I got up to leave the telephone rang and the secretary gestured to me to wait. 'It's a call from Jaén,' she whispered. A few minutes later she was telling me that a new house had just been placed on their books, and that it was situated outside a village called Frailes, 'about half-way between Jaén and Granada'. The house had been an old spa building, and she strongly recommended that I should take it.

The name of the village seemed familiar, but I could not think why. Looking at the map that was placed in front of me, I realized that I must have gone through the place a few years back while heading south from Jaén on a narrow, ill-surfaced road. I vividly recalled the dramatically empty mountain scenery, but could not picture either Frailes or any of the other humble communities I would have passed on the way to the district capital of Alcalá la Real.

'You're going to have to make your mind up fairly quickly,' the secretary persisted as she observed me inwardly debating the wisdom of renting a house I had not seen in a village I could not remember. I continued hesitating for a good few minutes, but in the end I stopped trying, for some inner voice had forced me into an abrupt and irrevocable decision. 'I'll take the house,' I told the secretary with an uncharacteristic firmness of manner.

And so, barely one month later, in a car driven by English friends, I set off again on the mountain road from Jaén. In the intervening weeks I had determined to read up as much as possible on the district to which I had blindly committed myself for the summer. But there was little I could find. Beyond Alcalá la Real, with its eloquent vestiges of a once indomitable citadel and abbey, the area known officially as the Sierra Sur de Jaén appeared to have been largely forgotten by travel books, not to mention by history itself. A former no man's land between Moorish and Christian Spain, it had been heavily depleted in later centuries by massive emigration. As for Frailes, I was able to glean from a nineteenth-century encyclopedia that this had been a community populated mainly by shepherds and charcoal-burners before being developed after 1830 as a small spa. However, as for what had happened to the village in more recent times, I uncovered nothing.

In an Andalucía where 'rural tourism' was spreading to ever more remote corners, the very absence of information on Frailes and its surroundings was cause for selfish hope. Isolated from the main roads, as it had been from the main currents of history, the place held the promise of a rural Spain that had yet to be tamed and prettified. What is more, I realised as I headed back into the mountains south of Jaén, it was even encouraging me to indulge in that ultimate and most implausible of traveller's fantasies: I was fantasizing about approaching some lost world.

Conditions certainly suited my mood of mounting anticipation. A light breeze, unexpectedly cool for a mid-August afternoon, had cleared the dust and heat haze that had accompanied us for much of our journey that day. By around five o'clock, when we had left behind the last of the high-rise surroundings of modern Jaén, the colours were so clean and sharp as to have the strange unreality of a vision. The empty side road was narrowing all the time as it ascended in hairpin bends through steep terraced fields, workable even then only by donkeys and ancient-looking ploughs. The rows of olive trees that turn so much of Jaén province into a rolling and interminable chequerboard blanket began soon to fragment into a rugged and threadbare patchwork of parched meadows, clusters of cherry and almond trees, forests of holm-oaks, stony ochre expanses studded with wild herbs, and bleached rocky peaks as picturesquely shaped as the mountains in a Japanese print, as monumental as a panoramic canvas of the American West.

The odd isolated white farm building, makeshift goat sheds in corrugated iron, and the distant gleam of the radar tower crowning the massive white profile of the Sierra de la Pandera, were the principle man-made distractions until our arrival, in the midst of this sublimely empty landscape, at the small town of Valdepeñas. The town's large, unappealing blocks of buildings, dating from the 1950s onwards, belied its remote character, reminiscent of some colonial outpost from the Franco era. We lost ourselves in its poorly signposted streets before breaking free again into the wildly beautiful surroundings, where, almost immediately, we found ourselves deviating from the newly repaired road onto one that was smaller still, pitted with holes, and marked, in corroded lettering, 'FRAILES, 15km'.

We climbed up into a hidden valley. The line of stones from a dried-up river bed lay ever further beneath us as we ascended, past a barking guard dog tied to a solitary kennel, then the dark-stained plaster walls of a collapsed cottage, then, far below, a great drop where an impressive waterfall would surely have been cascading down in times of rain. Finally, after the last of the trees had given way to a bare and yellowing summit, and the road had begun to descend, we turned a corner and saw before us paradise.

Excitement at the vastness of the panorama was matched by a profound sense of peacefulness. Beauty was not tinged by terror but by a feeling of enormous relief on attaining some long-awaited goal. The whole composition appeared to radiate a divinely ordained harmony. To the west the faraway towers and walls of Alcalá's citadel floated like a medieval mirage against an orange-tinted background of hills and mountains. To the east meanwhile, a faint full moon rose above olive-covered slopes framed by the distant Elysian profile of Granada's Sierra Nevada.

And, in the middle, so peaceful in its green protective mantle of trees and fields, was the village to where I had been drawn, I would soon conclude, for reasons other than mere chance. Reasons I am still struggling to understand.

Part One

In the Shadow of the
Santo Custodio

I

I WASN'T QUITE sure if I had heard correctly when he introduced himself to me as 'Custodio'. Was this really his name, or was he perhaps the 'custodian' of the house I was renting rather than its owner? I knew no one else in Spain with such a name; but neither had I known any Spanish caretaker who looked quite like him. Tall and athletic in appearance, and with a confident if not wholly natural smile, he gave the impression of a successful young professional with sporting tendencies and a proselytizing belief in the virtues of the healthy outdoor life. His behaviour too was in keeping with this image, and set him apart from the spontaneously trusting and easy-going Andalucían villagers with whom I had had previous financial dealings. Barely had we exchanged the usual introductory pleasantries than he was asking my friends and me to pay in advance the balance due for the rent of the house, which, it was soon confirmed, he did indeed own. There was, in short, nothing about Custodio, other than his unusual name, that seemed to fit in with my wishful vision of an exotic and self-contained rural world firmly wedded to the past.

But then nothing about Frailes itself lived up initially either to this vision or to my idyllic first impressions of the village from afar. The descent from the Jaén road turned out to be an anti-climactic process, if not also a bathetic one. A large and incongruous modern house in the style of a Swiss chalet had marked the entrance to the village, which was soon revealed as long, sprawling and badly affected by recent development. Traditional whitewashed dwellings stood out as scarred survivors alongside squat new homes with pretentious and ill-proportioned detailing. Several other buildings, some apparently in use and even inhabited, had been left in a half-complete state, and revealed their innards of bricks, breeze-blocks, and metal frames.

The annual August fair had just come to an end, and fairy lights and a carousel were being removed from a parched patch of ground near Frailes's northern outskirts. Further down, beyond two savings banks, an olive-oil factory, and a prominent roadside sign indicating the way to 'La Raya Pub', a group of elderly men with berets and walking sticks sat staring at our passing car from the benches of a concrete park. This lay under the shadow of a cliff partially covered by structures built directly into the rock. At this stage in our transit of the village I was still hoping that we would soon emerge into a shaded old square lined with welcoming cafés. But as the main street street drawled on, between unattractively tiled houses and a near-waterless stream choked with rubbish and a chaos of spiky vegetation, this ever fainter hope had finally to be abandoned altogether. We had reached the further end of the village, and all that caught the eye was a sign that quashed any remaining daydreams about an unchanged rural Spain: 'El Bar Lady Diana', it read.

For a few moments I contemplated the possibility that the British colonization of Andalucía had reached as far as Frailes. But it seemed highly unlikely that foreigners of any kind would wish to settle in a village as lacking as this one in obvious picturesqueness. The bar, in any case, gave no sign of life, in contrast to the 'Pub Guaneiro', which stood a few hundred metres further on, amidst the disorderly scattering of lamp-posts, chalets and building sites that was gradually taking over the outlying fields. Chaotically parked cars, strolling teenagers, and at least one middle-aged drunk were gathering there, lured by the loud Latin sounds appropriate to the painted panel hanging outside, which depicted palm trees and a tropical sunset. As we drove quickly past, disconcerted by the thought that the supposedly tranquil rural retreat to which we had committed ourselves for the rest of the summer could possibly be near by, we missed our turning. Five minutes later we were back at the Guaneiro and heading onto a rough track that lay between the bar and a large ceramic plinth which greeted visitors arriving from the south with the words: 'Welcome to Frailes, an Inland Paradise.'

Little dogs like enraged, oversized rats rushed towards our car as we bumped our way across fields of maize, tomatoes and melons towards a wooded enclave, from which a white tower protruded, suggesting some Moorish-inspired spa building from earlier and more elegant days. The entrance to the property was marked by a small plaque describing it as a *casa rural*, and acknowledging assistance for its restoration from organizations ranging from the European Community to an association (known as ADSUR) promoting 'the rural development of the Sierra Sur'. We had clearly come to the right place, so we stepped out of the car, and walked tentatively into a garden shaded by a giant walnut tree. An unseen hound, of comparably intimidating size, let out a sudden and ferocious bark, and strained violently on his chain until reduced to his former placid state by shouts from afar of 'Hermes! Hermes!' And this was when I had my first meeting with the man who referred to himself as Custodio.

Hermes was an entirely harmless creature, the smiling Custodio assured me, displaying what I interpreted as the amused and slightly patronizing attitude of an old country hand when faced with the timorous response of the effete city-dweller. However, within a few minutes of being in Custodio's company, I began suspecting that he was in many ways as awkward and alien a presence in the country as I was. He talked about Frailes from the point of view of a curious if not particularly impassioned outsider, and revealed unmistakable traits of the city-dweller in his obsession with the signposted walks and cycle trails that had recently been established in the area. At the time I failed to find much significance in the fact that he was not from here but from Sant Ana, a village barely eight kilometres away, and that he and his Frailes-born wife had chosen long ago to live in Alcalá la Real, where he worked in the town hall. Only in later weeks would I begin properly to understand what, in Frailes terms, it meant to be an 'Alcalaíno', and, even worse, an adopted Alcalaíno involved in local politics.

At the time I was merely conscious in Custodio's company of the persistent slight disappointment that had set in the moment we had entered the village. The house he lovingly showed us was undeniably beautiful – light, spacious, comfortable, and pleasantly decorated with objects that reflected a love of flea markets and the tastefully esoteric. Yet, like the village itself, it did not initially fulfil my expectations. I had half-imagined an old spa building steeped in a faded *belle époque* atmosphere, with evocative original detailing such as a stained-glass conservatory, or a sweeping stairwell balustrade in intricate wrought iron. And I had been assured of a place that was completely isolated and undisturbed. Instead what we found was a drastically modernized structure situated between a pallet factory and a half-built chalet, and within earshot of the Pub Guaneiro, from which we could now clearly hear playing the latest Spanish hit, '*Un movimiento sexi*'.

'You'll find this the perfect place to work,' Custodio smilingly insisted once he found out that I was a writer, and that one of the reasons for my coming here was the promise of a tranquil location. 'The factory', he added, seeing me maintain a rather worried expression, 'scarcely functions in August, at the most for a couple of hours a day. As for the bar, well it's the first Sunday afternoon after the *feria*, and people are still in a holiday mood, they'll have calmed down by next week.' While he was telling us all this a large car crammed with passengers approached the chalet opposite, which was separated from Custodio's property by a crude wire fence, and from a distance had the appearance of being little more than unplastered walls provisionally roofed with corrugated iron sheets. Looking more closely, I noticed that the only part of the site to be completed was an adjoining swimming pool. Within minutes of the car having stopped, children were splashing noisily in the water, while their young father, portly, smiling, and with a thick moustache, ambled over towards a shed, and pulled out a drill.

'He sometimes comes here with his family in the late afternoon,' Custodio drily commented. 'He works on his house whenever he has the chance.' As if overhearing us, the man gave a friendly wave in our direction before embarking on a drilling session that almost succeeded in drowning out the shouts of the swimmers. That was the final touch. What with the trite music, the screaming children, and, now, the sounds of building work, we could have been in a typical Spanish holiday resort rather than in a place which – as Custodio went on to remind us – had so far been untouched by tourism.

'You are', he said emphatically, hoping perhaps to distract us from the surrounding irritations, 'the first foreigners ever to have stayed in Frailes.' Judging by what I had so far seen of the village, this statement did not altogether surprise me. However, as he dwelt further on this subject, he brought back for an instant my fantasies of stumbling across a virgin Spain that according to travel writers such as Laurie Lee and Norman Lewis had disappeared altogether. 'You mustn't be surprised,' he chuckled, handing me over finally the keys to his house, 'if you find yourselves a great centre of attention. The eyes of the whole village will be upon you.' I waited for him to elaborate on this, but, in a way I would soon think of as typically Alcalaíno, he made sure that Alcalá rather than Frailes got in the last word, insisting that we come over one day to see him so that he could show us the town's famous citadel. Then he shook our hands and left.

Later that evening, when dusk was rapidly settling in and a raucous family barbecue was starting up in our neighbour's chalet, we walked out across the murky fields towards what appeared now as a pyramid of shimmering lights. We could not have chosen a better way to draw attention to ourselves, for it soon became apparent that virtually no one in the village went even the slightest distance without some form of vehicle. The entrance on foot into Frailes of a motley group of four foreigners had probably been widely announced long before we had reached the Lady Diana, where we were met by some incredulously staring teenagers. As we speculated whether we were the first English people ever to have stood on the threshold of this mysteriously English-named institution, one of the onlookers approached us with a grin to say that the place was no longer running, 'just like the princess herself.' He looked slightly puzzled when I told him that we were in fact aiming for a bar called 'La Parada', which Custodio said produced the village's finest home cooking. 'Ah, you mean El Choto,' he eventually concluded, before pointing us in the direction of a bar that lay a few hundred metres further on, at the beginning of a side street that climbed steeply up into the higher part of the village. We made our way towards an illuminated neon sign that clearly read, on close inspection, 'La Parada'. By now I had seriously begun to wonder if Frailes was quite as straightforward as it outwardly appeared.

But barely had I time to reflect on this than I became aware of what seemed like the whites of fifty or so eyes fixed on us as we awkwardly took up our positions at one of the unlit tables placed on the sloping street. To this day there are villagers who still tell me of that night when, to their great surprise, a party of English people sat down outside El Choto. Though I can scarcely conjure up a single face from the mass of shadowy, anonymous forms that were then so blatantly spying on us, they can still vividly recall 'that blonde-haired English friend of yours with the Sevillian accent', 'the serious, waif-like girl whose hair he was constantly stroking', and that 'other woman, large and dark-haired, with the lively expression and constant smile'.

The surrounding voices, so animated when we arrived, went briefly silent when the time came for us to put in our order. Self-conscious in the knowledge that all eyes were upon me, I asked the young waitress for the home-made salami and dish of garlic-fried goat that Custodio had described as the house specialities. 'The one with the beard and glasses speaks Spanish,' 'they seem to be talking English among themselves,' 'the two women don't have wedding rings,' were among the comments I overheard before the food was brought to our table, and we had our first taste of what I would only later appreciate as a truly virgin cuisine, untouched by fashions, fads, preservatives and shop-bought products. On this first visit to El Choto, however, I was too distracted by the gossips around us to register much more than the striking appearance of the waitress, who had the calm bearing and tightly cut black hair of some imagined handmaiden from ancient Egypt. In a village where everyone I had seen so far seemed as ordinary-looking as the place itself, and so much homelier than the slender and mysteriously dark-eyed Andalucíans of the popular stereotype, hers was a beauty that lingered in the memory.

Perhaps it was lingering still when, later that night, on the pretext of making a phone call, I went off on my own into the higher part of the village and had my first glimpse of a Frailes that travel brochures could almost have described as magical. Isolated couples and family groups, sitting talking on chairs outside their houses, observed my progress as I walked up an endlessly ascending street, in the course of which traces of crude modern reconstruction and alteration became ever less in evidence, until suddenly I was flanked by rows of near-intact, old, white houses. The street lamps were scanty and mainly broken-down, leaving just the light of the moon to illuminate, near the top of the hill, three grand homes arranged on three sides of a pleasingly simple parish church. One of these buildings was a neo-Renaissance structure crowned by twin towers with belvederes; another, less imposing from the outside, had a large wrought-iron gate through which you could see a garden with ornamental ponds, jasmine, and a walnut tree more splendid even than Custodio's.

But it was the palace on the opposite side of the street, protected by a high wall both from the church and the two other showy residences, that instantly caught the imagination. Part of its mysterious aura was due to the building being largely hidden within its enclosure, and to the way the silence of the night was broken now only by the sounds of water gushing from a mosaic-encrusted niche hollowed out of the outer wall. Almond and cherry trees spread their branches over the parapet, beyond which I could just make out a conservatory, attached to a building of indeterminate age but unquestionable stature. Only on slightly retracing my steps and heading on to another street did I finally discover that the main façade had been built as the centrepiece of a small and deserted square. It was a façade of restrained elegance, and would not have seemed out of place amongst the palaces of some aristocratic resort from the turn of the nineteenth century. Yet on closer inspection it also had a pared-down look, as if there had been ornamentation which had either been stripped away, following years of neglect, or else had never been completed as a result of some intervening tragedy. Speculating fancifully about the history that lay behind its walls, I went back to rejoin my friends. I was already dreaming long before I got to bed.

The next morning I woke up in an optimistic mood. Frailes, seen from across fields, its hill crisply profiled against a background of olives, and its white houses gleaming in the rays of the sun, had once again become beautiful in my eyes. And I could not even understand what had disappointed me at first about the house we had rented. While the others were still sleeping I went out into the long shaded garden to sit drinking coffee at its furthest end. From here the view of the unmistakably Andalucían-style house, rising above flower beds and a shaped swimming pool, could have been an illustration from some glossy magazine about country living. Though another hot day was looming, the night had been pleasantly cool, and there was a freshness in the air as if some unseen, silent presence had recently been watering the ground.

Before the sun had risen much further I walked again into the village to investigate its shops and to return to the places I had been the night before. Inevitably the upper district which had so impressed me under a full moon had in daylight lost some of its enchanted aura, especially as I now realized that immediately beyond it there extended an uninspiring area of recently constructed buildings. These included a school resembling an Inner London comprehensive, and a town hall whose clock tower appeared to have been assembled from a Lego kit. Yet, for all this, Frailes had an appeal that was beginning to grow on me. Though it was not the stunning, flower-bedecked white village foreigners expect from southern Spain, it was like one of those communities in the west of Ireland whose unmistakable charm eventually shows through behind the blight of bungalows and other artless additions. There was the setting, and there were the unfailingly friendly and helpful people whom I had met as I asked my way round, bought a newspaper, or entered a bar. And there was something else I could not for the moment define, if indeed I would ever be able to do so.

I was only going to be staying in Frailes for three weeks, I reminded myself, and I doubted whether I would be spending much of that time in the village itself. I would try and find out something more about its spa, and about its more distinguished monuments; and I would of course be coming in to buy provisions, and to have the occasional meal. But for the most part I envisaged my stay to be taken up largely by working on a pressing commission to translate a play by Lope de Vega, Shakespeare's prolific Spanish contemporary. The play, which I had entitled in English *The Labyrinth of Desire*, was one of the many works by this theatrical pioneer that had been unfairly neglected over the centuries, and seemed to me ripe for modern reassessment: it was a comic, bawdy masterpiece that touched on sexual ambiguity, lesbianism, and the intellectual power of women. A London theatre director had been urging me for ages to show him an English version, and this seemed exactly the sort of enjoyable, undemanding writing task suitable for a summer retreat in Spain. I determined to embark on it on my first morning in Frailes.

I laid out the manuscript on the garden table as soon I had got back from my outing into the village. For a good half hour or so I skimmed its numerous, densely printed pages before coming to the disheartening conclusion that the task was going to be infinitely more exacting than I had anticipated. I joined my friends in the pool, took out a novel, prepared a long lunch, had a siesta. The arrival later on of visitors from Granada put a final end to any hopes of continuing the translation that day. I would get up early the following morning, I resolved, accepting as I did so an offer of the first gin and tonic of the evening. The summer was already settling into the usual predictable pattern.

It needed all my diminishing reserves of self-discipline not to lie any longer in bed the next morning. I knew from experience that if I had not made a good start on my work before ten o'clock the rest of the day was likely to be similarly unproductive. In any case I have always loved those early hours when no one else is around, and there is still the promise of great achievement ahead. Wiping the sleep from my eyes, pouring an orange juice in the hope that it would clear my head and body of the effects of last night's drinking, I set up again at my garden desk and stared once more at the opening page of Lope's play. When I had first read this page over a year before I had been struck by the exhilarating freshness of the language, so typical of Lope's work in general. But now, when it came to putting this in English, I discovered that even the simplest-seeming line did not appear to follow on from the preceding one, leading me to conclude that either crucial words and phrases had gone missing, or that my grasp of seventeenth-century Spanish was just not up to the task. As I struggled to achieve a single coherent exchange of dialogue, my tiredness returned and my eyes began increasingly to wander from the page and out into the garden.

I noticed some cherry tomatoes discreetly tucked into one of the beds, then a patch of wild strawberries growing beneath an outer wall. The murmur of a stream in the wood beyond gave way briefly in my consciousness to the disturbing buzz of a hornet before that too was eclipsed by the starting up of the pump used to irrigate the adjacent fields. Daydreaming had turned to dozing by the time I became aware that I was not alone in the garden, and that some discreet and secretive presence had been there all along. In my drowsy state, unsure exactly of where I was, I had the distinct sensation that someone had been sent to be my guardian.

2

MY BLURRY EYES slowly focused on a man holding a hosepipe a few feet from where I had been trying to work. He had blue worker's overalls, a portly waist, and a peaked black cap covering a large head which proved to be bald. Even though his back was turned to me, there seemed something quiet, dignified and self-effacing about his manner. He was watering the garden with the pensive stance of a fisherman, and, wary perhaps of disturbing my reverie, he responded merely with a hint of a smile when finally our glances met. His round, large-featured face was kindly, reassuring, and so tantalizingly familiar that I tried desperately to remember where I had seen the man before. In Hollywood films, I suddenly recalled. I had mistaken him for a middle-aged Ernest Borgnine.

I stood up to say hello, and found out he was called Miguel. There was already a bond between us: we were namesakes. 'I come here every morning to look after the garden,' he said, 'I hope I won't be getting in your way.' He was concerned that he was interrupting me in some vital work. Nonetheless he appeared keen to talk and, after a hesitant start, was soon doing so with ever greater enthusiasm and expansiveness. In a way that is so typical of Spain, our conversation soon became exclusively concentrated on the subject of food. With that same passion with which many Spaniards claim that their country's cooking is the best in the world, Miguel extolled in vivid detail some of Frailes's specialities. He spoke of the idiosyncratic local taste for raw sardines; and he pursed his lips with pleasure as he described a dish called a *remojón*, little more than a salad of tomatoes and salt cod but with a transforming ingredient made from figs, chocolates, almonds and anise.

'I'm a cook, you see, that's always been my profession,' he said with much pride. 'I'm only helping out Custodio for the time being, it's just something to do in August.' He paused for a moment, then lowered his eyes towards the ground. 'The problem is,' he murmured, 'there's virtually no work in this village. Most of us are forced to leave.'

Many of the villagers, he said, had emigrated to Barcelona, many others had moved to Seville, following in the footsteps of a Frailero who had become head of the Renault factory there. Miguel himself had lived for twenty years in the Balearics, where there was also a large community from Frailes, mainly in hotels and restaurants. 'I hope I'm back here for good this time,' he said in a wistful voice as he thought of a way to change the subject.

'Have you been to the bakers just up the road from you?' he suddenly asked out of the blue. 'They were in Mallorca for many years, that's why they make Mallorcan specialities from time to time. You should try their *enseimada*, though it's not of course as good as the real thing.' His eyes, with their faint suggestion of melancholy, were beaming once more as he launched again into his favourite topic of food.

'I'd love to come here and cook for you one day,' he enthusiastically announced before listing the many tempting dishes he would be happy to prepare for us. 'It doesn't matter how many people you invite,' he added, 'Twice a year I prepare food for the whole village. I've got a pan large enough to cook *paella* for 2,000 people.' Then, putting down the hose as he decided to call it a day, he turned to look me fully in the face. 'Maiquel,' he said, pronouncing my name in a way that would soon become adopted by the whole of Frailes, 'You must tell me if there's anything else you need. You can always count on my help.' His expression indicated that this was no empty promise.

The aura of goodness that emanated from him seemed to stay on in the garden long after he had left, as if transferred to the shining beads of water on the grass – a satisfying sight in an Andalucía suffering, some said, from one of the worst droughts in recent years. I returned invigorated to the first lines of Lope's play, and within minutes thought I had a way of rendering the opening dialogue in reasonably lively English: '*I'm telling you the truth . . .*' says the courtier Ricardo, to which the aggrieved heroine Laura replies, '. . . *And I cannot take it.*' These simple phrases, like a banal melody, would echo repeatedly in my head over the following days, mirroring perhaps my own growing confusion in the face of a world that was rapidly becoming, as the Spaniards say, 'improbable but true'.

That there was something unquestionably special about Frailes became clear in the immediate wake of my first encounter with Miguel, when villagers kept on turning up at our house carrying gifts of food. The first one to do so was our neighbour with the drill, a cheerful man with a thick moustache and bright pink cheeks, who arrived bearing a basketful of tomatoes and cucumbers as abundant as a Rubensesque still life. A few hours later, on my return from a short walk, I was told that someone else from the village whom I had just had a brief conversation with on the street had made a donation of two giant marrows and a large jar filled with goat's cheese marinated in oil. The following morning Miguel himself knocked at our door, weighed down by pears, watermelons, and squash, 'all grown in my garden'. Within a few days I was envisaging the whole house being gradually taken over with produce from every single household in Frailes.

Hospitality is endemic to Andalucía, but the sheer accumulation of gift-bearing visitors was something entirely new to me, as were such other experiences as our first visit to the supermarket, when we ended up receiving far more than we had bought. We had gone inside to look for figs, but, on discovering there were none for sale, were sent with an assistant to a nearby garden, where we were told to help ourselves to as many as we wanted. Then we went back to the shop for drinks, and were given as a present a jerrycan of home-made wine. On our way home we entered a bar, where the coffee we ordered was immediately paid for by a customer on the far side of the room. Soon it would become difficult for us to go anywhere in Frailes where we could pay for ourselves or leave empty-handed. Even changing money involved a visit to a bank whose manager refused to charge commission, and then insisted on inviting me to a bar to celebrate this 'first transaction with a foreigner'. By now I was inevitably wondering whether there was some ulterior motive behind all this generosity.

Rumours that I was a writer, and that I had even been seen interviewed on Spanish television, lent weight to my suspicion that I had been mistaken for somebody famous. I remembered the time in the Alpujarran village of Yegen when two giggling schoolteachers had begged me for my autograph only to realize, too late, that I was not the Irish-born Hispanist and Lorca biographer Ian Gibson, a celebrity in the Spanish media. The situation now was potentially far worse: whereas in Yegen the consequences of the mistake had been the embarrassment of just two individuals (and the spoiling of a beautiful poster I was asked to sign), in Frailes there was the possibility that the whole village would feel defrauded and made to look silly. Eventually, however, my fears that I would suffer the same ignominious fate as the impostor protagonist of Gogol's *The Government Inspector* had to be discounted. The villagers I had known seemed so utterly genuine and free of pretension that I could scarcely imagine them behaving any differently towards someone they thought of as important than towards someone who clearly was not. Frailes, I could only conclude, was unlike any other village I had ever known. It was one of those endearingly fantastical communities that I believed existed only in fiction.

The person who did most initially to influence this vision was Miguel, whom I perceived increasingly as a man with an otherworldly presence. His solid, down-to-earth appearance was balanced by his uncanny ubiquity whenever I went into the village or needed to ask for something. With characteristic discretion he slipped into the role of my unofficial guide to Frailes, and helped me to get to know better its inhabitants. 'How could a village produce so many unfailingly kind people?' I was continually asking myself, the more time I spent with Miguel. I was also becoming steadily more confused. Most of the women I met seemed to be called either Mercedes or its diminutive Merce, while a surprising number of the men had the same unusual Christian name as my landlord, Custodio. Miguel eventually explained to me that the most important votive image of the area was the Virgin of Mercy in Alcalá, which accounted for the popularity of the name Mercedes. But no one could tell me at first why such a disproportionate number of the men here were known after the Ángel Custodio or Guardian Angel, and why they abbreviated this to Custodio rather than to the far more common Ángel. The existence in Frailes of so many Custodios remained for the moment a mystery, albeit one that was very much in keeping with my growing sense of having been inexplicably taken under someone's wing.

It was at this time that I had also my first inkling of Frailes as a place of miracles. Miguel was once again the catalyst. He had agreed to prepare lunch for us all on our first Saturday in the village, when friends were due from Seville. He went with me in the morning to get some olive oil from the oil cooperative in the centre of the village, but, finding this place shut, drove me on to a privately run mill lying in impressive isolation in the middle of a rolling landscape of olive trees. The journey back gave him time to talk at length about the 'extraordinary qualities of olive oil', and about the almost religious respect in which it was held in Frailes. He repeated the now conventional wisdom that olive oil was so much better for you than butter, and that it did not clog the arteries, but was instead a source of 'good cholesterol'. He told me as well that it was an 'excellent laxative', made 'wonderful soap', and was still favoured by many of the village women as a cosmetic ('Some of them mix it with lemon to make what used to be called "Cleopatra's Milk"'). And then he came out with a truly surprising revelation.

'I am convinced,' he said, 'that olive oil has something that cannot easily be explained in scientific terms. Maiquel, you probably won't believe this story I'm going to tell you but it's true. It's about my eldest son. When he was only twelve or so all his hair started falling out. There was little we could do, the doctor told us, there was no conventional cure for what he had. But then I was advised by a man living in the Sierra to rub oil into the scalp. This wasn't so far-fetched, I thought. After all, just think of all the people who swear that a few drops of oil with the shampoo helps to strengthen your hair. So I gave it a try, and within days my son's hair started coming back. It was miraculous. He's now in his twenties, and has got healthy dark curls.'

I stared at Miguel's shiny bald pate and wondered if he himself had ever considered this remedy. However, once we had got back to the house, the culinary rather than the healing properties of olive oil soon became uppermost in my mind. Vast quantities of the oil ('Frailes quantities,' someone would later remark, 'not your miserly English ones') were being poured by Miguel into a giant *paella* pan, which stood sizzling over a wood fire in the garden, ready to receive onions and rice, home-grown peppers and tomatoes, a rabbit which had been hunted that dawn, and a newly killed chicken from a neighbour's garden. Everything was shaping up for the kind of day only too typical of my Spanish experiences: a day of gastronomic indulgence in the company of a large and uninhibited group of people.

My Sevillian friends arrived, bottles of wine were uncorked, and a table laid out under the cooling shadow of the walnut tree. 'How Esperanza would have enjoyed this,' I commented, referring to an absent and now very ill friend from Seville who had first introduced me to the sybaritic excesses of Andalucía. Her sister Loli, one of those who had come to see me that day in Frailes, nodded her head as we began eating and drinking, recalling past times with Esperanza, including lunches that had lasted from midday to the early hours of the morning. Miguel, who insisted on maintaining a professional detachment from the proceedings, stood in the background, and finished preparing the last of the food before beginning to pack up his equipment. After a while I noticed that Loli had gone over to join him.

'Did you know,' she asked, once Miguel had said goodbye to us all, 'about the faith healers of the Sierra Sur? According to Miguel, there's a route one can follow in their footsteps. It's known as the "Route of Miracles".'

Loli had obviously been deeply affected by her conversation with Miguel. I was not surprised. The sadness of witnessing her sister's recent decline, combined with the almost pagan approach towards Catholicism that she shared with so many people from Seville, made her particularly susceptible to ideas about faith healing and spiritual forces. Nonetheless, many hours later, with the conversation still in full flow, I could not decide whether it was this or just the effects of drink that led her unprompted to say, 'Michael, I can see what you mean, there's something definitely unusual about Frailes, I don't know what it is, but it's something positive, reassuring.'

The sun was already high in the sky by the time we had all roused ourselves from sleep the next morning. Any ideas I might once have had about a regular work schedule had been abandoned shortly after coming to Frailes, and I was now getting up later every day. As I drowned a piece of toast with olive oil, I had a vague memory of Miguel telling me about some villagers who had tried twice during the week to pay us a morning visit but had found everyone still in bed. I wondered for a moment who these people could be, and whether we could expect them again. Then I took my breakfast out to the garden and sat down at a table only partially cleared of wine glasses and cigarette ends. Loli was examining a flower bed, while another friend was dreamily rocking on a swing. The 'Englishman with the Sevillian accent' was sitting reading on a deckchair before distractedly looking up towards the horizon. 'I think there are some gypsies coming to see us,' he murmured.

If these were gypsies they could not be from Spain, I thought, as I saw three women advancing along the path towards our house. They had clothes that appeared more suitable for winter than for a hot Sunday morning in August. As they advanced you could see that their brightly colored pinafore dresses were worn over black, heavy-looking garments stiff with embroidery. When I saw too that they were carrying in their arms wickerwork baskets laden with goods, I thought I recognized in them the women gypsies who gather these days around the train stations at Vienna and Budapest, desperately trying to sell their trinkets. Why a group of gypsies of Central European origin, possibly from Slovakia, would want to come to Frailes was of course beyond rational comprehension. The fact they had done so, however, only confirmed my belief that I had landed in a village where anything was possible.

Hermes the guard dog, whose barking seemed to be reserved almost exclusively for visitors from outside the village, became quite uncontrollable at the approach of these strange apparitions from the east. He lunged at the gate as they walked towards it, and was roused to even further fury when one of them shouted at him in a voice that managed to be husky, childlike and commanding all at the same time.

'Hermes! Hermes! Don't you know who we are?' said this voice, thus immediately dispelling my theory about Slovakian gypsies. 'He's never like this normally, but then he's never seen us in these costumes,' she smiled, the dog finally calming down when I went to the gate to find out what was happening. The woman who had spoken had wavy light brown hair tied up in a bun, a fair complexion, and restless pale green eyes that countered any suggestion of weakness in her features. She had obviously taken on the leadership of the group, and, once the subject of Hermes had been dealt with, embarked on what would have easily been an awkward rehearsed speech had it not been delivered in a completely natural and spontaneous manner devoid of any hint of pomposity.

'We are from Frailes,' she began, 'and we have come here to welcome you to this village of ours that we love so much.' Her tone had an engaging mixture of humour and heartfelt conviction. 'We want to give you the best that our land has to offer,' she continued, gesturing towards her basket which, like those of her companions, was decorated with a scattering of wild flowers. 'We have brought you figs, goat's cheese, tomatoes, chorizo sausage, pears . . .' she sensuously recited, letting out an occasional purr of pleasure to indicate the excellence of a particular product. 'And, of course, we have some olive oil,' she added, releasing one of her hands from the side of the basket and then using it to dangle before my eyes a miniature bottle ingeniously shaped like an olive.

'Aren't you going to let them in?' shouted Loli from behind, conscious that this most surprising of all our visits had left me in a daze. She herself responded to the women as if they were friends in flamenco costume who had made an appearance at a private *caseta* in the Seville Feria. Taking control of the situation as her sister Esperanza would have done, she hurried inside to get them food and drink, leaving me and the others in the house to keep our unexpected guests entertained. A few moments later, and without any awareness of how this had occurred, I was alone with the woman with the light brown hair, oblivious of her companions and indeed of anything else around me. I felt an empathy between us even before any dialogue had been exchanged.

'We tried a couple of times during the week to come and see you,' she said, breaking a pause in which I stood transfixed by her smile. 'We came with our good friend Manolo, who's very keen to meet you. He loves writers, and has a large collection of books dedicated to him by the authors. I know he'd love to have one of yours.' I saw little point in trying to lie about how I made a living, or to play down any illusions she might have had about my literary importance. The wink she gave me was surely a sign that there was nothing I could hide from her. She knew the truth.

'We had all been sitting at El Choto when you turned up there on your first night. I said you must be the foreigners who had rented Custodio's house. We thought of talking to you there and then, but Manolo and the others were worried about disturbing you. Then, a couple of days later, I heard that you had all been trying to buy figs at the supermarket. These people, I said to myself, obviously haven't learnt yet that in Frailes you take anything you find growing on the trees. So that's when I decided that we really must come and see you. Well, we're finally here. My name's Merce, I know yours is Maiquel.'

Laughter in the background brought suddenly to an end our brief isolation from the others. My friends were serving drinks to Merce's two dark-haired companions, both of whom had been asked to sit at the now cleared garden table. 'And after two failed attempts to drop by your house in the morning,' giggled one of them, who was plump and had a loud voice, 'we thought we'd give you just one more chance. "We'd better do something spectacular this time," said Merce, "Why don't we all dress up?" Yes, why not, we thought, but in what? We considered flamenco dresses, but Merce said that was too obvious, and that it had to be something from Frailes. This whole conversation, I must add, was taking place about three o'clock last night, it was nice and cool, and we'd had a fair amount to drink. Of course, when morning came, I was all for chickening out. We're going to melt in these costumes, I said, and we don't even know whether the foreigners will appreciate all our efforts, they could even turn us away. But Merce was all for going ahead, she can be quite stubborn at times . . .'

And so she went on, filling us in with the down-to-earth details of how their unusual visit had come about. Curiously, knowing about these did not seem to diminish the beauty and mystery of the whole event, or even the feeling that we had witnessed a traditional rite peculiar to this village. But hardly would I have guessed then that the story of the encounter between three costumed women and a group of bemused outsiders would soon enter the mythology of Frailes. Inevitably the story would become ever more distorted over time, with one embittered Alcalaíno even telling me directly to my face that the Fraileros had so little respect for individual privacy that they had frightened away an English family from the village by turning up well past midnight at a house these poor people had rented. Slightly closer to the truth was the version of the story recounted almost two years later in a local newspaper:

When Michael Jacquoc [sic] first came to Frailes, in the summer of 1999, he had intended just to spend a short holiday. What determined otherwise was a Sunday morning visit paid to him by three village women dressed in traditional local costume. Without them Frailes would not have had an English writer in its midst. And without him, would the village's history have taken the strange turn that it has of late?

3

WE WALKED IN the glare of the mid afternoon sun towards a bar
that, we had been told, was situated in a cave. I had been along
Frailes's main street almost every day for the past week without
having ever been aware that such a place existed. Now, during the
hour of the Sunday siesta, there was no one in the village to direct us
there, or indeed to confirm that we had not been the victims of some
practical joke. With everyone cursing the heat and my feigned insistence that I knew exactly where we were going, we went up and
down the section of the street that lay between a cliff face and a small
recreation area with balustrades in ageing concrete and a children's
slide in rusting metal. Only after my friends had threatened to give
up the search did one of us finally notice the words 'Bar La Cueva'
peering faintly behind a covering of ivy. A bead curtain obscured the
broken pane of a glass door that we had reckoned to be the entrance
to an abandoned dwelling. A firm push, however, led us into the
gloom of a cavern filled with smoke and mumbling voices.

Dazed by the contrast with the brilliant light outside, my eyes took
time to take in all the details of the scene before us. A red-nosed man
with a shy and kindly expression was pouring out a glass of anise
behind an L-shaped counter built between grease-stained plaster
walls that opened up into the cave proper. Hams were hung like stal-
actites from the blackened rock of a rounded chamber, while an old
ceiling fan swirled like a hovering, monstrous bat. A flickering television, suspended above a background of giant earthenware vessels,
occupied the place where one might have expected the image of a
pagan deity. However, none of the people who crowded into this
mysterious space seemed to pay any attention to it. Seated at tables
that disappeared into the darkness of a further, hidden chamber, some

of them looked up briefly to stare at us as we made our noisy arrival through a slamming door. But their attention was mainly absorbed by a matter of infinitely greater importance: they were playing cards.

We had entered this tenebrous domain to look for Merce, who said she came here every afternoon around four o'clock, and that the place was 'magical', 'phenomenal', and that I would love it. I said that we would all go and see her there that very Sunday, after we had finished lunch. It was now well after five, and I could not see a single woman among all the drinkers and card-players. Nor could I imagine any woman, let alone one of youthful and independent spirit, easily fitting into this traditional male world that could have been lifted straight from Franco's Spain. Then I heard her unmistakable laugh, the laugh of someone who did not restrain her instincts, who behaved exactly as she felt. A laugh comprising a rapid repetition of raucous whooping sounds that shook the whole cave.

I squeezed my way past grunting old men with caps and clothes that blended in with the crumbling ochre plaster. And then I found her, dealing out cards in the recess of the cave that was not visible from the entrance. Dressed in shorts and a T-shirt, without make-up, her long hair flowing freely like a tumble of straw, she looked obviously a different person to the one I had met in the morning. Yet her presence and unconventional beauty were as notable as ever, and overcame the plainness of her features when glimpsed unadorned and in their rare moments of repose. Merce dominated the cave in the same way as she had stood out among her woman companions. She was like a benign witch ruling over a male coven.

As soon as her eyes caught mine she let out a joyful shriek, dropped the cards, and threw her hands into the air. She introduced me to the three men at her table. 'This is Manolo, the person I was telling you about,' she said, indicating a trim elderly man with a mischievous smile, fine features and a high forehead supporting a shock of white hair. 'And this is Santi the village chronicler, he's writing a history of Frailes.' 'And I'm a person of absolutely no importance,' butted in loudly a man with bright red cheeks and an incipient pot belly. 'I'm only Merce's husband, I'm also called Manolo.' Contorting his whole face with laughter, he slapped his left hand hard against mine, and proposed we should all go and continue talking at the bar.

Pressed up tight around the now crowded counter, my new acquaintances mingled with my friends from England and Seville.

The beam in the elderly Manolo's eye became ever more pronounced as he indulged his evident passion for meeting new people, whom he insisted straightaway should address him by the informal '*tu*' rather than by the '*usted*' automatically used while speaking to strangers of his age. Though his primary interest had been to get to know the 'English writer', he flitted excitedly from one person to the next, leaving me for a long while caught in an awkward conversation with Santi, a man of ascetic and slightly troubled appearance whose shyness exceeded my own.

I told Santi that Miguel had often spoken about him as the person I should go and see if I was interested in finding out more about Frailes. Santi chuckled and said that he and Miguel had been close friends since childhood. Then the timid smile that gave him such an endearing and approachable look vanished as quickly as it had come, to be replaced by the silent, distracted stare of a depressive. Other attempts to get him going met with similar halts and splutters, until finally Merce came to help us out.

'Few people love their village as much as Santi,' she said, placing a hand tenderly on his shoulder.

'I work in Frailes, I'm writing about the place, and I come every afternoon to La Cueva. The only thing I don't do any more is live here,' he joked quietly before explaining for my benefit that his wife found it more convenient to have a flat in Alcalá, and that they had been there since marrying five years ago. Merce, watching my response to this, put on an expression that seemed to say 'Poor Santi!' Then she shrugged enigmatically, directed towards me one of her penetrating smiles, and clutched the arm of the red-nosed man behind the bar.

'This is my brother Pepín,' she said, 'he's one of six.' Pepín asked me if I wanted to try a wine pressed by his own feet, and then, without waiting for an answer, pulled out a plastic Coca-Cola bottle and began pouring me a glass. Shuddering at the recollection of the acid-like local wine that I had been given at the supermarket, I put my mouth warily to it, and recoiled immediately. This wine was even worse, far worse. Pepín, Santi and Merce laughed as they saw me grimace. 'It's better earlier in the year,' she commented, 'though I like it at any time. I'm sure you'll get a taste for it.' I gave it another try, hoping that it might improve once the initial shock had passed, but shook my head. It was definitely not an aspect of Frailes that would ever grow on me. But I took a further sip all the same, believing as I do that the ability to withstand gastronomic torture is an essential attribute of the traveller.

The next moment we were all out on the street, though I could not at first understand why. All I knew was that I had enthusiastically endorsed the proposal to do so, and was now gripped by a great sense of elation. '*Andalucía intoxicates like alcohol or opium,*' wrote the Sevillian poet Luis Cernuda. I remembered these words as I calculated the odds against my being made drunk by just three sips of wine. It was ages since I had been unable to control the effects of alcohol; but Pepín's drink appeared to have had the immediate impact of a strong drug. A bit of exercise and fresh air would probably do me a lot of good, I thought to myself as our now extended group from La Cueva started to climb a steep, overgrown alley lined by the shells of at least three or four collapsing old houses. I felt carried up by a force other than that of my body.

'It's a completely pure wine, uncontaminated by chemicals, so you won't suffer from any hangover,' Merce assured me, as the elderly Manolo strode nimbly past us, arm in arm with Loli. 'Look at him,' she commented as the two of them rushed ahead, 'you wouldn't think he's almost eighty.' They were almost out of sight by the time the rest of us had reached the top of the alley, where we found ourselves next to the parish church. 'We're not in such a hurry,' said Merce, stopping to comment on the most majestic of the three grand houses surrounding us. It had been built in expectation of a visit to Frailes by none other than Alfonso XIII, she said. 'That was when Frailes still had its spa,' she added, tantalizing me with another snippet of the village's history.

With my romantic taste for monuments steeped in melancholy decline, I was hoping that a visit inside this palace would be part of our impromptu excursion. But my fascination with the building had to be kept once more in abeyance. We had already entered the modern part of Frailes that lay beyond, and were descending a small street separating the village school from the town hall, with its funny clock that seemed permanently stuck at a quarter to ten. Blocking off the lower part of the street was a large ironwork gate where Manolo was standing, key in hand.

Manolo's house, apparently, was the whole purpose of our outing. I presumed we had come here on the pretext of seeing the books he collected, and prayed our visit had nothing to do with the tasting of more local wine. The building itself, an ordinary-looking structure in the middle of a large garden with a bare and dusty central area, did not promise from the outside huge riches or surprises. But it would provide at least a means of getting to know Manolo better; and its charms, whatever they were, would undoubtedly be brought out by the mood I was in, and the company I was with. I had of course not the slightest inkling then of the house's emblematic importance within the context of Fraile. Nor had anyone warned me that a tour of the place was an obligatory ritual for every visitor to the village.

The ritual, which I would get to know so well over the next two years, began at the porch where Manolo's two diminutive sisters, alerted by noises at the gate, and the barks of their dogs Curra and Rasputin, were scanning the driveway to see who was coming. Carmela, the younger and more silent of the two, had a long, angular nose and a face whose heavy lines expressed a mixture of bewilderment and quiet resignation. Mercedes, a fine-featured woman who must once have been a great beauty, had the look of someone instinctively wary of strangers and ready to be critical. Fortunately, on this first visit to the house my friends and I appeared to have been favourably judged. Soon she had put on the sweetest of smiles, encouraging Carmela to do the same. The two of them together, glowing beatifically as we approached, struck me as porcelain dolls that had suddenly been given the gift of life but not of immortality.

Once past this welcoming committee, Manolo led us through a wooden door into a tiny vestibule, and from there into an adjoining kitchen where the sisters hovered for a while behind us, muttering between themselves, and asking Merce in whispers who the visitors were. Then we proceeded into a white-tiled amenities room that served also as an antechamber to what was the outstanding feature of the ground floor. There was not enough space for us to see this at the same time, Manolo said, so I volunteered to wait, and was soon shaken by violent sounds reverberating from what seemed to be a space little bigger than an outside toilet. Laughter and applause soon followed. I awaited my turn with greater curiosity than ever.

Entering the miniature chamber, I was confronted by what Manolo proudly described as 'the smallest olive mill in the world'. It could have been designed by Heath Robinson. The engine from a motorcycle propelled two blades inside a sliced and perforated beer barrel where the olives were given a 'first pressing'. The pulp was then transferred to the upright drum of a washing machine and placed under a press taken from an old printer's; the oil, left to ooze out from the holes of the drum for several days, was collected in further barrels capable of storing an annual production that Manolo calculated as being around fifty litres.

'This is not a commercial enterprise,' he said with a smile. 'I only make the oil for myself and my friends.' Then, his eyes twinkling more than ever, he said that perhaps it was wrong to call his mill the world's smallest. 'There have been others that were smaller and more primitive still. In the village where I grew up, in the north of Jaén, day labourers would steal olives from their masters' fields and put them at night under a sock weighed down by a heavy stone.' Watching me shake my head with amazement, he followed up his anecdote with one of the homespun truths with which, I would soon discover, he loved to pepper his conversation. 'Necessity,' he said, 'inspires the greatest ingenuity in human beings.'

Back in the antechamber Manolo opened a cupboard to present us all with small bottles of oil, on which he had stuck labels marked '*Serenolivo*'. 'Everyone in Frailes knows me as "El Sereno",' he commented after I had asked him about the name of the oil. 'In the fifty years since I've been living in this village,' he added, 'I've worked in almost every capacity. But when I first came here I did a job that was not unlike that of a *sereno*.' Compared with many other village nicknames which I would eventually come to hear, that of El Sereno, as I now came to call him, was not unappealing – he had been fortunate in merely being called after the Spanish word for a night porter. The name might not have been a strictly accurate description of his former profession; but its double meaning of 'serene' seemed highly appropriate to what I was already gathering of El Sereno's character. Though incapable of staying still for any length of time, he nevertheless projected the serenity of an elderly sage who refuses to become embittered or cantankerous, but maintains instead a constant fascination with the world, a tolerance of other people, and an openness to new experience. As he continued showing us round his house, offering us as he did so revealing snippets about his past, I could not help marvelling at how this man, apparently unmarried and without children, had all the enthusiasm of an optimistic young person looking forward to a long, happy life before him.

We stayed so long on the ground floor that it soon became clear our tour was not going to leave even a single broom cupboard unvisited. From the kitchen we went into a small sitting room, where the two sisters had now taken refuge on a sofa. Ignoring their presence, El Sereno pointed to a framed, blown-up photograph of his father, 'a wise but illiterate man' who had struggled to find ways of raising his nine children. Then, after we had made suitably admiring noises about a spotlessly clean but otherwise unremarkable ground-floor bathroom, we were taken into a similarly immaculate little room with two beds arranged with cell-like austerity. 'This is my sisters' room,' he said in a perfunctory tone. 'They've shared the same room since they were children. Like me, they never married.' To our slight consternation he then insisted that Loli lie down on one of the beds. 'Don't move,' he shouted to his amused but protesting subject as he turned on a switch that raised the bed to any height or angle that was required. 'There's more to come,' he grinned, before admitting that he was only joking and that he had not got around yet to buying the 'massage attachment'.

From the vestibule a staircase climbed into a domain that appeared to be exclusively El Sereno's. We saw his own sparse sleeping quarters, and two other bedrooms of far more welcoming appearance which, he said with a grin, were kept for his ' "nieces" and other special guests'. The most lavish of these rooms had a king-sized double bed with brightly polished brass fittings, and a mahogany built-in cupboard. He urged us to take a closer look at this after he had opened one of its doors. Peering inside, I was greatly surprised to find a large and luxurious bathroom that an eccentric millionaire might have made to hide his lovers.

What we had yet to see was any book, and I wondered whether at this pace we ever would. But when we reached a darkened suite of rooms, encouraging me to think that we were entering some inner sanctuary, I felt that some form of climax was imminent. El Sereno pulled up the blinds to reveal in turn a columned dining area that seemed never to have been used, a room displaying old apothecary jars and oil reproductions of red-nosed clowns, and, finally, a study where the first thing that caught my eye was not the books but rather the most state-of-the-art television set I had ever seen. I would later learn that El Sereno had not only a love of up-to-date gadgets but also a mania for purchasing objects promoted by his friends. As he inexpertly fiddled with the controls to try and show us all the inter-national channels and image magnifications that his set was capable of, Merce slapped her thighs and cried out, 'Incredible! Incredible! Did you ever think that you would have to come to a village like Frailes to encounter such modern technology?'

By now El Sereno had put down the television's remote control and had moved over to a large coffee table covered with a dozen or so books and newspaper cuttings. A few crammed shelves facing this contained the rest of his renowned library, the fame of which was clearly due to something other than its size.

'I never had any schooling,' said El Sereno by way of introducing us to his books. 'I taught myself to read and write, but picked up most of what I've learnt in life from being with other people. I've been fortu-nate enough to have had a number of writer friends.' He bent over to reach from the table a book by someone called Juan Eslava Galán, 'one of the greatest writers today in the Spanish language, perhaps in any language'. I faintly recognized the name, possibly because it was the one to which El Sereno had already alluded several times in the course of the afternoon. However, it was not until I read the book's title, *In Search of the Unicorn*, that I remembered the author as the winner of Spain's Premio Planeta, the Spanish equivalent of the Booker or the Prix Goncourt. He was a schoolteacher from Jaén whose books covered every possible subject and genre, ranging from historical studies of Spanish sexuality to medieval mysteries published under the pseudonym Nicholas Wilcox. Every one of these works was on El Sereno's shelves, and every one of them was duly removed by him for our perusal. As I looked at the cover photograph on a work entitled *Country Breakfast*, El Sereno pointed out that the portly bearded man seated eating at the table was the author himself. 'And do you see what oil he's using?' He chuckled as I read out the word '*Serenolivo*'.

The effusive praise that El Sereno heaped on Juan Eslava Galán was extended to many of the other writers whom he had known, all of whom, with the exception of one Jesús Torbado (whom I vaguely knew for his travel articles in *El País*) had reputations that probably reached little further than Alcalá la Real. Such was his tendency to inflate talents that I was seriously tempted for a moment to appoint El Sereno my literary representative in Spain. I thought it prudent though to discover beforehand how he judged an author's worth. It did not take me long to find out that his litmus test for any book was its handwritten dedication, without which no work for him could be complete. Every time he removed a book to show me, he turned straight away to the dedication, which he recited in a way that dwelt lovingly on every word. This was, I confess, a literary genre which I had previously undervalued. Under El Sereno's influence, however, I would learn to read the comments scrawled on a book's title page and either murmur approbations such as, 'How beautifully expressed!' or else come to critical conclusions such as, 'He might be a magnificent researcher, but you can tell from this dedication that he lacks both feeling and a way with words.' As for those authors who contented themselves with a mere 'Best wishes', well, they had little right to consider themselves as authors at all.

'You're going to exhaust Maiquel!' shouted Merce after El Sereno had placed in front of me a dedication by Juan Eslava Galán which stated, 'To my good friend El Sereno, my best reader.' My concentration, it was true, was failing, and I had started looking up with longing towards the study's panoramic window, with its enticing views north towards the mountains of the Sierra Sur. Merce, intuiting my thoughts, proposed we should all go out into the garden.

Outside again, and refreshed by the early evening air, I came to appreciate El Sereno's property as a world of its own that dominated Frailes both literally and symbolically. Cut off from the village by its large gate, and yet adjoining the community's administrative, medical and educational facilities, the property crowned a sheer outcrop of rock that offered glimpses into almost every corner of Frailes. We studied the views carefully as we walked slowly along a pergola-covered path hugging the edge of the cliff. Frailes, seen from this elevated angle, surprised me by appearing so harmonious and unspoiled. Instead of being an unplanned and confusing conglomeration of the old and the new, it became an overall composition of white walls and reddish brown roofs hemmed in by ochre slopes liberally daubed in olive green.

For the first time I began to grasp Frailes's complex layout. The backbone of this long-drawn-out village was its now sadly depleted stream, which created a deep, curved indentation as it etched its way sharply down from the sierra. It separated the hill we were on from village's northern half where, among the mass of rooftops that rolled away toward the mountains, stood a tall building identified for me by El Sereno as the 'olive-oil factory'.

'And there in front of it,' he continued, pointing to some broken tiles suspended above the ragged, desiccated green ribbon formed by the stream, 'that was once the cinema. It closed down over thirty years ago.'

Just below this the stream reached the village's main street. It then changed direction, following the street in a barely perceptible descent along the narrow valley between El Sereno's cliffside promenade and a steep hill directly opposite. As I looked across the valley in the fading light, I saw two women laboriously climbing a winding path that led up to a white-walled cemetery guarded by cypresses. The rest of the hill was carpeted with olive, almond and cherry trees that I later learnt were mainly El Sereno's.

'And do you know where we are now?' he asked, urging me to lean over the railings and stare down at the street far below. Without leaving me time to answer he said that we were immediately above the Bar La Cueva, and that he used to descend to the bar from here by rope. 'The difficult part was getting up again,' he noted, enjoying the incredulous look on our faces.

The gap between the hill opposite and the cliff we were walking on gradually widened as we looked south across broadening fields towards the distant and now dark pink mountains of Granada and Córdoba. We came to a part of the garden that seemed to be used as a picnic area or an open-air bar. Below the branches of one of those massive walnut trees so characteristic of the village, a group of conical millstones had been placed upright in the ground to act as tables. There was also a pedimented white garden house resembling a miniature Greek temple, which El Sereno insisted on opening for us. Inside was an untidy little space with a sofa still protected in plastic, a broken-down television set, shelves packed with old newspapers and discarded files, and a large brick fireplace with a chimney breast decorated with a ram's skull, an old shotgun, and two gas cylinders dating back to the Spanish civil war.

Before I could properly assimilate the building that would one day be at the heart of my own imaginative world, we were back outside, following the promenade's final short stretch alongside a narrow strip of vegetable garden that bordered the walled grounds of the town hall. El Sereno, making brief but repeated forays in search of strawberries, walnuts, apricots, peaches, figs, cactus pears, and other ready-to-eat riches from his garden, helped stimulate our taste buds as our other senses succumbed to the spectacle of the setting sun. I stuttered out in a low voice to Merce that I had never seen Frailes look so beguiling as it did that evening.

She took my words of praise almost as a personal compliment. It heartened her that a foreigner could find in Frailes a beauty she thought only those who lived here could perceive. 'And not even many Fraileros really understand how special their village is,' she sighed. 'I mean, can you imagine when you look at this scene in front of us that there are villagers happy to leave their beautiful old homes here and go and live in expensive modern flats in Alcalá?'

Alcalá la Real, I inferred from teasing comments she had made earlier to Santi, was a small and conservative town with pretensions to be a large city. 'I know there's far more work to be had in Alcalá, but the place is only a quarter of an hour's drive away. My husband, who's a teacher there, is perfectly happy commuting. The only reason these other people want to live in Alcalá is that they think it's a fashionable location, they don't want to be thought of as country boors.'

Then she repeated in a serious tone what Miguel had already told me about Frailes's history of poverty and emigration. She herself had had to spend most of her twenties living away from here. She had loved seeing new places, and getting to meet new people, but she had been so relieved when, eight years ago, she and Caño had been able to move back to Frailes, apparently for good. For her Frailes had everything she could possibly want. 'Maiquel,' she added, 'you might find this difficult to believe, but I cry every time I have to say goodbye to my village.'

Was it all the accumulated emotion of this eventful Sunday, the evocativeness of the evening light, or the aftermath of local wine that made my own eyes water as she told me this? I was a rootless urbanite and cosmopolitan who had always been wary of rural nostalgia. Nonetheless something was happening to me in Frailes that was clearly softening my brain. I was becoming envious of those like Merce and Miguel who had such a strong sense of their roots. I wished that I too had been born in a village which I could love as passionately as they did. Merce, seeing me so pensive and stuck for words, broke the silence with a smile. 'I can see,' she said, 'that you too have fallen under the spell.'

4

MERCE'S ENIGMATIC WORDS instantly came back to me as I drifted back into consciousness the next morning. Far from suffering from any hangover, I was conscious of having undergone some wonderful experience whose bewitching effects had managed to survive the night unscathed. To fall in love with a place was perhaps something more than just an overused figure of speech; and perhaps the symptoms of this condition were not so different from those of falling in love with another person. I was excited, rejuvenated, and perhaps also slightly frightened. I was succumbing to emotions beyond my control.

The day ahead promised further revelations, of a more esoteric kind: the time had come to introduce me to the Route of Miracles. The idea had been Merce's, but was keenly supported by El Sereno, who loved any excuse for showing visitors his adopted land. The impossibility of doing anything on one's own in Frailes was fast becoming apparent. By four in the afternoon, when we had agreed to meet up again in the Cueva, I realised that at least six others were going to join us on our spiritual tour of the Sierra. Among these was the youngest of Merce's two children, Alejandro, a blue-eyed eight-year-old with the same teasing smile as his mother, and a comparable ability to become immediately close to strangers and to know what was on their minds. There was also Merce's young sister Isa,who had dyed orange hair and a past reputation in Frailes as a hippy and rebel. Another, and for me more puzzling, addition to the group was my landlord Custodio, whose wife, I now learnt, was a childhood friend of Merce's 'who encouraged my interest in tarot cards and magic'.

'What's happened to your companions from England?' Custodio asked, 'and what about those many other people who I hear have been staying with you?' I said that a woman friend of mine from Seville had been very keen on coming but that she had had to go back home that morning. As for the others in the house, they had decided to have a quiet day recovering from the weekend activities. I did not want to admit that they neither shared my enthusiasm for large group outings, nor did they quite comprehend the degree of fascination I was developing towards Frailes and its surroundings. They knew me well enough to have witnessed the many other short-lived obsessions I had acquired in the course of my travels. They recognized that the inhabitants of the village were unusually friendly, but teased me for trying to find some deeper significance behind this. The idea of being in a land ruled by miracles and guardian angels was of course too ridiculous to be worth even discussing. 'What a shame your friends couldn't come,' said Custodio. 'I think we're in for an interesting afternoon.'

We set off in a trio of Land Rovers headed by a battered yellow Suzuki driven by El Sereno. I elected to be in the latter vehicle, together with Isa and Custodio. 'I hope you're not a nervous passenger,' joked Isa. I assured her that I was not, and as someone who had never learnt to drive himself had absolute confidence even in the worst of drivers. 'But Manolo is something else,' she laughed.

El Sereno merely smiled to himself as he lifted his foot from the brake in so sudden a way that the car sped off like a rocket. My seat was forced backwards and my head almost touched the dented roof. 'I don't know why he's always in such a hurry,' commented Isa from the back seat as I made sure that my safety belt was tightly fastened. My gesture in touching the belt inspired El Sereno to put on his own, which he did without stopping or even slowing down. The one hand that remained on the wheel struggled to keep control as the car veered towards the other side of the street and then swerved immediately back. 'The belt isn't really necessary,' he calmly said. 'There won't be any *Guardia Civiles* where we're going, and in any case they're all my friends.'

El Sereno's confidence in his driving abilities reminded me of my Irish grandmother, who finally had had her licence withdrawn in her early eighties after a multiple pile-up at some traffic lights. But El Sereno was at least able to see the funny side to his notorious reputation. Characteristically delighted by my expression of mounting panic, he related a story of how he had once given a lift to the director of a parachute jumping school. 'After only half an hour of being in my car he said, "in more than forty years of jumping from planes I've never known moments of fear as great as I've had today." ' Laughing more than ever as he repeated the punchline, El Sereno narrowly avoided hitting a pedestrian – through the side mirror of the car I saw the near victim throw up his hands in shock. A few hundred metres further on I turned around to see an old woman making the sign of the Cross. The route we were on had better be miraculous, I thought, if we were to survive it.

Once past the village we left the road on which I had first entered Frailes and headed off to the right into a miniature valley cultivated with orchards. 'Manolo, Manolo, take it easy! Don't rush!' implored Isa as the car persevered in its rally up a series of hairpin bends ascending rapidly through a landscape of oaks.

'Up there,' mumbled El Sereno, briefly taking both hands off the wheel as he talked, 'is the Cave of the Treasure. There is a legend that a terrifying old woman lived there, keeping watch on anyone making their way into the Sierra . . .'

'Keep your eye on the road!' shouted Isa, as El Sereno switched to another story involving his own exploration of the cave. Caves had always fascinated him, he continued regardless, and he had acquired such a thorough knowledge of this particular one that he had been woken up once in the middle of the night to go and search for a local boy who had got lost inside. Thanks to him the boy had been found, after which a television film was made reconstructing the whole incident. 'The cameraman was too frightened to come down with me into the cave,' El Sereno beamed, making me aware for the first time of his enormous potential as a media star.

The car halted as violently as it had started, and the other Land Rovers eventually pulled up behind us. We had stopped next to a fountain within sight of the hamlet of Los Rosales, a tightly packed cubist composition in white, with a commanding position high above the yellow-green, steeply sloped valley that descended towards Frailes. Merce's husband, whom everyone seemed to refer to by his surname Caño, seemed highly amused by my pallid appearance. 'Are you all right then?' he asked rhetorically.

'The people in this hamlet', Merce interrupted, 'are among the kindest, most generous and selfless people you're ever likely to meet. It must be something to do with their healthy lifestyle. They're mainly in their seventies, but they enjoy themselves so much. They play bowls, they all make the most beautiful basketwork . . .'

'And their goat cheese,' added Caño, 'is outstanding. As with all the best products, it doesn't fulfil any of the EEC sanitary regulations. Every couple of years or so there's a fatal case of brucellosis, but such is life . . .'

'Come and try the water, Maiquel, it's delicious,' shouted El Sereno at the head of the small queue that had formed next to the fountain. At this time of drought, the many springs and fountains of the area had become an especial source of local pride, and essential stopping-off points for all visitors. 'This one is a mineral spring,' noted Custodio. 'Mineral waters are abundant in the Sierra. They might have something to do with the miracles performed by the faith healers.'

I drank the cool bubbling water in the hope that it had special qualities that might protect me during the next stage of the drive. Then I climbed into the car, and had barely time to close the door before El Sereno was racing up the road again. A few moments later we were at the top of the pass, which was marked by a solitary roadside chapel overlooking an immense panorama of woods, lost valleys, and bare rounded peaks. We turned on to a side road pock-marked from years of damage caused by heavy snowfalls. 'This is it,' exclaimed Isa. 'This is where our route really begins.'

We followed a valley lined in its lower reaches by holm-oaks and elms. Though fields of olive trees, financed by substantial grants from the district authorities of Jaén, had begun to make incursions into the Sierra, this was, as El Sereno described it, 'essentially a virgin land-scape'. An impenetrable forest of oaks covered the hill in front of us, which had the evocative name of La Maleza, a word meaning 'under-growth' but with suggestions of primeval darkness. The farmsteads we passed were few and far between, and mainly in ruins or given over to goats. The occasional signpost indicating tracks leading to further farms turned out to have been painted nearly fifty years earlier by El Sereno himself. He had made them, he said, after seeing how difficult it was for anyone wanting to find their way around this once barely accessible area.

'When you come to such a wild place as this,' he reflected, 'you can see why its inhabitants took so readily to faith healing. You have to bear in mind that for centuries this was a part of the world isolated from the rest of Andalucía, without doctors, and where the nearest medical help was up to a day's journey away.'

That faith healing flourished in remote rural areas where superstition was rife and medical resources scarce was beyond any doubt. But already I sensed that this phenomenon in the Sierra Sur was underlain by factors that were less easily explicable. Ever since hearing about the 'Route of Miracles' I had tried to find out as much as I could about the district's faith healers. Santi, who had become now more relaxed in my company, had talked to me about them, and promised to bring me a book on the subject by a locally born doctor called Manuel Amezcua. From what I could gather, faith healing here was not only more widely embraced than in other, similarly isolated parts of Spain, but was also distinguished by a particularly idiosyncratic religious and mystical aspect. In this former border zone where Christianity and Islam had repeatedly replaced each other, faith healing seems to have emerged as an alternative religion. I did not know anywhere else in Spain where there were so many healers with the reputation as saints. Nor anywhere where the powers of saints were said to be handed down from one individual to the next.

My thoughts about faith healing had not just been limited to the Sierra Sur. I recalled the Irish actor Patrick McGee giving a swansong performance in a mesmerizing play on the subject by Brian Friel. And I remembered meeting witch doctors in Mali, and even a man in London who claimed to be a psychic vet. Yet, surprisingly, it was only now, as we drove deeper into the Sierra Sur, that memories slowly came back to me of the story told to me in Slovakia by the millenarian couple from Australia. Had not their faith healer been from Jaén, or was it Extremadura? And what on earth was his name? I knew it was something strange and unusual, and I was convinced that the Australians had referred to him as a *Santo*. The face was unforgettable, but all the other details about him had still to be dislodged from my subconscious.

In the meantime, as we skirted La Maleza and bumped our way across a deteriorating road towards the bare profile of the Sierra's highest mountain, the Perón, Custodio revealed the fruits of his own researches into the faith healers of the area.

'Michael, you should read this book by Manuel Amezcua, it's quite fascinating. I had a look at it last night when I knew I was coming here. Apparently faith healing is documented in the area as far back as the fifteenth century. Soon it came to be associated with the Moors who stayed on in Spain and made token conversions to Christianity.

Today it's still widely believed in. I've heard myself of people who go to their doctor and then have a further consultation with a healer, or vice versa.

'Amezcua has in any case identified four different types of modern healer. There are those who use prayers or incantations to cure such common ills as toothache or warts. Then there are the so-called "sages", reputed psychics to whom people turn to be rid of the "evil eye" and other curses. A third type are the specialists in back problems and the like, who generally have a wide knowledge of the healing qualities of plants. Finally there are the "saints", divinely ordained healers who are like intermediaries between the earthly and supernatural realms. They are people endowed with the power to see the future, and who usually have embarked on lives of miracle-working after having had a vision. They have all the trappings of devout Catholics but are not recognized by the Church. That's why perhaps there's so much secrecy surrounding their cult. Amezcua confesses to have been threatened with death if he did not abandon his researches. Curiously, while faith healing in general is on the decline, these "saints" are more popular than ever. I think we're coming now to the hamlet of one of the most important of them.'

As with yesterday's visit to El Sereno's house, I had set off on the Route of Miracles without much idea of what I was letting myself in for. Now, observing Custodio's fresh-faced look as he studied his surroundings, I wondered if he was any wiser than I was. Had I misunderstood what he told me next, or was it really true that we were on the point of meeting an actual 'saint'?

'You don't know how lucky you are to have El Sereno as your guide,' he said, as we left the road and jogged frighteningly from side to side over a track leading up to the diffuse hamlet of Cerezo Gordo. 'Without El Sereno we'd never get into the house we're going to. The man we're going to see is really strange, he doesn't admit anyone into his presence. Fortunately he'll always greet any friend of Manolo. Manolo is a man who opens many doors.'

I was becoming definitely uneasy. The growing possibility that my encounter in Slovakia had been the starting point of some much larger journey into the supernatural, together with the imminent appearance of a madman capable of revealing disquieting truths about my future, were an unsettling combination of thoughts.

'This is as far as we're going to get by car,' announced El Sereno, after we had reached a point where the track had become indistinguishable from the rocky field. We continued on foot up to the highest farm of the hamlet, pausing near the top to look back at a view in which the craggy, sharply delineated peaks of the Sierra Nevada had suddenly appeared in between the softer profiles of the Perón and La Maleza.

'You can imagine what this place is like in winter,' muttered Isa behind me, speaking from the experience of someone who had spent a Christmas trapped for days in a nearby estate. A few moments later, as we entered the upper farm, I suddenly froze on becoming aware of a thickset man with a bald head staring directly and fixedly at the two of us. Was this the 'saint' whom we had come to meet? And was he looking straight through us and into our minds and destinies?

'Domingo!' shouted El Sereno, encouraging the man's impassive, sculpted features to accommodate a faint smile, 'I've come here this time with an English writer and some other friends.' The man nodded slowly, then led us up to a patio with fig trees, a well, and flower-pots adorning a parapet overlooking the valley we had just climbed. For several minutes he and El Sereno engaged in inaudible conversation, as if involved in some conspiracy. Finally I caught something of what was being said.

'I'll come back later for the cheese,' were El Sereno's words.

By now a woman with a face as open and smiling as it was wrinkled had appeared on the threshold to greet him with a kiss. Introduced to us as Domingo's wife Ana, she welcomed us all with the same warmth and friendliness she had shown El Sereno. Ana and everyone else I would come to know in the Sierra, including the quieter and shyer Domingo, would disprove my fears of closed and suspicious mountain types, such as those whom I had met in the Alpujarra. They might have been devotees of the unofficial cult of *santos*, but there was nothing secretive or sinister about them. I reassured myself with the thought that if there really was some mysterious spirit ruling these mountains, then surely this was a force of good and not of evil.

Domingo, in any case, was clearly not the man whom Custodio had described. He and his wife were merely the custodians of the place we had come to see. Our destination lay far further away, on top of the wooded ridge that rose in front of us. El Sereno pointed to a solitary white building standing just above the trees, and Domingo mumbled something about the owner being there, and that other visitors had preceded us.

We followed a footpath across a field of stubble and up into a near-vertical wood obstructed by boulders and bramble. Breathing hard we fought our way up into the ridge top clearing across which were spread the scattered ruins of Cerrillo del Olivo. 'This is the farm of the Santo Luisico,' said Merce. 'He has followers from all over Spain.'

A Land Rover with a Barcelona registration plate was parked at the end of a track El Sereno had forsaken in favour of our shorter but far more arduous approach. I did not have time to ask either him or Merce whether the Santo Luisico was still alive and about to receive us when the two of them went off to join a group of four people who stood outside the entrance to a small white courtyard. Among them was a tall old man with crutches and wild, staring eyes. 'Who's that?' I asked Custodio, who shook his head, and then confessed he had never been here before.

I wondered whether the old man was the Santo Luisico, and whether he was old enough to have been the healer visited by the Australians in the early 1960s. But these thoughts were interrupted by his disappearance into the Land Rover, assisted by two young men who could have been his sons. A middle-aged woman, not much older than myself, was waving them goodbye.

'This is Maiquel, an English writer,' said El Sereno, presenting me to her. Her name was Mercedes, and she had delicate features and sparkling deep brown eyes. 'She's the great-granddaughter of the Santo Luisico,' whispered Merce, as we crossed the crudely plastered brick courtyard towards an open door. There, in a miniature white room with a painted beam ceiling, the saint was waiting for us – in the form of an old sepia photograph, surrounded by a polychrome lava flow of devotional images, ex-votos, plastic flowers and other floral offerings as densely packed as the plants in a tropical forest.

'He died in 1912,' Mercedes explained. 'This photo was taken towards the end of his life, when he was in his mid-eighties.'

Luisico had been an ordinary shepherd boy who one evening had failed to return from the fields at his usual time. His worried parents went out to look for him and found him happily playing, but strangely different from his normal self, as if transformed by a divine visitation. All that he told them was that from then on there was nothing he would ever lack. The special powers he had acquired that day became widely known, and people travelled from afar to tell him their problems and ask for his help. They did not have to talk for long. He sensed immediately what was wrong with them. He refused to charge for his services, and the presents he received would always be given away to those with needs greater than his own.

Most of his recorded miracles, as far as I could make out, seemed largely to have been in response to those who had doubted or had tried to curb his miraculous powers. On one occasion a group of strangers had attempted to kill him with a poisoned cigar. As they sat down to watch him light it, he cut off the cigar's affected part, and calmly smoked the rest. On another occasion, after he had been denounced by doctors, two officers of the *Guardia Civil* went to arrest him, but were literally stuck to their seats and unable to rise until he decided he was ready to accompany them. Later, after he had been brought to the police station in Valdepeñas, the two officers fled on seeing a crucifix mysteriously replace his squiggled mark on a document he had been forced to sign.

Another miracle helped perhaps to account for the structural decay of the house where he had lived for most of his life. During a terrible storm he had taken refuge in his bedroom, the roof tiles of which had remained completely dry. Neighbours who observed this later carried away many of the tiles as relics, some of which have survived to this day as talismans against bad weather. The miracle that the house did not afterwards fall entirely to the ground was due greatly to Mercedes herself, who, though living for most of the year in the town of Jaén, had always maintained the building as a shrine to her great-grandfather. Numerous people, such as the Barcelona family who had just left, continued to come here in the hope of the saint's posthumous assistance, and to thank him for what he still managed to achieve from beyond the grave.

I asked Mercedes if she minded my photographing the shrine. 'Of course not,' she replied, before adding, with a smile, that if the face of the Santo Luisico remained a blank in my photo this meant I was a person of no faith. This was what apparently had happened when a sceptical contemporary of the saint had tried to photograph the man himself. And history had repeated itself only a few weeks ago, when Andalucía's main television channel had been filming inside the building, only to discover later that nothing had come out. I was not quite sure how seriously I was meant to take Mercedes. She seemed a down-to-earth, sophisticated, no-nonsense woman with a good sense of humour. Could such a person really believe the story she then related about the Santo Luisico's hands?

She made me first of all look carefully at the photograph of her great-grandfather, who was shown sitting on an upright wickerwork chair, with his hands resting on either knee, one of which was covered by the broad-brimmed hat he was holding. Over the last twelve years or so, she said, the hands had been changing position. 'They are moving,' she said, 'so that the left, free hand can grasp the hat as well.' There seemed little point in asking her why this should be so, or indeed in suggesting that the ghostly outlines marking the original position of the hat and hands were the result of a long exposure, during which the subject had moved. I just murmured with interest and went ahead to take my own photo of the Santo Luisico. A few weeks later, when I had this developed, the saint's features were reproduced with the sharpest of clarity. My faith was obviously strong enough to withstand a healthy degree of scepticism.

There was little else of the house to be seen. Stooping, as I had to whenever I visited any old house in Frailes, I entered three miniature white rooms, including the saint's bedroom, which was as cell-like as El Sereno's. 'Even at the height of summer,' Mercedes told me, 'you have to sleep here covered in blankets.' Yet, for all the Spartan nature of living conditions at Cerrillo del Olivo, the place projected a sense of calm, contentment, coziness, as if truly nothing more was needed to improve it. Even the wild surroundings were far more hospitable than they were threatening.

While the others in our group lingered talking, I went briefly outside again, past the isolated walnut tree that stood in the middle of the clearing, and over to a large rock at the very edge of the ridge, where oaks clustered in profusion. The rock formed a comfortable throne on which I sat dreamily, enjoying the sensation of being suspended in a realm of my own. It was not until nearly two years later, after numerous return visits to this most relaxing of sites, that I found that the rock had been the favourite seat of the Santo Luisico himself. Here he prayed for hours, and here he received his visitors, offering them consolation that I imagined must have drawn strength from the beauty of the surroundings.

Before venturing further along the Route of Miracles, Merce waved me back inside the shrine again to show me a framed print whose full meaning had only just been revealed to her. It was a crude devotional picture I had seen a couple of times before in Frailes, and which I had interpreted as a representation of some saintly local priest blessing a parishioner. The standing man wearing what I took to be a dog-collar was the Santo Luisico, while the elderly-seeming person with a full head of hair kneeling before him was in fact a poorly drawn shepherd boy known as Custodio Pérez Aranda. Lying on the ground between them was the former's hat, which was tilted at an angle towards the spectator.

'If you look closely at the hat,' said Merce, 'what do you see?'

I could have been doing a Rorschach test, for all I could see at first was what I reckoned to be the ink smudges of a bad first impression of the print.

'Come on, look carefully,' she urged.

On staring for a few more moments, a head began to take shape before my eyes, a rounded head with a distinctively cropped fringe that provoked a chill of recognition.

'I've never found this head here until today,' she said, 'though I've seen the print a hundred times.'

Then she told me what she had learnt that day from the great-granddaughter of the Santo Luisico. The print depicted the saint two years before his death, when he was visited by the young Pérez Aranda. The two of them had conversed for hours, and established such a special relationship that when the boy kissed the saint's hands, the latter did the same to him. Those who witnessed this scene knew then that the Santo Luisico had found his successor, the person who would one day inherit his powers. In the print the artist had rendered this moment of realization by portraying the face of the man whom Pérez Aranda would one day grow into.

'You are staring,' said Merce, tantalizing me with the longest of pauses, 'at the face of the most revered saint of them all. The Santo Custodio.'

I could not as yet be sure if this was the person I had heard about in Slovakia, but at least I had solved the mystery as to why there were so many Custodios in this area. What I could not understand was why no one, seeing my interest in the name Custodio, had been able to tell me before that its popularity here was due to the veneration of a local healer. The discovery of the face in the hat, however, would prove to be a symbolical turning point. It was like my initiation into a cult that brought me new insight into Frailes itself, and which I was able both to joke about and to take deadly seriously in almost equal measures.

The skeleton facts of Custodio's life were given to me by Merce as we stayed a few more more minutes in the shrine. In the following days I would try and supplement these with what I could find in the village library. But his was a life that had been recorded mainly in people's memories, and even the supposed facts varied according to the source. The general consensus was that he was born in 1885 and died in 1960, on the 15th of August, the very day celebrating the Assumption of the Virgin. For all these years he had barely strayed from the hamlet which we were now going to visit, La Hoya del Salobral. His particular way of healing involved rubbing a person's back and scribbling on pieces of cigarette paper, which were then swallowed by the patient. As with the Santo Luisico, he gained the disapproval of doctors, never accepted money, and was always willing to work a miracle to confound the sceptical. On the day of his death hundreds from Frailes and the vicinity rushed to La Hoya to carry the saint's body over the mountains to its final resting place.

'And who was his own successor?' I asked.

'The Santo Manuel,' Merce replied. 'He lived in a village near Alcalá, and died there in about 1982.'

'And who has the powers now?'

'No one knows, though of course there have been many rumours.'

We strolled the slow way back to Cerezo Gordo, Merce and I taking up the rear, together with her son Alejandro and sister Isa. The idea of a mountain dynasty of miracle-workers, and the question of their as yet unrevealed successor, had seized my imagination. Of all the people I had met in Frailes Merce, with her evident status as uncrowned queen of the village, had the right degree of mysterious charisma and universal appeal to be the most likely candidate. And if she were not the one then it might one day be Alejandro. He had his mother's compelling presence, a fearlessness unusual for his age, and a sweetness of manner that both helped him get what he wanted, and gave him the aura of a child possessed by godliness.

In a moment of sudden inspiration, I then blurted out El Sereno's name. 'Could it be him?' I asked in a half-jesting tone. 'He certainly seems a saintly person.' In the twenty-four hours since knowing him I had already heard a wealth of anecdotes that lent weight to all that I had observed myself about his character. No one apparently had done so much for Frailes as he had. His creation of the road signs in the Sierra Sur typified the thoughtfulness of someone who had devoted much of his life to helping people, whether ensuring the well-being of visitors such as myself, donating parts of his property to the town hall, doing errands for anyone who asked him, visiting the sick in hospital, or even distributing ice creams to children on the annual village procession honouring the Eucharist.

'I'm not sure if he's a saint,' smiled Isa, who had been good friends with him long before her sister had. 'But I agree that he's a very unusual and special person. I mean, what other villager do you know of his age and generation who's so open to new people and experiences? It was only a year or so ago when he was happily mingling with the nudists and hippies of Almería.'

The story of El Sereno's Almerían experiences, involving his being asked to soap the back of a completely naked young German woman, and then accepting an invitation to spend a night beating drums in a cave, was one of the many I would soon be hearing from the man himself. It might not have enhanced his saintliness, but it helped further my increasingly fantastical image of him. His tales, embellished with each telling, and already part of Frailes lore, would soon be as vivid in my mind as any of the stories connected with the Sierra's saints.

'He must have special powers,' Isa pointed out, 'to have survived so many years of dreadful driving.'

'That's nothing to do with him,' interrupted Merce, 'he's just been lucky enough to have driven always in a land protected by the Santo Custodio.' She laughed as I looked at her as if to question the seriousness of her statement.

Almost exactly at this moment a widow in black with unruly hair and restless eyes joined us as we walked down the track. 'The Santo Custodio and the Santo Luisico,' she said, seeing that we were obviously returning from a visit to the latter's shrine, 'there's never been anyone like them since. They really had the powers; today's healers are merely charlatans.'

Back once more on the road, we returned to the chapel above Los Rosales, from where we headed off this time towards the hamlet of the Santo Custodio. A pale crescent moon was visible in the sky as we skirted fields and woods that had been reduced to darkening shadows. Ahead of us, and made sharper and more brilliantly orange by contrast with the sea of gloom below, projected a rocky outcrop shaped like Cape Town's Table Mountain, and as ethereal as Australia's Ayers Rock.

In the darkness at its foot was the elongated hamlet of La Hoya del Salobral which, to many of the followers of the Santo Custodio, was known simply as La Joya (the jewel). This hamlet, a far more sizeable one than the handful of farms comprising Cerezo Gordo, had been described to me by El Sereno as a place of extraordinary poverty. But when we arrived both he and Isa, who had not been here for some time, were amused and amazed by the spread of prosperous-looking chalets (in keeping with the last, newly surfaced stretch of road), and by the presence not only of a shop but also of a branch of the *Caja Rural* of Jaén. When Merce and her husband Caño got out of the car behind us, they were almost shaking their heads in disbelief. Such was their response at finding a *Caja Rural* at La Hoya that I began envisaging some future painted scene depicting the bank's miraculous appearance to the shepherds.

We had parked in a miniature square, next to a free-standing monument encased in railings and topped by a bronze statuette of the 'Ángel Custodio'. This memorial to Custodio Pérez Aranda stood directly in front of the house that had been the place both of his birth and of his death. Though there was not a glimmer of light coming from it, El Sereno knocked hard on the large, forbidding old door. 'He won't be wanting to see visitors at this hour,' pleaded Merce, too late to stop him.

'He's definitely in there,' replied El Sereno, after several ineffectual attempts to rouse this mysterious being. Caño, teasing El Sereno for his insistence, explained to me that the 'he' in question was the Santo Custodio's son Enrique.

'Enrique,' he said, 'is a living corpse who has suffered all his life for being whom he is. People are convinced he must have some of his father's powers.'

A passer-by told us that Enrique was indeed at home, but that he turned a deaf ear to anyone who came knocking outside of the morning visiting hours. I was not too disappointed. A sensational sunset seemed imminent, and everyone was keen to reach the top of 'Ayers Rock', from where we would be able to enjoy the spectacle from outside 'the cave where the Santo Custodio used to pray'.

A road marked simply '*Ermita*' set us on our way. Climbing sharply in its early stages, it passed next to a fountain where a sign clearly indicated that the water was not drinkable.

'Not drinkable perhaps, but miraculous yes,' laughed Isa, pointing out to me a group of women lining up in the semi-darkness to fill their containers with water blessed by the shadow of the Santo Custodio.

In Custodio's day the only way up to the rock's bare, exposed heights was by one of the many sheep tracks created by the animals that the saint himself had guarded. Now a modern road had been cut directly into the cliffside, making the ascent feasible in little more than a matter of minutes. On its final bend the road went through a metal arch wrapped in the tattered remains of a floral festoon. The flattened ridge beyond was covered with what seemed like modern white barrack buildings arranged in parallel lines on either side of an equally new chapel, whose main portal stood above a small flight of steps.

'The Catholic Church,' said El Sereno, warming to what I soon found to be one of his favourite themes, 'always wants to be the protagonist.' He then made clear his atheism, and his hatred of the Church for hoodwinking people, and for persuading the poor and gullible to hand over all their money.

'Every time I come here,' he said forcibly, 'this place gets more and more commercialized. There was nothing here once except for the memories of a simple man whose hold over people began to frighten the Church. When they saw that the death of this man did nothing to curtail his popularity, and that more and more people came to La Hoya to visit this mountain, then they began to get frightened. They didn't want to be left in the shadow, so they constructed this large chapel and dedicated it to the famous votive image of the Virgin of La Cabeza. Every year, on the last weekend of April, more than than 10,000 people come here as part of the festive pilgrimage in honour of the Virgin. That's why there are all these buildings. They're for the different Brotherhoods who organize the event.'

The rest of our group had caught up with us by the time we reached the entrance to the chapel, which we decided not to enter in the interests of catching the sunset.

'The pilgrimage is of course just an excuse to pay homage to the Santo Custodio,' intervened Caño after we had started to ascend a concrete path built into the rock behind the last of the shrine's buildings. 'Naturally you couldn't put that in print,' he continued, 'everyone would be up in arms. The whole cult of Custodio is still very secretive.' I confessed that La Hoya and its shrine did not appear even in the most detailed guidebooks to Andalucía I had seen.

We were all pausing for breath when Caño came out with a revealing story.

'I'm not a believer in these saints, nor am I a practising Catholic. My wife's different, well you know she's a bit unusual . . .' He laughed before launching again into his tale. 'But my parents are believers, they've got better reason to be so. When she'd only just married, my mother developed this strange affliction, she began feeling this numbness in her legs, then she could barely walk at all. The doctors in Jaén couldn't do anything at all, so she and my father decided to go and see the Santo Custodio. She was carried to La Hoya on the back of a donkey, and when she arrived . . .'

There was no need for Caño to finish the story, I knew exactly how it would end. Every detail of the conversation I had had with the Australian couple in Slovakia came suddenly back to me.

'. . . The Santo Custodio, without asking what was wrong, said you must get off the donkey, and you'll find you'll walk again as before. And this is exactly what happened,' concluded Caño, echoing almost word by word lines that had been lost for so long in my consciousness.

A tall, emaciated man dressed entirely in white, who looked after a religious knick-knack stall at the bottom of the path, was now hanging around us. 'He drives me mad,' whispered Merce, 'he's always standing next to you, totally destroying the magic of this spot.' We tried to forget him as we stared out across a deep valley at the now crimson Sierra Nevada which, as in the culmination of a symphony when all the instruments and musical themes come triumphantly together, was stretched along the horizon in its near unimpeded entirety.

'This is what it's really about,' murmured El Sereno for my benefit only. 'The emotions we feel here are really nothing to do with religion or the esoteric. What really matters is the beauty of nature, that's why the people who come here are so moved.'

The man in white, who seemed to have overheard some of these words, accompanied us like a gaoler as we dragged our tired bodies up to a rock shelter topped by a totem-like crucifix wound with ribbons and flowers. Carved in primitive joined-up writing, which at first I mistook for runic script, was an inscription recording this was the cave where the Santo Custodio 'came to pray and contemplate'. A metal ladder led down inside, where candles were burning and offerings and portrait photos had been placed by those whom the saint had cured.

'You'll find all sorts of things down there,' said El Sereno. 'I've even found a bra and pants.'

I descended up to my neck, which was as far as it was possible to go. Then, bending down to survey the walls and ground below, I felt the warmth and smell of scented candles against my face. And then I saw it: the final proof. The same pumpkin-like head. The geometrically cropped fringe. The pasted-on eyebrows. The impassive stare. The proof perhaps that I had been making fun of the forces ruling my destiny.

In the darkness that followed we carefully trod our way down to the souvenir stall next to the chapel. I scrutinized all the objects featuring the Santo Custodio: the keyrings, the bumper stickers, the necklaces, the heart-shaped caskets, the ceramic water stoops, the medallions showing the saint's face as the obverse of the Virgin of La Cabeza. And then I picked up the passport-sized photo that I had first seen so long ago in distant Slovakia. 'You can have that,' said the man in white, opening his mouth for the first time.

And I put it immediately in my wallet, where it has remained to this day.

5

A T THE TIME I thought of it as a miracle. It happened a few days
after my rediscovery of the Santo Custodio, when I was trying to
see if I could make further progress with my Lope de Vega translation. I doubted whether this would be possible, but thought that at
least the attempt would assuage the occasional pangs of guilt caused
by my ever more indolent lifestyle. By midday, to my surprise, I had
already completed the difficult first scene, and was well into the
second. It was as if a key to unlocking the meaning of Lope's text had
mysteriously become available to me.

With this key apparently in my possession I began translating with
a fluency that made me wonder at times whether my hand was being
directed by some other spirit, perhaps even by the author himself.
Long poetic speeches, rich in metaphors and double meanings,
flowed from my pen with baffling ease. And when eventually I
reached a section of the play so complex that I thought I would never
be able to make my way through it unassisted, I discovered that one
of Spain's leading experts in the textual analysis of Lope's plays spent
his weekends at nearby Sant Ana.

I would certainly have finished my translation had I not been constantly distracted by the very world I now held responsible for rescu-
ing me from my difficulties. After our excursion to the Sierra, El
Sereno and his friends kept on suggesting activities that would bring
us altogether again, and reduce my available time for working to a
healthy minimum. Once they all invaded my rented house to cook
lunch for us all, believing that my friends and I would be incapable of
organizing such a feast ourselves. The one notable absence was the
house's owner, Custodio, who, for all his knowledge and theoretical
interest in local faith healers, had seemed very much the outsider on

our journey along the Route of Miracles. Afterwards he had tried unsuccessfully on two or three occasions to invite me over to Alcalá, after which he never again took part in any of our group activities. The gulf that separated the Fraileros from the Alcalaínos was broadening in my imagination, in parallel with my increasingly childlike vision of a world reduced to the simplicity of a fairy tale.

Our lunch in the garden was copious, and had to be followed by a walk on foot to the Cueva, along an overgrown path Merce was sure I had yet to discover. Soon we were all scrambling through the wood at the bottom of the garden, which led down to a stream whose little remaining water formed a series of pools shaded by brambles and elms. El Sereno, with Merce's two children closely at his heels, boldly led the way across a rotting tree trunk that served as a bridge. Once across, we followed the stream into an opening carpeted with mint, nettles, and the faded yellow of wilted daisies. Further on, some of us stopped to collect blackberries from a bush that marked the edge of this wild patch. As we did so, El Sereno told us a story.

'At the end of the nineteenth century,' he began, 'when the garden where we've just been eating formed the grounds of a fashionable spa, there was a poor shepherd's boy who went to the spa every morning to sell goat's milk to those taking the cure. One day a wealthy woman from Madrid asked him for a special favour. She had a craving, she said, for blackberries. The boy went off to get some, and threw them into the pannier strapped to his donkey, but then realized he would have to find a more attractive way of presenting them to her. So he placed the berries in a basket, which he decorated with a pink ribbon tied into a large bow. The woman was so delighted that she invited the boy to come back with her to Madrid. She promised to provide him with an education, and to treat him no differently from her own children. The boy grew up to be a professor of philosophy, and a rector at Seville University . . .'

This mythical-sounding tale, in conjunction with the flow of poetic images that was running through my Lope-steeped mind, helped give an additional romantic tinge to my perception of Frailes. As we continued on our late afternoon walk, with El Sereno leading us on like some benign Pied Piper, I became gradually more conscious that this romantic world through which I was treading had, like the best of tales, an element of pathos.

'If only you had known Frailes then,' said Merce, referring to the days when she had walked along this path as a schoolgirl. We were now approaching the village across the narrow band of fields that lay between the cemetery hill and the cliff crowned by El Sereno's garden. Framed now by foreground trees, and forming a picturesquely variegated silhouette rising above a patchwork of fields, the place seemed if anything at its unspoiled best. But Merce was not thinking of the recent urban changes to Frailes, but rather of the drought whose potentially disastrous consequences had only now begun to be fully apparent to me.

'Even at the height of August,' Merce continued, 'everything you see in front of you was green, bright green. It was a paradise.'

'Frailes,' agreed El Sereno, 'was a village that everyone envied. Everywhere you went there was rushing water, the place was famed for the abundance of its springs. But now the springs are drying up, the river below us is just a trickle. I've heard some of the more elderly villagers say that this is the worst drought in living memory. It hasn't rained since October of last year.'

The lament that Frailes had never been the same since the recent drought was one I would keep on hearing. During what remained of this first summer in Frailes, it served as a reminder of a darker presence lurking in a world which in all other respects was becoming for me ever more idyllic and Arcadian.

In the company of my village friends I would devote longer and longer hours to picnics, evening strolls, and drives in the surrounding Sierra, which I recognized increasingly as one of the most beautiful mountainous areas of Southern Spain still untouched by tourism. In the course of these outings the boundaries were slowly being mapped out of a personal domain centred on a handful of locations to which I would continually return, such as the shrine of the Santo Luisico and the cave of the Santo Custodio.

The most important new addition to this magical geography was a huge estate known as Puerta Alta, which was left as the last major trip of the summer. It was a place which El Sereno had been promising to take me to ever since we had stood outside the Santo Custodio's cave and contemplated the sublime panorama crested by the Sierra Nevada.

'There,' El Sereno had said, pointing to one of this landscape's deep, hidden folds, 'is where a friend of ours has an estate. You couldn't imagine anywhere so beautiful, so cut off from the outside world. There you'll find pure-bred horses and animals of every description. We must go there one day.'

And so, on the last afternoon of August, the by now familiar convoy of Land Rovers assembled once again outside the Cueva. I opted this time not to travel in El Sereno's Suzuki: I took fright on hearing that one of the ways to get to Puerta Alta was along a track clinging to a sheer precipice. Instead I went in Caño's car, together with Merce and their two children. El Sereno was nonetheless allowed to be at the front of the convoy, which we soon realized was a terrible mistake. 'Where on earth's that madman going to?' exclaimed Caño as the Suzuki turned unexpectedly on to a track that led off from the isolated olive-oil factory where Miguel had once taken me.

It had been Caño's and Merce's idea to go to Puerta Alta by a less direct but safer route than the one I had originally heard about. But the gently ascending road through olive groves on which we had started out had clearly proved too unchallenging for El Sereno. Now we found ourselves following him at great speed along a track covered by rubble from landslides, and permanently tilted, so it seemed, at a forty-five degree angle. Under these circumstances it was difficult to give our full attention to the beauty of a changing landscape in which ever steeper slopes broke wave-like into cliffs falling down into the deciduous woods below.

We entered the woods and finally rejoined our original route, after one final, gravity-defying movement of the car. El Sereno had got out of the Suzuki to wait for us.

'What did you think of my short cut?' he asked, beaming like a child.

'You're sacked as leader,' said Caño, shaking his head with amused disbelief.

We went to the head of the convoy, and continued climbing up a valley where rows of elms stood out above large patches of straw-like grass and dense areas of holm-oaks so dry that they looked as if they might ignite with a single spark.

'Just look at those trees,' sighed Merce. 'They're yellowing from lack of water. They've survived for hundreds of years, and now they'll die if it doesn't rain soon.'

We stopped the car at what appeared to be the top of a pass. A large metal gate blocked our entry to a track that deviated off to the left.

'We might have to go back all the way we came,' Caño informed me, as Merce went off to search for a key 'which might or might not be there'. Then she pulled up a stone and turned to face us with a broad smile. 'It was in its usual place,' she said with relief, before letting us pass through into what were apparently the uppermost limits of the estate we had come to visit.

Before descending to the heart of the estate we veered off cross-country along a bare and narrowing ridge which formed a spectacular belvedere. The antlers of deer could be seen rushing away from us as we approached, to disappear down the near-vertical slopes that came to face us on three sides. Caño, who had a mischievous, childish streak comparable to that of El Sereno, pretended to chase the deer in our car, and drove at accelerating speed towards the void.

'Stop! Stop!' implored Merce as a smiling Caño pulled up yards away from the precipice.

We walked out to see the views. El Sereno, more agile and daring than ever, encouraged us to slide down to a large rock that jutted directly above a terrifying cliff. I felt like one of the diminutive figures in a romantic landscape by Caspar David Friedrich as I stood there, my stomach turning, looking towards the entire range of the Sierra Nevada. Merce, shouting to me to be careful, urged me to turn back and come with her to enjoy the views in the opposite direction, towards the distinctively shaped rocky outcrop in which the Santo Custodio's cave was situated. We sat down on a slope of herbs to observe a steep-sided valley guarded at either end by dramatic gorges. Far, far below, between cliffs and a small patch of fields extending to the other side of a dried-up river, was a large, white *cortijo* built by the owner of this wilderness.

This person, it turned out, was a cousin of Merce, Santiago Pérez. He was an entirely self-made man who had accumulated his money in property speculation, pinball machines, discotheques, and olive oil. Yet he had remained, according to Merce, a person with a warm and simple heart who loved nature. When it came to business he was someone who 'turned to gold everything he touched'. But his luck had not extended to his personal life. His first wife, and the child they were expecting, had died while she was giving birth. Now he had married again, to a tall and blonde Alcalaína who did not share his enthusiasm for the country, and never went to Frailes, but mingled instead with the social elite of Alcalá. Amazingly, claimed Merce, she never came to her husband's estate. It was his private passion, a place to entertain his hunting friends, and to escape for the odd day or so from the small-town world where he lived.

'If I were him I would want to stay here all the time,' commented Merce as I sat silently watching an eagle soar in and out of the gorge immediately below us.

Later, as we snaked down in the car towards the *cortijo*, we caught repeated glimpses of deer, mountain goats and ibex.

'If we're very lucky we might even see a wild boar,' said Caño, who then added, presumably (I thought) as a joke, 'there are also wild bulls around, they're one of the hazards if you decide to go for a walk.' At the bottom of the track Merce stopped to open another gate, on which was written on the other side, 'Danger, Keep Out, Wild Bulls'.

'To be accurate,' corrected Merce, 'I think there's only one left now. There were originally three or four that the owner decided to keep here for his own amusement.'

We drove past stables, a caged enclosure with a solitary boar, kennels for hunting dogs, a couple of dozing mastiffs on chains, a gaggle of geese, strutting peacocks, dozens of staring goats, and a miniature bullring. Then we came to a halt in a large, gravel-covered forecourt that surrounded the *cortijo*'s main building. A formidable coat of arms carved in stone was attached to one of the walls, and confirmed my hunch that the building must date back at least to the seventeenth century. However, I found it difficult to imagine what sort of eccentric aristocrat of that period would wish to create an estate in such a remote and agriculturally unproductive location.

As we all waited outside for the massive front door to be opened from within, I asked El Sereno if he knew anything about the building's history.

'Yes,' he affirmed, 'the place was built five or six years ago. The entwined S and P on the coat of arms stands for Santiago Pérez, the cousin of Merce who owns the estate. Before he came here there was just a tiny farm. I remember once in the 1960s, when I had begun working in the Frailes pharmacy, the farmer's wife fell seriously ill, and there was no available doctor to go to such a faraway place. So I had to go myself and decide what was wrong with her. That was my first visit to Puerta Alta, and perhaps my first medical diagnosis. Miraculously, the woman recovered.'

The door was finally pulled ajar by a large-featured young woman with a bewildered, slightly shy expression. She had the unusual name of Leticia, which struck me as the sort of name Lope de Vega might have chosen for one of the buxom maids in his plays. Her husband, Juan Pedro, made his appearance shortly afterwards, astride a thoroughbred horse on which he was practicing dressage. Lithe and handsome, with a confident poise, light brown beard, and elegantly tilted cloth cap, he seemed the perfect courtly companion for any Leticia. Already I was envisaging Puerta Alta as the setting for some theatrical drama.

El Sereno, whom I noticed had a weakness for young women, began chatting away to the perplexed Leticia. Merce meanwhile asked Leticia's husband how long they had been looking after the estate. Juan Pedro answered that they had taken over a month ago from his uncle and aunt, and that there could not be a better place for a newly married couple to live.

'Once you experience the sort of peace you get here,' he said with a smile, 'you would never want to live again with lots of other people.'

'But doesn't it ever get lonely?' I asked.

'Never', he firmly replied.

We all now turned to look at El Sereno, who was touching Leticia's arm and telling her a joke. Then he rounded us all up to take us on a tour of the building, which he treated almost as if it were his own property. From the broad vestibule, with its traditional cobbled floor, he led us into a dining room that had something of the character of a Scottish baronial hall. A massive chimney breast, with a roasting spit placed right in the middle, spread across the whole width of one of the walls, while all around were hunting trophies, at least two of which must have been acquired on an African safari. Gothic-style metal candelabra hung from a wooden-beam ceiling, immediately above a chunky dining-room table made from a single piece of oak of sequoia-like proportions. The only obvious sign that we were in Andalucía was the abundance of framed photographs on the walls, which revealed that Santiago Pérez was a lover of flamenco and bull-fighting. In some of them a smiling, bald-headed, middle-aged man, whom Merce identified as Santiago himself, could be seen next to two of the leading bullfighters of the moment: one of these was the child prodigy 'El Juli', the other was the gallant Jesulín de Ubrique, who had once famously fought a fight for women only. Jesulín, I gathered, was a regular guest at Puerta Alta. He came here to escape the attentions of the press, and to be able to lead a private life unobserved.

Images of secret seductions and romantic weekends gave an additional appeal to the next part of the tour, which involved climbing up the wooden staircase that led from the dining room into the bedrooms above. In a way that I had already begun to discover was special to Frailes, there was no part of the house, however minor and uninteresting, that was not included on our visit. El Sereno made us examine and admire cupboards, toilets, light fittings, bedside tables and other such details as he went from one room to the next, each of which had the name of a local beauty spot. The room that best aroused my fantasies of an idyllic love nest was *El arroyo de oro* ('the golden stream), which had a four-poster double bed, and an en suite bathroom, where El Sereno, like a magician performing his greatest trick, revealed to us a jacuzzi.

From the darkened interior, with its overall impression of heavy wood and sombre ceramic floor tiles, we moved into the brilliance of an unmistakably Andalucían courtyard. There was an old well in the centre, and white walls that vividly showed up the exotic birdcages and colourful flowerpots that had been placed against them. Off one of the sides was a chapel-like space functioning as the *cortijo's* bodega. I felt a slight wariness as Juan Pedro poured out from an oak barrel a sherry glass of 'home-made wine'. But this proved to be wholly unlike the acid, drug-like liquid I had known in Frailes. Smooth and refreshingly cool, it helped further lighten our mood as we took in a decoration consisting entirely of bullfighting mementoes, including the stuffed head of a bull that Jesulín had killed in a fight in which he had been awarded the animal's two ears. The bright cape that had been used in the same contest was also on show, and was of such thick material that it stood up of its own accord, like some phantasmagoric apparition. El Sereno, after making us all feel the great weight of this object, then took it out into the courtyard and treated us to a remarkably skilful display of the art of the *capote*. Caño gave a convincing performance as a charging bull.

The shadows were lengthening as at the conclusion of a real bullfight when Merce hurried us all outside to take us to a site we 'simply could not miss'. Walking down to the river we stumbled along its stony, dry bed towards the narrow gorge that opened up a few hundred yards away from the *cortijo*. I looked up to see the same eagle whose flight had so entranced me from above. It was soaring now towards the cliff, where Merce directed my glance towards a huge natural arch, which she said was the reason why the *cortijo* had been named Puerta Alta, 'The High Gate'. The eagle glided right through the middle of it, then swooped sharply upwards as if threading the eye of a Brobdingnagian needle.

A different type of gate, in barbed wire, closed off the entrance to the gorge, and featured another warning of wild bulls beyond. Juan Pedro, over our glass of wine, had told me that the estate's one surviving bull was a giant creature who had last been spotted in the pastures on this gorge's further side. I was assured that 'he was rarely seen', but I was glad of the relaxing effects of the wine as we pursued down a gorge that would have made the perfect setting for an ambush in a Western. The sunlight now was touching only the crests of the sheer cliffs that closed in on us on either side. The scenario of some real bull rushing towards us in this place of no escape was one I preferred not to contemplate. Suddenly Merce nudged my arm. I prepared to run, but she merely wanted to show me the cliff-top tree to which her brother Pepín, paralyzed with fear, had clung for several hours after losing his grip while hunting for birds. 'He's never come back to Puerta Alta again,' she said.

We emerged into the warm colours of a late afternoon to see the river bed disappear behind reeds and thickets. El Sereno, stealthily guiding the way like some native American scout, gestured to us to remain absolutely still. I almost let out a shriek when, a few moments later, the bush directly in front of us shook violently to release from its protection a huge beast.

'It's ages since I've got so close to a deer,' El Sereno calmly commented as the antlered animal leaped in great bounds towards the horizon.

Once we had made our way back to the *cortijo*, Merce announced that we only had the horses left to see. Juan told us that they were out to pasture, and pointed to a distant sloping field on the other side of the river bed. There, below rocky crags, grazed about fifty horses which El Sereno claimed were among the finest Spain had to offer. We went towards them on foot, eventually to slip under a corrugated iron fence and enter their field. El Sereno made a clicking noise with his mouth, a sound he used indiscriminately to attract the attention of all animals, including the odd human. Within a few seconds horses were stampeding towards us from every direction.

For a timid urbanite who had been known to run away from an advancing flock of sheep, the sight of these speeding horses was disconcerting. 'They're harmless, noble creatures,' said Merce and El Sereno almost in unison. Yet it was not until they were a few feet from us and had slowed down as suddenly as they had started to gallop that I was able finally to relax. What I had interpreted as savage fury turned out to be merely curiosity in their new visitors, and a desire to be stroked. These were truly special animals which made me understand, for the first time in my life, how humans could develop such strong equine passions. Gentle and affectionate, with smooth brown skins and magnificently groomed black manes and tails, they had the stature and unreality of horses from ancient mythology. As I stood patting and stroking them, and receiving in return the odd kiss on the back of my neck, I realized the extent to which my whole attitude to nature had recently begun to change. Until coming to Frailes I had seen nature essentially as a series of potential hazards and inconveniences, balanced by the odd aesthetic experience. The idea of achieving oneness with it was not only sentimental nonsense but also, in my case, wholly unimaginable. Now I was not so sure.

The knowledge that my stay in Frailes was shortly coming to an end certainly contributed to my mood. Regret at having soon to leave behind so much beauty had by the end of the afternoon at Puerta Alta superseded every other emotion, even my anxieties about being driven by El Sereno. On our return journey to Frailes, I was feeling sufficiently emboldened to climb into his Suzuki, even though we had opted to return to the village the precipitous way. Despite repeated sharp manoeuvres that threatened to hurl us down to the fast diminishing *cortijo* below, I was able to absorb myself in an expanding panorama in which the orange red profile of the Sierra Nevada eventually made its appearance above the darkening valley. And as I did so, I searched for excuses other than the pull of destiny to bring me back as soon as possible to a corner of Spain I was coming to think of as my own.

The following evening, when only two of our party remained in our rented house, I gave my first interview to the *Ideal de Jaén*. Santi, the village chronicler, had been responsible for arranging this, and came to see me with a young woman journalist from Alcalá with ambitions to be a poetess. Their combined article, when it eventually appeared, would take up an entire page of the paper, and have as its title the words 'No place so welcoming'. It contained descriptions of the costumed visit of Merce and her friends, the impact on me of Miguel's 'traditional cooking', my fascination with the area's saintly faith healers, and my budding friendship with 'the popular local personality El Sereno'. At the end of this article, which unquestionably assumed I would become from now onwards a regular visitor to Frailes, I was asked if I would ever consider writing about the village. In the unlikely event of my doing so, I replied, I could assure the readers of *El Ideal* that my portrait of Frailes would be an entirely favourable one, penned from the heart.

My difficulty in replying to this last question stemmed from a genuine conflict within me. As with so many British lovers of Spain, I had been seduced at an early age by the Hispanist Gerald Brenan's *South from Granada*, his account of moving in the 1920s to the then obscure and exotically remote Alpujarran village of Yegen. The idea of trying to follow in Brenan's footsteps was one that had perhaps taken root in me as a teenager. However, I now knew how impossible it was to write up one's experiences of a place without offending those who had taken one into their confidence. What is more, I was wary of perpetuating the genre of rural Mediterranean escapism that Brenan's pioneering and unsentimental book had unwittingly inspired.

It would take many more months of exposure to Frailes to enable me to resolve these doubts. For the time being, however, my interest in the village was not so much as a subject in itself but as a place ruled by a kindly spirit that seemed very favourable to writers. The breakthrough in my translation of *The Labyrinth of Desire* had been persuasive evidence of this, and had also spurred me on to pursue a literary project I had been toying with for some time. For almost a year now I had been planning a novel in which Lope de Vega's unbelievably complex life would be related by an elderly Spanish actor exiled at the start of the civil war to Buenos Aires. Now I was convinced I had the perfect place in which to write this.

The thought of this kept me at least pleasantly distracted after my interviewers had gone, when I sat pensively in an armchair, contemplating the imminence of my departure from Frailes. Eventually I fell fast asleep. When I woke up several hours later, in the middle of the night, I was conscious of having had a vivid dream in which my friend Esperanza from Seville appeared before me. She had become young and beautiful again, and indeed very unlike the person who was now dying in a Seville hospital. A few days earlier I had travelled from Frailes to see her, and had found her in an almost comatose state, her features swollen from months of chemotherapy for a rapidly progressing cancer. I had tried talking to her about Frailes, but I was not sure if she registered anything that I said. Only after I had started to leave had she muttered that she would love one day to visit the village. Now, in my dream, she had finally been able to make the journey.

The next morning, as I was pottering in the kitchen, I heard a knock on the door. I opened it to find Miguel, together with the manager of the local *Caja Rural*, a lifelong friend of his with the face of a cheerful angel and the suitable name of Rafael. But Rafael had lost his normal smile, and Miguel had an expression that made me know immediately what had happened. Esperanza had died in the night. As there was no phone in my house, her sister Loli had had to leave a message at the bank. On receiving this Rafael had immediately closed shop so that he could come and look for me.

I rushed off to Seville for the funeral. But returning to the city that had once summed up for me all that I loved about Andalucía proved an unsettling experience. The place, proverbially so seductive and exotic, seemed now airless, claustrophobic, and alien. The drive to the cemetery, through the scorched, American-style urban landscape that characterizes so much of Seville away from the orange trees, colourful tiles, and narrow white streets of the old town, was disconcerting enough. But stranger still was being reunited with all those friends of Esperanza with whom I had once enjoyed so intensely an Andalucía that had lived up to all the stereotypes – an Andalucía where pleasure was pursued almost to the point of self-destruction, and where much of life seemed to be spent preparing for and then recalling the *Semana Santa* (Holy Week), the *Feria*, and the annual festive pilgrimage to the Virgin of the Rocío.

This world took on an almost grotesque aspect later in the day, when a small group of us decided to dispose immediately of Esperanza's ashes. A family argument ensued as to where we should leave them. In the end we chose a place that had had joyful, magical associations for Esperanza: the hamlet of El Rocío, in the middle of the marshes, dunes, and pine-covered sands of the Gualalquivir estuary. The exact spot we had in mind, however, directly below the sanctuary of the Virgin, had been transformed from a reedy, watery expanse into a parched wasteland littered with beer cans and horse shit. We attempted afterwards to take the ashes into the nature reserve of the Coto Doñana, but were refused permission to enter the park. Eventually, in an illegal gesture Esperanza would have thoroughly approved of, we surreptitiously crawled under barbed wire to reach a pair of isolated pines. The emptying here of the urn was a moment of deep, symbolical resonance for me. More than just a parting tribute to a close friend, it was like the severing of an important link with the Andalucía that had first awakened my imagination.

I got back to Frailes before sunset, and when the bus from Alcalá left me at the top of the track leading to Custodio's house I felt almost relieved, as if a new phase of my life had begun in replacement of the old. The sight of Miguel watering the garden with his hose was a welcoming one, as was the view of a Frailes that looked, on this brilliant summer evening, like a manuscript illustration depicting the bounties of nature. I experienced a sense of homecoming greater even than if I had been coming back to my real home.

The farewells the next morning, when I was due to depart, were as drawn-out as time permitted. El Sereno filled the car with olive oil, boxes of peaches, pastries, and a good kilo or so of his 'fig bread'. Caño and Merce arrived with cheese, salami, and chorizo. It was no good explaining that I would have difficulties passing this off as hand luggage on the plane, nor that most of this was technically not allowed through British customs. No visitor to Frailes could leave without being loaded down in this way.

Miguel, still without a job, and fearing more than ever that he would have to return to Ibiza, offered to come in his own car so as to guide ours to the fast route to the motorway. Leaving the passenger door open while I went to open the gate of the house for a final time, I discovered Hermes the dog had profited from my brief sortie to make his own contribution to our departure. He had cocked his leg, and pissed over my seat.

Miguel led us through a jewel-like hamlet I had never seen before, a dark wood of elms I never knew existed, vast empty stretches of landscape whose beauty I had never suspected. Even as I was leaving it, the world of Frailes kept on growing before our eyes. Then, as we finally reached the junction with the motorway, Miguel stopped his car to wish us goodbye. Hugging us, he repeated what he had said to me in the garden on our first meeting.

'Remember, Maiquel, if I'm still here in Frailes, you can always count on me for help.'

A few minutes later we were speeding among juggernauts towards Madrid, hurtling into a dangerous new world beyond the protection of the Santo Custodio.

Part Two

The Englishman Sang

I

I HAD SLEPT for only two hours, my luggage had been lost somewhere between London and Seville, and all I had with me was a laptop, a bottle of whisky, and a handful of gifts from the food hall of Fortnum and Mason. The important thing was that I was back at last in Spain, and on my way to Frailes. It was 6.30 on a dark, late February morning, and I was setting out from an area of central Seville which had once been notorious for pickpockets and prostitutes. The person driving me was one of the numerous middle-class intellectuals who had been settling recently in this increasingly gentrified corner of the city. A minor celebrity in his native province of Jaén, he was one of the world's greatest writers in the eyes of his friend Manolo El Sereno: he was the Planeta-winning novelist Juan Eslava Galán.

Juan, according to some observers, could have been mistaken for a slightly older and rather balder brother of mine. Bespectacled, tall, and broad of features, he had a commanding presence but a gentle smile. Meeting him now for the first time, I was reassured that Galán was a man of flesh and blood and not the mythical being I had begun to believe. El Sereno, who peppered his conversation with what Juan had said and done, had told me so much about him in the summer that I was surprised to discover that they had met on only a handful occasions, and that their friendship had been maintained mainly by telephone. The initial point of contact was Juan's home village of Fuerte del Rey, where El Sereno himself had been brought up. Whereas El Sereno had abandoned this place on discovering Frailes, Juan had done so after becoming used to life in Granada, Seville, Madrid, and even London, where he had studied history.

'A place such as Fuerte del Rey, or Frailes for that matter,' said Juan, 'might be fine for a weekend or a short holiday, but I could not imagine living there for any longer period, I would hate all the gossip and lack of privacy.'

'I've lived for more than forty years in London,' I replied, 'but I'm curious now to see for a while what life in a village is like.'

Juan turned his head away from the steering wheel to look at me with a face full of pity and bewilderment.

It was no use explaining that for my friends in Frailes my decision to return was not simply a sane one, but might also make a difference between life and death. Since the summer I had been sent the occasional email by way of Caño's school computer, and had managed a weekend visit from Seville. But my continuing delay in coming back for a longer stay was apparently cause for growing concern. Merce, in one of her messages, told me that her son Alejandro had become worried about me after hearing on television that the Thames flood barriers might soon be in danger of breaking. A few days later, with the news of the Paddington train crash, a message came signed by her, Caño, Santi, El Sereno, and at least three other Fraileros. Was I alive? Had I lost any friends or family in this terrible tragedy?

The ties that were developing between my world and theirs had been considerably strengthened by my weekend return visit, which had taken place barely a month before the Paddington disaster. Caño and Merce had given me a lift back to Seville, where they had a wedding to attend, and as I guided them through the city centre, they stopped the car to greet a young woman whom I too recognized. She had recently become on very close terms with one of Esperanza's daughters, and I was surprised they knew her.

'Of course we know her,' Merce explained, 'she's from Frailes!'

From now onwards coincidences such as these involving Fraileros were to become a regular feature of my Spanish travels. It was if I had been welcomed into a secret support group whose members were everywhere.

Now Juan turned off the motorway at the Seville town of Estepa. We had reached what I considered the home stretch, and the sun was rising over the new, empty road that would lead us in little more than an hour to Alcalá la Real. As we climbed gradually into the Cordovan mountains, the sun exposed a landscape of yellow fields and dusty slopes. An unseasonably hot day was building up. For someone just emerging from an almost uninterruptedly wet and cold

London winter, these were joyful signs. For an Andalucían villager these were portents of impending catastrophe.

'I don't think it's ever going to rain again,' commented Juan. 'It's now almost a year and a half since the last drop.'

Alcalá's famous citadel was coming into view, but it no longer rose in isolation above the hidden town below. A sight unchanged since medieval times was now altered by a row of mobile telephone masts bristling on the hill beyond. My own newly acquired mobile chose this moment to respond with a snatch of Beethoven's *Für Elise*. It was El Sereno calling to find out where we were. I assured him we would be arriving at Frailes within less than fifteen minutes.

'I'm sorry for interrupting you,' I muttered to Juan. Mobiles were still a novelty to me, and I thought that the ringing of them in public was a rudeness for which one had to apologize. I had purchased mine with extreme reluctance, and would be constantly criticized for having one by Merce, who had a loathing of new technology. In vain I would explain to her that I wanted the local *Caja Rural* no longer to close its doors while the manager went to look for me. I needed a more efficient way of being contacted.

'It's extraordinary,' said Juan, 'how mobile mania has taken hold of Spain. The last time I came to Jaén, I was having a walk in the mountains when I saw a shepherd sitting under an oak tree minding his goats. It was one of those timeless scenes that made me wish I had a camera. Then suddenly a ringing sound was heard. The man reached for his pocket, and – I couldn't believe what I was seeing – took out a phone. "Hello," he said, "I'm sitting under a tree." '

By now we had passed the hamlet of Rivera Alta and were driving between fields of asparagus, olives and vines towards a Frailes that shone brightly in the early morning sun against its back-cloth of dark ochre sierra. I found it hard to accept that my long-protracted return to the village should be taking place today of all days, the day when Frailes was celebrating what I thought to be its least attractive product: its home-made wine, or *vino del terreno*. And whoever had heard of a wine festival at the end of February? Juan, who had given a talk at the village's first such festival, in 1997, explained.

'The wine, of course, is made in the autumn, but is not drunk until the beginning of December or so, and probably reaches its peak about now. But the reason for the festival at this time of year is that it coincides with the end of the olive harvest, which is always concluded with what we call a *remate*, or finishing party.'

A small crowd was gathering at the entrance to the village, around a group of buildings that included the imposing 1950s headquarters of the *Guardia Civil*, the ill-fated Bar Lady Diana, and a similarly unsuccessful place opposite that advertized itself in faded lettering as a bar, restaurant and wedding salon. Half blocked-up now by bricks, and looking like an incomplete car showroom, this last establishment bore the grandly urban name of La Avenida. It had apparently closed down almost before it had opened, the expected wedding parties having continued to frequent the more conveniently situated salons of Alcalá. Today, however, it had been briefly resuscitated as the focal point of the '*IV Jornada de vino del terreno*'.

El Sereno stood on the Avenida's steps like a mayor receiving visitors to his village. As soon as he saw our car he rushed down to the road, causing a mild flutter of excitement among some of the bystanders. The full extent of his involvement in the festival would not be appreciated by me until the following year, when I was able to witness closely all the preparations leading up to the event. Allowed by the town hall to invite anyone he liked from outside the village, he spent weeks beforehand telephoning and sending letters to friends and acquaintances whom he considered 'important' – university graduates of any description, but in particular doctors, pharmacists, politicians, lawyers, and, most recently, writers. By associating himself with 'important' people in the past El Sereno had cleverly succeeded in advancing his own concerns. But now that he was retired and comfortably well-off, he did so purely out of a disinterested love for his adopted Frailes. He believed that the presence of illustrious outsiders at the wine festival would transform a mere drunken exercise into an event that would heap prestige on the village.

Watched by many, he embraced the Jaén writer whose regular attendance at the festival had so far been his greatest coup as the village's unofficial publicist. After being warmly greeted in turn, I wondered whether my own standing in Frailes would now be enhanced as a result of association with Juan Eslava Galán. However, as became clear in the course of the day, the people who had shown an especial interest in Juan's arrival, and had come up to him with books to sign, were mainly officials from the town hall of Alcalá. The village of Frailes, which I had perceived as a perfect writer's haven, appeared sensibly to be a place that paid little attention to conventional notions of literary importance.

One person who was certainly unimpressed by them was Frailes's mayor, a short stocky man with a disproportionately large head and an inability to keep still. Whatever his faults, sycophancy was not one of them. Muttering greetings indiscriminately, he flitted from group to group, merely stopping at ours to urge us to take up our seats as soon as possible in the basement of the Avenida, where the speeches were about to begin. We walked from the hot sunlight into a chilly and uninviting room, with exposed brick walls and plastic ceiling tiles that were coming unstuck. Facing us, on top of an improvised platform, was a long table on which the names of the day's speakers were placed.

Some mumbled words of welcome by the mayor were followed by a glumly delivered introduction from Santi, who was clearly shyer and more uncomfortable than ever in his role as public speaker. To his credit he dispensed with the habitual preamble of 'Most Excellent this . . . Most Illustrious that', which was a characteristic of official meetings such as these. But his failure to include such vapid forms of address was more than made up for by the first of the invited speakers, who wasted at least five minutes with these courtesies before launching into a detailed history of wine-growing in Jaén. I got as far as the increased annual production of the *crianza* reds of Torreperogil before the symptoms of last night's lack of sleep began to take effect. The second speaker, an oenologist from Murcia, was scarcely more exciting, but revealed the interesting news that Frailes was shortly to have its own wine cooperative. I was about to doze off again when the meeting's one moment of humour was provided by the spontaneous arrival on the platform of the speaker's young son. 'Come on papa,' he wailed, pulling his father's arm. 'I'm bored, I'm bored.'

Longing by this stage to move on from theory to practice, no matter how bad the wines proved to be, I was delighted when the mayor put an end to the proceedings by inviting us all to a tasting in El Sereno's garden. Outside the Avenida a festive mood was mounting, with growing numbers of people congregating around stalls that sold bottles of home-made wine marked with the label, '*Vino de Frailes, Paraíso Interior*'. Reunited with Merce, Caño, and many others whom I had got to know in the summer, I found myself chatting away enthusiastically to several people simultaneously before being interrupted by the sounds of folk music. I turned round to see players dressed in the costumes I had once mistaken for those of Slovakian gypsies. Among them was the bank manager Rafael, who looked more cherubic than ever dressed up in a colourfully braided black jacket, and strumming a mandolin.

We all streamed up the hill for the wine tasting.

'Remember this is a wine that goes straight to the head,' Caño reminded me, as I debated the wisdom of drinking it on a stomach that had yet to have any breakfast. By now at least 500 people were talking loudly in El Sereno's property, below the walnut tree that stood in front of the temple-like garden hut. Like ants drawn to a single giant morsel, they swarmed around a central cauldron where rings of black pudding as big as an elephant's intestines were bubbling away in the water. A moist slab of the sausage was handed to me on a piece of bread.

'Eat!' ordered Caño. A glass of wine came next, and then another. Once you got used to the idea that this was a wine unlike any other liquid that would go under the name, it came to seem quite attractive. After many glasses it began to be as satisfying as a mature Rioja.

'Just shut up and drink!' shouted Caño.

From the scrum that had developed around the black pudding I edged my way in a daze towards the cliff-edge promenade facing the hill where El Sereno had his olive, cherry and almond trees. Was I imagining things, or was it really possible that since my last visit to Frailes three unsightly mobile telephone masts had grown up alongside his property?

'You're to blame,' said Merce, glancing at the mobile that protruded from my jacket pocket. 'They went up a few weeks ago, just after those of Alcalá. Now that important people like you are coming to Frailes our communications with the outside world have to be improved.'

Pilar, the plumper of the three 'Slovakian gypsies' from the summer, roughly pushed her way through the crowd to join us. She introduced me to a tall man with a moustache whom she said was the head of the 'rural accommodation agency' through which I had first found a house in Frailes. He was a German called Klaus who had been living for more than twenty years in Almería. 'I'm thinking,' he told me, 'of moving my agency over here, this is an area that is almost virgin as far as rural tourism is concerned. It has great potential.'

I had no right to be alarmed by this announcement, which disturbed me more than the telephone masts. I had been a beneficiary myself of Klaus's agency, and was also realistic enough to know that there was nothing which would stop the eventual spread of tourism to the Sierra Sur. Such a development might even be necessary if a village like Frailes was to survive at all. But there was something patronizing and proprietorial in the way Klaus spoke.

'Pilar was telling me about your summer stay in Custodio's house,' Klaus continued. 'I had clients like you in mind when I founded the Andalucían rural accommodation agency. It's very important to break down the barriers of mistrust that country folk often put up when confronted by outsiders. Friendly relations need to be established between the two worlds if the locals are to realize that people like us are actually doing a great service to their communities.'

Pilar, who was nodding as he said this, was soon revealed to me as someone rather less straightforward than the down-to-earth, fun-loving person I had originally imagined. She broke into the conversation by talking about all the old and abandoned village houses she was hoping to purchase and restore with a view to promoting 'rural tourism'. Already she seemed to have made considerable progress in the village.

'There,' she said, pointing to a group of buildings on the hill behind us, 'there's one of my properties, and there's another one over there. And that also belongs to me, and so does that . . .'

The next moment, oblivious to the surrounding merriment and confusion, she went on to talk about how many square metres of property it was possible to buy for how many thousands of pesetas. And she was promising to continue interminably in this vein until Merce suddenly came to my rescue.

'Pilar,' she said, as if to explain to me her friend's behaviour, 'is not from Frailes.'

Depressing thoughts of a future Frailes given over to 'rural tourism', and in the hands of opportunistic outsiders, fortunately receded as the wine took increasing control over the festival, which was now entering its third major phase – a lunch given in the Avenida for nearly 2,000 people. The drinkers gradually dispersed from El Sereno's garden, and formed a long-drawn-out procession slowly making its way down the hill. Back at the Avenida, I found Miguel standing outside at the back of the building, stirring with what appeared to be a broomstick the contents of the giant *paella* pan he had once vividly described to me. Indoors meanwhile the sea of benches that filled the smoky gloom seemed almost to sway with arriving guests already replete with wine and black pudding.

Contemplating the impossibility of a British village inviting all its inhabitants and a few hundred others to a day-long feast of free food and unlimited drink, I lost sight of El Sereno and his circle. In the midst of all this noise and flow of people I paused for a moment to talk to a young and tiny lady, a divorcée called Paqui who, unknown to me then, was soon to become my landlady. Paqui sat at a table entirely occupied by members of the *Guardia Civil*, who encouraged me vociferously to come and join them. But after hesitating there for a while, I was pulled down forcibly by complete strangers to an adjoining table, where I was welcomed like the returning prodigal son.

Shouts of 'Eat! Eat! . . . Drink! Drink! . . . Eat! Drink! . . . Drink! Eat! . . . Drink!' could occasionally be heard rising above the general din. I tried to raise my voice sufficiently to converse with my softly spoken neighbour, who turned out to be Manuel Amezcua, the author of *The Route of Miracles*. He worked now in a hospital in Granada, but had spent a long time in medical practice at Frailes, where his interest in local anthropology and faith healing had deepened. Dr Amezcua confirmed what I now wanted keenly to hear after a day in which the possibility of becoming disillusioned with Frailes had threatened to arise. The label on the wine bottles fast accumulating on our table did not exaggerate, he told me. Frailes, of all the Andalucían villages where he had lived, was perhaps the one that best qualified as an inland paradise.

Our conversation began to lose its coherence under the influence of wine, food, and the surrounding distractions, and I found myself repeating what Merce had so often told me: Frailes was an exceptionally difficult village to understand. I admitted to being fascinated by the strange coexistence here of modernity, legends, and what outsiders might consider archaic beliefs, such as the Santo Custodio. Then, as another bottle of *Vino de Frailes, Paraíso Interior*, was opened before me, I proposed defining Frailes in the same way that the poet García Lorca had characterized his beloved Granada: a paradise, yes, but a 'paradise closed to many'.

'So that's where you've got to,' bawled Pilar, dragging Klaus behind her. The meal was drawing to a close, people were moving from one table to the next, while others were gradually filtering off into what was left of the daylight. 'We were wondering what had happened to you, but we weren't really worried, we knew you'd be well looked after . . .' Pilar's loud voice was soon indistinguishable from the shouts around her as I veered light-headed towards the door, and from there to the place where I knew instinctively everyone would be waiting for me: the Bar La Cueva.

I had never seen the place so crowded. The drinkers far outnumbered the card-players, and eventually supplanted them in those sacred tables at the back where I had never dared sit before for fear of disturbing village customs. Seated there at last, in what I felt to be the very womb of Frailes, I anticipated the alcoholic ritual that would soon unfold. The coffee would be followed by the inevitable anise or cognac, and then perhaps a longer drink, after which we would be going to another bar in time for the evening *aperitivos*. There would be beer and wine, and the tapas that still automatically came with them in the provinces of Granada and Jaén. And then we would almost certainly be going on to a *bar de copas*, the Guaneiro, for instance, where there would be more gin, more whisky, more rum. This was a pattern of drinking that is often thought of in Spain as essential to true enjoyment.

Matters turned out exactly as I had predicted, with rather unfortunate effects in the case of Klaus. This essentially serious man became drunk in a way the Spaniards describe as '*pesado*' or 'heavy'. After a good four of five whiskies he became quite fanatical in his advocacy of rural tourism.

'What this area lacks is a proper tourist infrastructure, an information office, restaurants with reasonably priced set menus, decent places to stay, the possibility of guided tours through the Sierra.' His diatribe succeeded in making Caño as argumentative as I had ever seen him, and in forcing from Merce a succession of jeers, shouts, high-pitched laughs, and shrugs of the shoulder.

Klaus carried on obliviously: 'There are so many houses in this area that would be perfect as holiday residences. All you have to do is to strip away the concrete floors, the hideous modern tiles, and the other ghastly recent additions, and you'd be left with picturesque old homes that would attract the foreign tourist market. And the example of places such as these would make other villagers think twice before they carried out some unsuitable modernization, or put up a corrugated iron barn . . .'

'But we don't want our village turned into a museum!' interjected Merce.

'You're just incurable romantics!' Klaus shouted, before stumbling off ostensibly towards the toilet, only to disappear completely. He would never again be seen in the village. With his departure I could relax more in my newly acquired status as Frailes's only foreigner. At last I could indulge in self-deluding fantasies about having become the Gerald Brenan of the Sierra Sur.

We remained in the Guaneiro for only a short while longer. At around two in the morning, Caño and Merce said they were going home. They took me with them, to a house they had built themselves about two kilometres from the village, almost exactly on the frontier that divided the municipality of Frailes from that of Alcalá. This house, most unusually for the area, was constructed from exposed, roughly hewn stones, each of which, a Jaén poet once told them, was like a 'laid-down illusion'. The building's fabric seemed also to have absorbed much of the friendly, open character of its owners, who, with characteristic generosity, insisted I stayed there until I found a place of my own.

On entering the house Merce declared she was not tired, and switched on the television. Caño brought out a bottle of whisky, and placed a small glass of it into my half-protesting hands. 'Drink!' he said.

'Would you like to see our wedding video?' Merce asked in one of those sudden flashes of inspiration so typical of her personality.

My response was as hesitant at first as it had been when offered the whisky, but in the end I said yes. A wedding video seemed hardly what was needed after a day of non-stop drinking and eating on merely two hours' sleep. But Merce's whims had a way of judging exactly the right moment. Slumped in a comfortable armchair, I awaited the video with both wariness and curiosity, hoping I would not soon be struggling to keep awake.

To the accompaniment of a popular Spanish folk singer of the 1980s, the screen flickered with images of flowers and running water seen in ever greater close-up until finally dissolving into a sensual blur. Out of this there emerged slowly into focus a svelte young Caño in blue suit and lacy shirt, holding the hand of the twenty-two-year-old Merce in her bride's outfit, her long brown hair waving in the wind. The video, Merce explained, was made by a friend of theirs who wanted to become a film-maker. This was evident in the restlessness of the camera, which pulled back, panned in, and changed angle almost as many times as the happy couple moved around in the idyllic garden where they were being filmed. This bucolic prelude finally ended with a soft-focus kiss over which appeared the words 'The Marriage of Manolo and Merce, 6 September 1986'.

'We'd been sweethearts since we were young children,' commented Merce, as I realized the extent to which I was giving in to sentimentality. As we proceeded to an almost minute by minute record of the great day itself, I was soon as absorbed as if I were watching the most gripping of feature films.

'Look how green Frailes was then,' said Merce as the screen was filled with a view of the village seen from the cemetery hill. She provided a near-continual commentary as the camera toured the streets of a Frailes that seemed almost impossibly beautiful on this summer day sixteen years before.

'Look how much water there was in the river, and how incredibly clean it was. We used to bathe there as children . . . And look at the view from the Cueva when the river flowed freely in front of it, before our mayor built the ugly concrete park . . . And would you recognize where we are now? That's the part of the village where El Sereno has his house. It was all open fields then.'

Merce fast-forwarded the scenes inside the church to concentrate on the procession through the village streets, and on the reception that culminated with old and young alike dancing outdoors until the early hours of the morning. More than the changes to the village, what held my attention above all was seeing what the villagers themselves had once been like. Some, such as Rafael or Merce herself, had barely changed. Others had acquired in the intervening years what I would later dub the 'Frailes stomach'. Some I failed to recognize at all when they still had their slim figures and thick black hair. Others were unmistakable despite these differences, for instance Miguel, who could be seen stirring his giant pan with the same *gravitas* that he had shown today.

Then there were those whose whole character and even appearance had been subsequently marked by personal misfortune.

'You know who that is?' asked Merce. 'It's Josélillo, the shaven-headed man, with the scar and off-putting manner, who sometimes sits at the bar in La Cueva.'

The person I knew bore no relation whatsoever to the fresh-faced, cheerful young man seen always laughing on the screen, and talking openly to everyone.

'He's never been the same since the death of his mother. . . . And look there's Santi, how happy he always was when he went out with my sister Isa . . . and there's Paqui, the woman who was sitting today on her own with all the *Guardia Civiles*. She runs the village disco, which once had the wonderful roof terrace where you can see us all dancing. . . . And that tall, handsome man is her ex . . . I sometimes think she would have been better off if they'd stayed together.'

In the months ahead, when I had become increasingly immersed in the life of Frailes, and ever more aware of the village's inevitable secrets and sadnesses, I often thought back to the video and wondered why it had moved me so greatly. Perhaps it was the pathos in the contrast between past and present. Perhaps too I had been struck by the idea of a whole village coming to one's wedding, and by the enviable sense of continuity one must feel in knowing that one's childhood friends are likely to be present at every major phase of one's life. But perhaps it was simply because the video was a portrayal of the sheer happiness I hoped would always be foremost in my memory of Frailes.

Recollected scenes from the video and from the wine festival later merged together in my dreams, reinforcing my sense of disorientation on waking up the next day in a strange room and with no idea of how I had got there. I opened the shutters to be dazed by sunlight. Caño was already up, carrying buckets of feed to a population of ducks, turkeys, dogs, chickens, wild cats, and a solitary horse who all lived in apparent harmony around a swimming pool overlooking olive groves towards the faraway but now crystal-clear Sierra Nevada.

For a moment I thought I was back in the summer, and that the sybaritic days I had known then would stretch on forever. Then I realized it was a Sunday in February, and that I would soon have to experience the reality of a place I had perceived perhaps in too glamorous a light. For a start I needed somewhere to live.

After the statutory protracted lunch, and then coffee in the Cueva, my friends took me in the fading afternoon light to a house Merce was sure was going to be perfect for me. It was in the highest part of the village, in an old district which had survived remarkably unspoiled behind all the modern development spreading over the former fields near which El Sereno lived. The locally much-praised spring known simply as the Nacimiento stood at the entrance to this district, alongside an old washing place that village women still used in preference to the more solitary activity of throwing clothes into a machine. Driving past this we criss-crossed our way up steep lanes that would have taken us to sheer slopes of rock, shrub and gnarled trees, had we kept on climbing. Well before this we reached my potential future home – a tall, narrow building squeezed within a slightly decrepit row.

It was the sort of house that Brenan might have taken on. It was the typical Frailes dwelling that Merce remembered from her childhood, with tiny, whitewashed rooms, large fireplaces, and beds with wrought-iron fittings hidden behind draped alcoves. At the back was a dark, ramshackle area once reserved for sheep, goats, chickens, the odd pig or two, and the storage of hay and barley. To cap the house's romantic appeal there was a small shrine to the Santo Custodio, tucked away under a staircase.

'No, this is not the place for Maiquel,' El Sereno declared, seconded by Santi. Merce had perfectly guessed my aesthetic and sentimental tastes, but had underestimated the practical difficulties that such a run-down old place might pose to a solitary and not wholly competent urban dweller. There was the further consideration that I had no intention of spending an entire, uninterrupted year in the village, but would be coming here for relatively short periods in between other travels and occasional return visits to England.

'Then there's only one solution,' said Merce with another of her brainwaves. 'He should go and stay with Paqui in the *Mesón*.'

'The *Mesón*?' I queried, unaware before that Frailes had its old-style 'tavern'. If this were so, I was totally taken with the idea of renting a room above such a place. It conjured up the days of bygone travel.

'You saw the place in our wedding video,' Merce replied.

The penny dropped.

'But you're not sending me to sleep in a disco?'

'Not exactly,' said Merce, 'but almost.'

My heart sank even further as we headed to the village's modern outskirts, to a place immediately beyond the headquarters of the *Guardia Civil*. Behind a large tarmac forecourt protected from the road by a hedge and tall trees was a building resembling an American motel. There was no sign indicating this to be a disco, but neither was there any evidence of a *pension*.

'The *Mesón* has changed completely since I was young,' Merce said, once we had squeezed out of El Sereno's Suzuki. 'When Paqui's father was alive, this was the best place in Frailes for food. Then the property was divided between his two daughters. The older one got the tavern, and then promptly closed it down. Paqui inherited a new extension that the father had intended as a disco. It had a fantastic roof terrace, where everyone used to dance in the summer months. The place functioned really well until a few years ago, when more and more young people started getting their own cars and driving off on Friday and Saturday nights to Alcalá. Then someone gave Paqui the idea of building a *pension* on top. Well, you'll see the result for yourself. At least, I hope you will, if Paqui ever emerges.'

While Merce had been talking, we had all climbed up an outdoor staircase, and were now waiting outside a bubble-glass front door. A final ring on the bell at last met with some response. Paqui arrived in her dressing-gown, rubbing her dark-brown eyes.

'Oh, what a state I'm in, I was fast asleep, I thought it was about five, I should have been up some time ago, the disco's in a complete mess!'

Merce placed an arm around Paqui, and then tenderly stroked her hair. Paqui, whose head barely reached Merce's shoulder, responded by snuggling against her friend and smiling like a contented cat.

'Oh Paqui, Paqui, Paqui, what are we to do with you?' sighed Merce before facing me to explain that they had been 'the best of friends since childhood'.

Apologizing for being so unprepared for visitors, Paqui gave me a full tour of her *pension*, which, on a first impression, could have been described as comfortable, bland, and with an unlived-in character. Beyond the entrance area extended a long dark corridor hung with a job lot of gold-framed prints illuminated by picture lights. There were as yet no numbers on the doors, which made me assume that the place was still not properly functioning. When I then found out that it had been open for at least six months I began wondering if anyone had ever stayed there.

'A theatre company took over the whole place for a weekend last summer,' said Paqui, after she had shown me a couple of small twin-bedded rooms and had opened the door to a much larger room with a double bed and private bathroom. There were six of them in this room alone.'

I understood that there had been no other visitors before or since then, and that Paqui was not at all keen to rent out again the whole property. The root of the problem became apparent after we had visited the two remaining rooms, which were occupied by Paqui herself and her two young daughters, Inmaculada and Marta. They were the most comfortable rooms in the whole *pension*, and the only ones to face the front, and to have a view other than that of a back-yard. One of them even had a jacuzzi.

'When the theatre company came, we had to move to my mother's house next door. I don't like the idea of people taking over my home.' Paqui had clearly been unable to achieve a clear separation between home and *pension*, as a result of which the *pension* appeared as informal as a home, and the home as formal and provisional as a *pension*.

But the greatest conflict of interests was between the *pension* and the disco. Though Paqui assured me that the latter was open only at weekends, and that she was happy to turn down the music for the benefit of the putative guests upstairs, it did not require much common sense to realize that a *pension* which hoped to attract 'rural tourism' was unlikely to do so with a disco below, and that the most popular days of the week for this type of tourism were precisely the ones when the disco was officially operative.

Yet it was the disco rather than the *pension* that won me over to this hybrid, bizarrely thought-out establishment. When Paqui opened the disco's large glass and metal door I was soon overwhelmed by a world where touches of the absurd, the poignant and the unexpected raised the outwardly ordinary *Mesón* almost to the level of the poetic. I was aware at first of a cavernous dark space of surprising, seemingly infinite dimensions. Then Paqui turned on some dim lights to reveal to our left a debris of cigarette ends and sunflower seed husks, spread out in front of a long bar receding into a distant corner of the room. A solitary gas heater stood at one end of the bar, while at the other was the disco's glass control box, filled with panels, switches, and a messy array of tapes and CDs. The decoration of the bar was that of a sleazy nightclub, with a back wall of artfully arranged velvet drapes, and a handful of tiny lithium lights illuminating bottles that were suspended in isolation on brackets. Dangling cut-out hearts in red cardboard, an idiosyncrasy typical of Paqui, had been left over from a Valentine's Day party.

The dance floor extended into the limitless obscurity that opened up directly in front of the bar. Paqui disappeared for a moment into the darkness to re-emerge inside the control box wearing a padded headphone. The cold and eerie silence of the room was broken by a sudden burst of dance music. A large mirror ball began to rotate, casting a magical snowfall of light into a room where hidden corners and furnishings were picked out by flashes of what appeared to be an electrical storm of apocalyptic character. Swivelling spotlights cast a chaos of coloured beams, and ceiling panels switched violently from red to blue to green to yellow in time with the accelerating rhythms of the music. Where once had been total blackness there were now stroboscopic glimpses of painted fencing wire, plush red seating, pinball machines, an electric dartboard, an ancient table-football set, and even another bar, as long as the main one, and with a background wall splashed with luminous paints as if by a madman. The whole was as much of a relic of the past as was La Cueva. It could almost have been an intact provincial disco of *c.* 1985, when the influence of the fashionable, expressively free bars and clubs of post-Franco Madrid had finally made it into the Spanish countryside. But, once again, there was an incongruous feature. The psychedelic wall behind the second bar was hung with plastic moulds of bells, holly and reindeer. For a split second I could read the words, 'Happy Christmas'.

Then in an instant all again was silent and cold, as if midnight had come and the magic was over. The control box went dark, and the only noise was the shuffle of Paqui's feet as she walked towards me in the darkness. I said I would become her lodger. She offered me the room with the double bed and told me I could move in the next day.

The next day was Andalucía Day, a local holiday. My luggage had finally arrived, and I was feeling as sunny as the weather itself when I turned up once more at the *Mesón*. Paqui, her eyes full of sleep, said she already thought of me as part of the family, which was why I was entrusted with the pension's only key, and allowed freely into the kitchen and sitting-room – privileges she said she was unhappy to grant to other guests. I was introduced to her daughters, who were like yet smaller versions of herself, with neatly cropped jet-black hair and a certain resemblance to oriental dolls. Then we went next door to meet her mother, sister, brother-in-law and an oddly behaved six-year-old nephew, who appeared to live in his own dream world, and speak his own incomprehensible language.

Paqui's sister Mercedes shared with her younger sibling little more than her height. Punctuating her conversation with an irritating laugh that swung between nervous and the false, she was as bouncy and full of enthusiasm as Paqui was melancholy and resigned to her fate. Unlike her white-haired husband, an aloof man of few words, Mercedes spoke without the slightest inhibition. I gathered within a few minutes that she was the local representative of the Andalucían National Party, and was involved in numerous projects for the community, from carpentry workshops to language and computer classes. She was full of schemes, and, together with the slightly severe mother, could easily be imagined as trying to organize Paqui's chaotic life. I suspected that it was she who had given Paqui the idea for the *pension*, and that funds for this were found through the political connections that Mercedes was so obviously keen on cultivating.

It was in any case Mercedes who took full control of my moving into the *Mesón*. When I asked for a desk for my laptop and a comfortable chair, she immediately whisked me down to the cellar of her house, where, behind dust, cobwebs, and piles of firewood and furniture, there had survived to my astonishment the 'tavern' that gave the *Mesón* its name – a homely wooden-beamed space which had later been abandoned in favour of a now equally outdated disco. With Mercedes' help I fished out the most suitable chair and table, and installed these in my bedroom. Supplied afterwards by Paqui with a traditionally Spanish form of heating – a brazier to put under the table, and a heavy mantle to keep the heat in around my legs – I was all set to begin writing. Then an art historian friend arrived from Seville.

The friend was an expert in the traditional architecture of rural Andalucía, and was curious to see the village I had spoken so much about. She had thought of me teasingly over the years as the last in a long tradition of 'romantic travellers' to Spain, and wondered what new direction my spiritual journey through her native land was taking.

'You can't be serious?' she exclaimed, after meeting me at the entrance to the *Mesón*. 'You're going to be staying here, above a disco?'

I assured her I was.

'But surely you'll just be here for a few days, perhaps even a week or so, until you find somewhere suitable?'

No, I insisted, this was going to be from now on my base in the Andalucían countryside.

'This is no place for a romantic traveller,' she continued. 'You want an old whitewashed house with a small patio and garden, an elderly woman in black as a housekeeper, and a quaint gardener who turns up riding a donkey.'

As we walked afterwards around the village, she pointed in the distance to an isolated, ramshackle building higher up still from the house I had been to the day before. 'There,' she said, 'that's the sort of place you need.'

I argued that I saw myself essentially as a post-romantic traveller who had adapted to changing times. 'Whereas Gerald Brenan was obliged to bring musicians to his house whenever he wanted to organize a village party, I now have a whole disco at my disposal.'

We continued talking until well after nightfall, when she went off back to Seville.

'I hope the Santo Custodio knew what he was doing when he guided you here,' she commented as she waved goodbye from her car.

My own doubts about what I was doing had now begun to surface. When my friend had gone, I was left with a disconcerting sense of solitude for the first time in Frailes. I found little consolation in the disco's clientele, which consisted of two or three giggling teenage couples and a handful of mature drunks. This tiny number of people for so huge a space seemed barely to justify the deafening volume of music. I went upstairs to my room, and tried to sleep as the walls shook, and the bed appeared to move. Then I woke up in the middle of the night to a deadly silence in which I thought I saw ghostly forms rushing around in the total darkness. A few hours later I got up to raise the blinds, and contemplated a room that seemed then wholly lacking in warmth, human or otherwise.

Writing in such a room proved almost as difficult as sleeping. After a while of sitting at the table with the electric brazier lit, I decided to take up Paqui's suggestion and attempt to work outside on the terrace, where the sight of Frailes, olive groves, and a small corner of the Sierra Nevada promised at first to provide the necessary inspiration.

But the most pleasing sight of all turned out to be that of El Sereno's Suzuki, which, with a dangerous swerve, noisily made its entrance shortly afterwards into the *Mesón*'s yard.

'I've had an idea,' said my saviour. 'From tomorrow onwards you should come and write in my garden hut.'

This was the main moment of optimism in a day that got progressively worse. Never having lived before in a village whose main economic activity was the annual olive harvest, I had been unprepared for the mood of listlessness which sets in when the harvest is over. This mood, combined with the post-holiday hangover, and the fears of continuing drought, was palpable as I wandered at dusk through a village whose inhabitants were nowhere to be seen. Inside the near-empty Cueva I talked for a while to its owner Pepín, who told me that most villagers only went out at night at this time of year when it rained. I returned to the *Mesón*, where I almost would have been pleased had the disco been open.

I had resigned myself to an early night as I climbed up the stairs to the unlit *pension*, but a few moments after I had reached my room there was a knock on the door. Paqui was inviting me to have a drink in the sitting room. When I joined her there a fire was burning, and a bottle of whisky had been placed on the coffee table. I sat down next to her on the sofa, and answered her questions. Was I comfortable in my room? Was the desk the right height? Was it warm enough? Then, as the whisky took its effect, the conversation became more intimate. My sorrows soon disappeared as I listened to hers.

She spoke a lot about her father, and wished I had had the opportunity to meet him. He was a man of vision who had made an enormous success out of the *Mesón*, despite all the doubting villagers who thought he had been crazy to establish such a place. He was also, she said, a lover of life. Others who later told me about him would corroborate this with tales about his passions for socializing, gambling, smoking, drinking, and food. His days on earth had been full but tragically short.

'He was playing cards in La Cueva,' Paqui continued, 'when suddenly he keeled over with a heart attack.' I asked her how old he had been when this had happened, and was sobered by her reply. Only a year older than me, he had died when he was forty-eight.

The other men in her life had been disappointments, in particular her ex-husband Horacio, 'a tall man, just like you'. He had taken to disappearing for long periods, until eventually he went too far, and she had kicked him out. That had been about two years ago. He wanted to come back, but she was adamant that she would never let him. Her life, she admitted, was getting more and more difficult to manage on her own, what with her two daughters and an ailing disco.

'Business has never been the same ever since I closed the *Mesón* down while the pension was being built upstairs. I lost many of my clients to the Guaneiro, which opened during this period.' She looked at me earnestly, and asked if I had any suggestions. 'You have travelled around the world, you have written many books, I have great faith in your opinions.'

But all I could come up with was to ask her if she had she thought of moving to a larger place than Frailes.

'I couldn't leave Frailes,' she said, shaking her head. 'There's no place like this. That's why a man of your experience has ended up here, the village is unique. No other village is so supportive of its inhabitants.'

I did not want to point out that she herself had confessed earlier to having virtually no knowledge of the world outside of Frailes and Alcalá. Nor did I want to say I suspected her problems to be insoluble until she had a significant change of personality. Paqui did not seem cut out to be a businesswoman. She appeared to be someone who followed her heart rather than her mind, and her heart had clearly not got over the pain of her separation. Her current lack of energy had affected the atmosphere of the *Mesón*, and was perhaps putting people off from coming here. Certainly it had resulted in an inability to come up with schemes that would animate the disco, and bring clients to the *pension*. And, as I would find out the longer I remained her lodger, it was leading to a growing distractedness, which in turn would be the cause of numerous incidents and failings worthy of some Spanish *Fawlty Towers*.

From the time of our first talk in the sitting room, my awareness of Paqui as a 'disaster' grew in tandem with my awareness of her as an extraordinarily kind person. These two sides to her character made for a most endearing combination, and would soon inspire in me such an attachment to the *Mesón* that the only conclusion to be drawn in the village was that I had become Paqui's lover. I had not, but I had begun to look upon her and her establishment with the tolerance of a person in love, of someone who regards the physical imperfections of his beloved with such tenderness that they become eventually the focus of his attraction.

The imperfections of the *Mesón* became daily more noticeable to me, and never ceased to be a source of wonder. Everything had been conceived to the highest standard of modern technology, but nothing quite worked. The central-heating system, for instance, baffled even the most efficient of local plumbers. It could be on for twenty-four hours continuously without heating a single radiator, except perhaps in the very middle of the night when, after weeks of coldness, I would suddenly wake up sweating in a boiling room at three o'clock in the morning. But when the time came for getting up, the room would never be anything but freezing. I would rush to the shower and have to wait for a good ten minutes or so before the running water began to be tepid. Standing there naked, wet and shivering, I would then reach desperately for a towel, only to find that Paqui had taken it away and forgotten to replace it with another.

The electrical set-up of the *Mesón* was another story, and more complex still. Neither I nor anyone else who came to visit me here could quite come to grips with the multitude of switches that confronted you wherever you went. There were the basic switches, then the timer switches, and then the dimmer switches that you pressed gently if you wanted to increase or decrease the level of the light, or else gave a sharp push if you wished simply to turn the light off. Then there were switches of no apparent use whatsoever but which suggested, in conjunction with the numerous exposed wires protruding through the walls, that further electrical ingenuities would shortly be coming. I would have to wait for next year's olive harvest before understanding how so much effort had been expended in so many unnecessary details. It turned out that the person responsible for all this, and for the lighting in the disco below, was an electrician cousin of Paqui who was delighted to conduct electrical experiments in the *Mesón* in return for Paqui's help in harvesting his olives. I admired the extent of his professional ambitions; but I was also perplexed why, with so many switches around the building, he appeared to have forgotten the most elementary one of all: a switch to turn on the lights as soon as you entered the front door.

The performance of the simplest tasks was endlessly protracted by Paqui, and often abandoned at a half-way stage. She refused to allow me to do any of my washing for myself, but then kept my dirty clothes for days and weeks on end, until eventually some of them would mysteriously go missing, as happened once with no less than thirty pairs of underpants. Even the provision of such prerequisite basics of a *pension* as soap and toilet paper was something that Paqui was continually putting off, for no reason other than absent-mindedness. Of course there was always the excitement of surprise whenever something was achieved. I remember the euphoria of coming back one night to find a bath mat, after nearly two years of regular long stays at the *Mesón*.

Then there were other surprises, of a more intriguing kind. Shortly after first moving into the *Mesón*, I returned to my room to discover that a bracket had been placed on the wall with a view to installing a television. The television itself arrived a good three months later, and was a small, black-and-white set which produced only blurred images and crackling sounds. A year later it had been taken away, but not the bracket beneath it, which served now only one purpose other than as an unsightly obstacle on which I was constantly hitting my head. It supported, enigmatically, a straw hat.

The pathos of the establishment was compounded by the continuing absence of guests, despite all of Paqui's well-meaning efforts. After I had been there on my own for a couple of months, Paqui told me of her plans to create a website advertising the *pension*. Three months later, and with still no sign of a guest, she managed to get enough money from the Andalucían government to bring out a pamphlet. This was an attractive little publication which came with a text extolling the place's rural tranquillity, and photographs which showed a jacuzzi only she could use, a sitting room that was also officially out of bounds, a bedroom which belonged to her daughters, and another room that was almost permanently occupied by me. There was of course no mention of the disco underneath.

A further two months had to pass before Paqui finally got round to carrying out what was most obviously lacking in terms of publicity – a roadside sign that drew attention to the existence of the hitherto unmarked *Mesón*. Only after this had gone up did I realize that the *pension* and the disco had their own individual names. Though everyone in the village referred to them both regardless as the *Mesón*, the *pension* was in fact called the 'Hostal Ardales', after Frailes's former spa. The disco meanwhile had a triter if, for me, more appropriate name.

It was a name that echoed the reaction of some of my friends on discovering where I was staying. It was also a name that expressed the sense of marvel that only continued to increase the more I got to know Frailes and its people. The place was called the 'Discoteca Oh!'.

2

LIVING FOR THE first time in a Spanish village introduced me to a way of life I thought only existed in the sentimental recollections of writers such as Laurie Lee. Despite the mobile phones, the internet links, the 'rural tourism', the 'Discoteca Oh!', and other concessions to the modern world, life in Frailes had something of that proverbial 'timeless' quality which always made me cringe whenever I saw it referred to in print.

It was a life I had never experienced before as a Londoner, a life stereotypically described as lived according to the rhythm of the seasons, marked by unchanging traditions and age-old festivals, and the activities associated with the agricultural year. For many of the younger villagers this unvarying cycle of events must have seemed monotonous and oppressive. For others it enriched the year with the promise of a reassuringly familiar and reliable series of spectacles and distractions: the search for wild asparagus in the shadow of the depleted olive trees; the white bursts of cherry and almond blossom that announced the spring; the string of *fiestas* and festive pilgrimages stretching from Holy Week right into the summer; the ripening of tomatoes in July, and the making of fig bread when the summer was ending; autumn weekends with their hunting and mushroom-picking; and the coming of winter to the accompaniment of pig slaughters and the return of the olive harvest.

When I first went back to Frailes I had expectations of miracles and boundless inspiration, but few delusions about truly integrating myself into village life. For the first weeks I was indeed less of a participant than an observer whose evolving picture of what Frailes was like was based on fragmentary impressions and insights gathered incidentally in the course of following a daily writing routine from which I had hoped, unrealistically, not to stray too far.

There was the potential to be sidetracked at every stage of the day, beginning early in the morning with my walk from the lower depths of the Discoteca Oh! up to the Elysian heights represented by El Sereno's garden. This invigorating journey between the two poles of my Frailes existence was punctuated and protracted by encounters and revelations, sometimes necessitating reappraisals of familiar scenes. Thus, after a night at the disco in the company of someone downing gins and tonic, the sight the next morning of the same person riding off to the fields on top of a laden donkey was no longer so evocative of an unchanged rural world. Then there were the mental adjustments to be made after being finally invited inside houses whose owners had so often greeted me on my climb. An outwardly 'typical' whitewashed old building looked somehow different once you knew that its interior was entirely furnished on three floors with giraffe dolls, toilet-roll holders, and other such miscellaneous objects that had all been hand-crafted in a mixture of esparto grass and the green plastic tape used for packaging. Even more revealing was my discovery, behind another traditional façade, of an unmarked modern hairdressing salon as luxuriously appointed as Vidal Sassoon's. Aurori, the shy young owner, then surprised me by saying that there were no less than six other such establishments in this village of little more than one and a half thousand inhabitants. 'We're a very conscientious lot,' she explained. 'We go to all the weddings and first communions.'

As I walked every day up the street I sometimes indulged in a fantasy of mine that had been growing ever since my return to Frailes. I had begun thinking of myself as a detective determined to uncover secrets in a village I still perceived in terms of some deep, all-encompassing mystery. The main focus for these imaginings remained for the time being the trio of distinguished houses around the parish church, near the top of my daily climb. My curiosity as to what lay inside them had been heightened when Merce suggested, during the summer, a royal connection with the most intriguing of these structures, which she referred to as 'the House of the Armandos'. Since then the stories I had heard about this particular building had accumulated. There was talk about a man who had been confessor to Alfonso XIII, and about his eccentric nephew who had married the family maid, and had staged his own funeral in the village while still alive. The place was apparently still owned by the latter's two bachelor sons. They were said to spend several months of the year there with their mother, but I had yet to find any evidence of this. Their house seemed as permanently closed as the other two buildings, one of which, featuring twin towers and neo-Renaissance detailing, appeared so pock-marked outside as to have been abandoned altogether.

Strangely enough it was the last and most damaged of these three palatial houses that would prove my point of entry into this enigmatic trio. I was passing by it one morning when I saw an open door, through which I glimpsed a vestibule decorated with hunting trophies, ceramic tiles, and a fountain. A tall and distinguished middle-aged couple were standing there. The husband beckoned me in. He introduced himself as José Luis, and presented me to his elegant and nervously smiling wife Matilde, who could have been the subject of an English society portrait from the 1920s.

The two of them, I soon learnt, were Alcalaínos who had taken the near-unprecedented step of moving from Alcalá to Frailes.

'We came here because of this house,' José Luis explained. 'I've known and loved the building since I was a child. I finally managed to buy it several years ago.'

Only recently, however, had they been able slowly to begin its restoration. The original owner, a local doctor called Fermín Medina, had sold it to them as a very old man, and had then immediately regretted having done so.

'He said he wanted to die in the house of his dreams,' José Luis told me, 'so we allowed him to do so.'

Dr Medina had barely altered the house since the time he had had it built, in the early 1930s, and the new owners were themselves keen to maintain the place's faded, old-fashioned character. 'I hope you don't mind the mess,' murmured Matilde after the husband had volunteered to show me around.

A subdued, dappled light cast a nostalgic glow over rooms more resonant of the past than any I had so far seen in Frailes. As we paused in a sitting room painted in a sombre ochre, I could easily picture members of the village hierarchy playing cards around the velvet-lined table, or discussing politics while reclining on the now peeling leather armchairs. During the post-war 'years of hunger', when most of the villagers lived in claustrophobic, low-ceilinged dwellings without electricity or running water, the house of Dr Medina must have represented a world of unimaginable luxury. The extreme contrast between rich and poor that had once existed in Frailes was further emphasized when we reached the attic. Though now a storeroom in which a stuffed vulture loomed over a mountain of books and pamphlets, this had served before as a granary for the wheat regularly given to the doctor by his patients.

'That was the only way,' said José Luis, 'that most of them could pay for his fees.'

As the tour continued, I felt at last that I was beginning to make some headway with my still half-hearted researches into the more hidden areas of Frailes's past. The main revelations concerned the heated rivalry between Dr Medina, a lifelong liberal, and the staunchly conservative family of Dean Ezequiel Mudarra, the royal confessor responsible for the construction of the neighbouring 'House of the Armandos'. Dr Medina had unashamedly built his own house in the hope of outstripping in grandeur the home of his enemies opposite. His Republican views were fortunately in his favour at the start of the civil war, when the House of the Armandos was ransacked and left almost as a shell, while Dr Medina's was spared through being used as a hospital.

The tensions between the two families were highlighted by a grim anecdote told to me at the end of José Luis's tour, when I was shown the former consulting-room, which still contained the doctor's desk and swivel chair. It was while sitting before these that Ezequiel Mudarra's brother met a gruesome death. A few months into the civil war, a group of Republicans had taken him forcibly to the barber's, where his neck had been 'accidentally' cut. Being an old man, the skin on his neck was tough and resistant, and the job was botched, so he was dragged over to Dr Medina's. But by now there was nothing that could be done to patch him up, so they finished him off there and then with a shot to the back of the head.

'This is what happens in civil wars,' José Luis stoically noted.

After hearing this story I often wondered what other tales of the past lay buried in the buildings that lined my daily route. On a few occasions I broke my journey to look inside the cheerfully simple parish church, hoping to find further traces of the village's history. But recent modernization had succeeded in eradicating all evidence of the past, including, I was told, some late Gothic vaulting dating back to the time of the building's foundation. Once, as I scoured the walls in a futile search for masonry breaks, revealing inscriptions, and other such historical and archaeological clues, I met for the first time the parish priest, Alberto, an energetic young man whose energies were unfortunately devoted largely to finding money to 'prettify' the building in his care. As he described to me his current project of replacing the old tiled roof with a brand new prefabricated one, I knew I was dealing with someone with the same lack of architectural sensibility as the village mayor. A month or so later I walked by the church to find that the old roof had been taken down overnight, apparently without any official permission. El Sereno was incensed when I mentioned this to him on reaching his house that morning.

'To think of all the time I spent looking for suitable old tiles when the roof needed restoring before!' he complained, as we reflected over breakfast on the continuing disappearance of Frailes's past.

The prospect of my daily breakfast with El Sereno usually overcame all other thoughts once I had gone beyond the church and was on to the walk's final stretch, down the dead-end lane which led past the pharmacy, the school, the clinic, and the town hall, eventually to finish up at the large gate to my friend's property. However, these last 100 metres were fraught with potential further delays, especially if I had been distracted on the way there, and had not arrived in time to avoid what counted as the Frailes rush hour – a confusion of a dozen or so cars bringing children to school. The number of people whom I would then be obliged to greet was often so large as to add twenty minutes or more to my journey, thus making me run the risk of being late for breakfast, and causing anxiety to El Sereno's sisters.

Slipping as furtively as I could down to the gate, I turned the key that was left permanently in it, and entered the part of the village that had become for me a retreat within the greater retreat that was Frailes itself. Curra the dog rushed merrily around me, prompting the much grown and permanently chained Rasputin to leap out from his Polynesian-style kennel. To this chorus of welcome I walked up to El Sereno's house, where I would be soon sitting at a small round table under the gaze of his dead father. The pampering I received from El Sereno's two sisters was something that had taken me time to get used to. Refusing to let me do anything by myself, they scuttled in and out of the kitchen, patiently bringing and then taking away the components of a large breakfast. The climactic feature of this meal was a slab of toast on which I was encouraged to lavish home-made tomato preserve and a quantity of *Serenolivo* that must have constituted a significant percentage of its annual production. More than the awkwardness of feeling unable to lift a hand even to clear the table afterwards was the knowledge that El Sereno's sisters would never sit down to eat with me, or with their brother, or indeed with anyone. Never leaving the house now except to buy food, they were people who had devoted all their lives to the serving of others. But Merce rebuked me for referring to them as 'domestic slaves'. I was viewing them, she said, too much from a present-day perspective. They were doing what they had been brought up to do, and it would not have felt right for them to behave in any other way.

What I could confirm was the sheer pleasure they seemed to derive from their proximity to those whom the villagers knew as 'the pharmacist's family'. This was the last in the line of 'important' Frailes residents whom their brother had spent much of his life cultivating. El Sereno and his sisters, before moving to their present house, had lived for many years with this family, who were still constantly dropping by. The dominant personality among them was the pharmacist herself, who was known to everyone, even to the two sisters, by the formal name of 'Doña Inmaculada' or just simply 'Doña'. With her husky voice, corpulent appearance, and moon-shaped face, she was as formidable as her title suggested. A person with remarkable skills and talents, to whom people would often turn for advice, she wrote with an old-fashioned elegance, embroidered beautifully, and was the founder and leader of the village musical group, for whom she had collected many traditional songs that were in danger of dying out. Her retired businessman of a husband, a quiet, good-natured man with a voice that had been destroyed by years of smoking, appeared in comparison a shy and at times barely noticeable presence.

The immediate family was completed by their two sons, Pedro Jesús and Ernesto, both of whom had inherited their mother's musical talents and medical interests. El Sereno's sisters doted on them as if they were their own children, and in return were treated by them as second mothers. The elder of the two, Pedro Jesús, now worked as a GP in the nearby town of Priego de Córdova, and was to be married to his childhood sweetheart, but he seemed always to be escaping to Frailes to spend time with the sisters. Ernesto, mean-while, often confessed to me that what he missed most whenever he went away from Frailes was being fed and looked after by the elder sister, Mercedes, whom he still addressed by the name he had mistakenly used as a baby, 'Yé-Yé'.

Ernesto, who had largely taken over the running of the pharmacy from the mother, was the member of the family whom I got to know best. In fact, he was the only other person to breakfast with me daily at El Sereno's where, watched by a tenderly concerned Yé-Yé, he slumped every morning into an armchair, complaining always of tiredness or of the aches and pains brought about by his futile attempts to lose his bulging weight. Despite being a single man in his late twenties, and having the fresh-faced looks of a swollen cherub, Ernesto had the metabolism and personality of someone much older. He was altogether the perfect foil to his honorary second father El Sereno who, when in Ernesto's company, appeared increasingly as a young man hiding inside an elderly body.

When 9 a.m. struck on the grandfather clock, and Ernesto rose from his seat to go off to the pharmacy, I would often stay behind to listen to El Sereno's fresh and youthful views on life. Invariably managing to relate world affairs to village issues and his own personal experiences, his conversation combined idealism, breathless enthusiasm, and a mixture of naivety and curious perceptiveness reminiscent of Hasek's good soldier Schwejk. His thoughts touched on numerous subjects, from crop-spraying (to which he was vehemently opposed) to the importance of living in close contact with nature; but his repeated themes were hypocrisy and greed, which gave him cause to find endless fault with the Catholic Church, Americans, and politicians of all kinds and nationalities. When I knew him better, I noticed how he adapted his views according to his listeners, and how willing he was to spend time with people whom he should theoretically have despised. But I rarely questioned or interrupted him, and was merely content to let his outpourings of wisdom continue to flow from one topic to another.

'Look at the way the politicians have treated García Lorca . . .' ran a typical El Sereno monologue, 'first they kill him, and then they exploit his memory . . . it's just like the Americans with Vietnam, first they create a real war, and then they turn it into a Hollywood movie . . . I remember when I was doing my military service in Equatorial Africa . . .'

Listening to El Sereno became for me an excellent early-morning displacement activity, comparable to reading a newspaper. Fortunately, as far as my work was concerned, he was incapable of staying inactive for any length of time, so eventually he would get up and leave me to my brief daily contact with the world beyond Frailes. This was when I connected my laptop to the telephone line in his hall, and read my emails – to the great bewilderment of the sisters, who, as they stood there in their black clothes watching me at the keyboard, became like visitors from another century.

It was sometimes ten o'clock or later by the time I was finally settled in my garden hut with the intention of at last getting some writing done. The sisters were appalled that their brother had allowed me to work in a place that for them was depressingly untidy. 'Maiquel's a man,' El Sereno had argued, 'he doesn't mind a mess, it's what he's used to.'

The mess was in fact an integral part of the hut's charm, and provided numerous opportunities for nosing around whenever inspiration failed me. I had sometimes the sensation that I was delving into those obscure fragments of a person's memory that surface only in dreams. Studying closely, in moments of boredom, the chaotic shelving, the drawers so crammed they could hardly open, the decaying contents of the fridge, and the surprisingly deep recesses of a built-in larder, I searched for a story to tie together the miscellany of curiosities I uncovered: untouched account books from the 1950s, meteorological graphs, rancid olive oil, a magazine supplement about impotency, rusty utensils, a history of Spanish cinema, scraps of cheese resembling prehistoric shards. Much of what I found proved to have been placed here with some future, if often unforeseen, use in mind, as was the case with a blue plastic milk crate, which ended up as a means of raising my laptop to a practical level. As for the piles of magazines and newspapers, these came gradually to be depleted with the sudden return of a cold spell of weather, and the subsequent necessity of lighting a fire.

The lighting of the fire was another of the daily distractions that cut into my working schedule. Country weekends in Britain had made me erroneously believe that I knew exactly what I was doing when I set about placing first the crumpled newspaper in the hearth, then the twigs I had gathered from around the garden, and then the larger pieces of wood, and finally the firelighters. But every time I was on the point of putting a match to my creation, El Sereno would turn up to tell me that I had got it all wrong, and that I would need to start again. He was particularly contemptuous of the firelighters, which he thought unnecessary and a waste of money (a box of them could be bought for the price of a coffee at the Cueva). Eventually I learnt the Frailes way of making and maintaining a fire, which, needless to say, was a method impossible to replicate in Britain, involving as it did the rancid oil, kilos of discarded walnut and almond shells, and an element only available to those with immediate access to an olive mill – the dried crushed stones and olive pulp known as *orujo*. Such was the combustibility of the latter that much of my day would be spent pushing a wheelbarrow filled with wood from a pile within disturbingly easy reach of Rasputin's leash. A further complication arose when El Sereno suggested that the embers from the *orujo* would be ideal for the brazier which had once sat below the old wooden table at which I worked. Failing to find a suitable container among all the rusting items in the larder, we searched the garden until finally we rescued from Rasputin's kennel what seemed like a First World War helmet dredged up from the Somme. The filling and emptying of this sorry receptacle, which I was sure would one day set fire to the whole table, became from then onwards another addition to my daily routine.

With the fire lit, the embers burning in the brazier, and a decent stack of logs ready to be used, I sat down on my recycled office chair (which El Sereno had saved from the village dump) and enjoyed in retrospect the pleasures of the kind of 'useful toil' that Ruskin had been aiming for while building a road outside Oxford, or Gladstone while chopping up wood in his garden. Now, however, my real work had to begin, and I speculated how long it would be before El Sereno interrupted me. Usually I would have at least an hour to myself, and the visits, when they came, would be uncannily timed to coincide with moments when I felt briefly in need of talking. He would drop in on various pretexts: to report on his outings into the village, to relate his latest telephone conversation with Juan Eslava Galán, or to persuade me to taste some new fruit that had just ripened.

Every so often he would turn up either with a long-standing friend to whom he wanted to introduce me, or else with one of his growing number of newly-made acquaintances whom he had invited on impulse to see his property: the sight of an English writer at work in the garden hut was becoming an attraction of his guided tour second only to the library and olive mill. On at least three occasions he surprised me by arriving with a whole class of young children from the school. Their teacher had told them how privileged they were to have a native English speaker living in their midst, and a writer at that. Timidly they tried out their English on me – 'Good morning', 'How are you?' and 'What's your name?' – but my replies bore little relation to the English they had previously heard spoken. They sat perplexed until El Sereno came to the rescue with a large bag of sweets, whereupon all remaining interest in the English writer wore off.

For all these interruptions I could normally make good progress on my work if I stayed firmly put within the boundaries of El Sereno's property. Yet, as my detective-like fascination with Frailes only continued to deepen, the lure of what lay beyond the gate became difficult to resist. On the pretext at first of buying something, saying hello to a friend, going for a coffee, or visiting the *Caja Rural*, I would step outside for what I regularly persuaded myself would be 'just a moment'. Of course, I knew only too well that one of the charms and frustrations of Andalucían village life was the impossibility of doing anything quickly. This problem was compounded whenever I was joined in my outings by El Sereno, whose inability to walk or drive without stopping every fifty metres or so to talk to somebody, or to carry out an errand or series of errands completely unconnected with what he originally set out to do, was matched by an extraordinary capacity to get carried away in conversation. In the words of a Spanish expression frequently uttered by his sister Mercedes, he became 'as wrapped up in people as if he were a Venetian blind'.

Endlessly curious, frequently indiscreet, and not ashamed to ask the most intimate questions, El Sereno appeared just the person I needed to help me in my investigations into a rural world in which I too was becoming slowly entangled. Within a few weeks of being back in Frailes I had even begun, disturbingly, to ape certain aspects of his behaviour. In particular I had acquired his habit of going on morning rounds to the places of work in the immediate vicinity of his house, seeing what other people were up to, and occasionally joining them in the obligatory mid-morning break at the only bar in this district, the Charro.

As with El Sereno, these wanderings usually began with a visit to the town hall where Santi, my main informant on local news and politics, would hand over, with barely a comment or a smile, his latest outspoken article for the *Ideal de Jaén*, or even the most recent pages from the book he was writing on the village's history. Sometimes I would go on afterwards to discuss village matters with Santi's rival and right-wing propagandist Mari Tere, who ruled alone amidst the dusty files of the municipal archive. A consummate actress whose breezy, open manner concealed a stubborn pedantry, Mari Tere always tried to rid me of my more fanciful notions about Frailes, which for her was a quiet village no different from any other.

'I'm a historian and you're a writer,' she would conclude as I set off on my way, often with the intention of finding light relief in the unlikely setting of the village clinic. In this building I was likely to find the district nurse Antonio, a rotund man with a constant twinkle in his eye and a ready joke on his lips. He at least agreed with me that Frailes was a truly special place, though not for the deeper reasons I was hoping to find. 'What other village do you know whose inhabitants have such a healthy outlook on life?' he asked with a broad grin, lighting up a cigar next to a poster illustrating the dangers of smoking.

Perhaps, as Mari Tere had said, I had been taking Frailes too seriously, trying to read too much into this half-forgotten borderland where facts were few and myths plentiful. As my mornings became gradually filled with entertaining chat and banter, I wondered at times if the sense of well-being that the village inspired in me had little more profound a basis to it than the discovery, in middle age, of the pleasures of complete indolence. The idea of being on some elusive spiritual quest would certainly have been difficult to sustain had it not been for an ever more important element in my rural existence: my developing friendship with Merce. As a companion in my exploration of Frailes she had become almost as vigilant and indefatigable as El Sereno, but without the latter's compulsion to be the village's public spokesman. She was more interested in people's personalities than in what they did, preferring what lurked beneath the surface than what lay above it. Merce loved the irrational and the extraordinary.

On my very first day of trying to work in El Sereno's garden I had heard what I was sure was her voice calling to me as if from nowhere. The mystery of this dismembered greeting was solved when I realized that my writing hut was overlooked by her office in the town hall. She had roared with laughter as she watched me from her window walking about with a bewildered gaze; and she did the same again a few days later when she crept noiselessly into my hut, suddenly to appear before me as if she were a spirit. I learnt later to recognize her stealthy, almost ethereal approach, so different from that of the fidgety, loudly humming El Sereno. She often came to visit me in the hut, and I reciprocated by spending ever longer periods in the office where she had been happily employed for the past ten years as village social worker. The empathy I had felt between us the very first time I saw her was constantly re-confirmed. We really did seem to know what was on each other's minds. There were even moments when we surprised ourselves wearing almost identical clothes.

Merce did not mind me sitting in her office as she dealt with her clients, who likewise appeared remarkably unconcerned by my presence. All the time I observed her special way with people, her directness, her belief in acting according to instinct rather than through social obligation, her tolerance of everyone who did not suffer from grand pretensions. I also noted in her an attitude towards the rural world that was more what I would have expected from a city dweller. She did not believe that progress was necessarily for the best; she preferred instead to keep to dying traditions, and to preserve old buildings, so long as the act of doing so did not turn villages such as Frailes into showpieces for the delectation of the middle classes. Hers was a romanticism with which I was completely in sympathy, but to which I had always been reluctant to confess, at least not in a rural context. It had seemed tantamount to admitting that poverty in the countryside was picturesque. Merce, who herself had been raised in the most precarious circumstances, reassured me otherwise.

Some of the villagers whom she most admired were themselves romantics in their own way. Unmarried, heedless of social convention, often living in squalor, refusing to adapt to the modern world, and generally spending what money they had on drink, these people represented what might normally be thought of as the underbelly of society – to be pitied, helped or even shunned. They were not the sort of people to interest El Sereno who, for all his professed socialist convictions and hatred of elitism, had noticeably little time for those whom he considered unimportant. Merce, in contrast, had a philosophy of life in which real wealth and happiness were achieved through being true to yourself, even if this resulted, in conventional terms, in spectacular failure. Rather like the eponymous 'Holy Drinker' in Joseph Roth's tale, these unorthodox village drunks had for her an almost spiritual purity.

Periodically her job as a social worker obliged her to visit their homes. She knew they would refuse all offers of help, but she went all the same, just in case. Sometimes she invited me to come with her. Our first visit together was to the house of the local grand master of inebriation, a man in his late sixties with the ecclesiastical nickname of '*Cabildo*' (which means literally the chapter of a cathedral). Treated by the villagers like their much-loved mascot, he walked around Frailes like some cloth-capped Charlie Chaplin, making jerky, uncoordinated movements, and speaking in a slurred, near-incomprehensible fashion. In the late 1970s, when Frailes was visited by Franco's former Minister of Tourism, Manuel Fraga (then in the running for the Spanish premiership), Cabildo had extended his hand to hold Fraga's, and promised afterwards that he would never clean it until Fraga had become prime minister.

'He had once been a farmer who had inherited a large amount of land,' Merce told me as we drove to his outlying house just to the north of the village, 'but he gradually sold it all off to fund his love of the good life. He owns nothing now, not even a bicycle. He's been all alone since the death of his mother.'

I could not believe that anyone could possibly be living in the solitary farmhouse we eventually pulled up at, let alone the man whom I had always seen dressed in the frayed smart clothes of some former dandy. It stood off the side of the road like a pile of masonry and tiles discarded from a passing lorry.

'We've often offered to re-house him, but he doesn't even want electricity or running water,' said Merce as she shouted out his name to see if he was at home. After a few knocks at a door half-hanging from its hinges, we heard the groans of someone clearly in the midst of a deep alcoholic slumber. Merce saw little point in staying. I took a final look at the house. I saw it now as a touching epitaph to the man whom Santi, in one of his articles, had dubbed 'the last of the romantics'.

We had better luck a few weeks later with Gamazo, a drunk whose progress through life had been almost the reverse of Cabildo's. When Merce was a child, she had remembered him as an orphaned semi-tramp who had been allowed to live rough inside what had once been a tile factory next to the Cueva. When the factory closed down, the family who had owned it moved to Seville, leaving Gamazo the substantial house that was attached to it.

'He could have lived in all the comfort he wanted,' said Merce as we passed the now boarded-up mansion that was technically his, 'but he chose to remain in his bare room in the factory. He's never slept in a bed in his life. He says he never wants to.'

We found Gamazo huddled by a fireplace off the factory's court-yard. He was a tiny old man whose bald head was permanently covered with a peaked cap. I had seen him many times slumped drunk on the street in between the Cueva and a nearby bar, but he had no idea who I was. Merce, with the combination of prescience and spontaneity typical of her character, told him I was writing a book about Frailes, even though I had as yet no such project in mind. He did not register at first this misleading piece of information, so Merce had to repeat it. Then he directed towards me an amused and slightly crazed look. 'Whatever for?' he asked.

By the time Merce had set off on her rounds as a social worker, the mornings were usually drawing to an end. This was not the best moment for reflections on the purpose of literature, or on the ultimate futility of all human activities. Another, more concrete pre-occupation was about to divert me from my journey with Merce towards spiritual revelation. Lunch was approaching, and with it I could resume the one aspect of my researches into Frailes that was yielding abundant rewards: food. I took my leave of Merce and Gamazo and rushed back to my hut, where I knew that El Sereno would soon be arriving to prepare the *aperitivo*, an essential pre-lunch ritual.

He would come like clockwork at a quarter to two. Opening the larder door, he generally proceeded to remove one of the archaeological pieces of cheese that I would never have guessed were still intended for eating.

'Some find this a bit strong,' he would say, cutting up a greenish lump that he claimed was a good seven years old, and which had an initial paralyzing effect on the palate, as if all the taste buds had seized up in preparation for an attack.

'Have some wine,' he added, after inspecting the contents of half a dozen or so half-empty bottles that looked like the neglected remnants of an old chemistry laboratory. My unease the first time I had been offered such appetizers was viewed by El Sereno as the understandable response of a city-dweller who had become spoilt by too many additives, sell-by dates, and 'unnatural products'. I soon adjusted to my new culinary world, and began to look forward to the gastronomic surprises that El Sereno would manage to uncover after minutes of rustling in the larder. I only hesitated when he produced one day some mouldy crisps crawling with ants.

'Yes, aren't they good,' he said, misinterpreting my expression on tasting one. 'They've been fried in olive oil, that makes all the difference.'

The taste I was rapidly developing for Frailes's natural cuisine made the lunch that came after the *aperitivo* an unfailingly interesting experience. As the months passed I ended up eating all my meals in El Sereno's house, where his sister Mercedes treated me to the sort of simple, traditional and essentially vegetable-based food that could easily have been emulated by smart city restaurants: gazpacho with apple; salads of orange, tomato and sweet pimento; broad beans with ham; lentil stews whose secret, I was told, was the use of a certain spring water from El Sereno's native village of Fuerte del Rey. A concern for detail was the hallmark of Mercedes' cooking, which required constant words of approval from those eating it. Emerging every few moments from the kitchen she would stand over you with her apron to ask a continual stream of questions.

'What's the stew like? . . . Don't you notice the difference the water makes? . . . Is the meat tender? . . . What are the eggs like today? . . . Are the oranges good? . . .'

'Delicious as always,' was my ubiquitous but sincere reply, which had her glowing with satisfaction as she returned to the kitchen to prepare the next course.

Before these meals with El Sereno became an unchanging feature of my daily life, I tended to eat on my own at El Choto where, in the absence of the beautiful waitress who had worked there in the summer, I was able to give my undivided attention to the food prepared by this woman's mother Cari. For little more than the price of a couple of sandwiches in London you could stuff yourself on a meal made up of mounds of charcuterie, deep-fried vegetables of every description, goat cutlets swimming in garlic and olive oil, and a home-made sponge over which a triple English measure of whisky had been poured. All this was brought to the table by Cari herself, a woman with an invariably cheery demeanour, who waited on me like a kindly mother as I sat in a dining room that seemed like a provocative riposte to modern notions of restaurant elegance. The room was small, narrow, and garishly tiled, and had such echoing acoustics that it was difficult to talk above the distorted sounds of the television. I dreaded the day when the growth of rural tourism would oblige the owners to give their establishment a tasteful 'country look'.

The unrefined nature of the food and setting was reflected in the handful of regulars who stood for much of the afternoon at the adjacent bar. Sometimes, as I emerged from the dining room, they invited me over to join them for a drink. The person I knew best was a man who had inherited his father's enigmatic nickname of 'Pancanto'. Blonde, thickset and slightly brutish in appearance, with a large distorted nose, and pig-like blue eyes, he could easily be pictured as a laughing grotesque in a seventeenth-century tavern scene. Pancanto worked mainly as the driver of the daily taxi run to Granada, but was much in demand as a cook who slaughtered and prepared the animals himself. One afternoon, when I had given in to his offer of a post-lunch whisky, he asked me if I would go with him and his friends to kill some kid goats. I hesitated for a number of reasons, ethical and otherwise. Daniel, Cari's misleadingly surly-looking husband who ran the bar, egged me on, and filled up my glass. Merce and Caño would later identify as one of my main character defects an inability to say no.

I do not know how many drinks everyone had had before we all crammed into an ancient Land Rover driven by Pancanto. Daniel had come, as had the three others who had been with us at the bar: a one-toothed man with a walking stick and weather-worn face; an elderly, maniacally gesturing shepherd who collected foreign coins; and a burly policeman on brief leave from Granada. They all were cracking jokes and laughing madly, and I had the uncomfortable feeling that I was soon going to provide them with another source of amusement. As we rattled off into the sierra there was even something sinister and foreboding in the sky, which had a dull and silvery sheen as if from months of accumulated dirt and dust.

'Stop!' shouted Daniel, as he turned round to pick up a shotgun and aim it through the window at a couple of pheasants scurrying terrified across a field. They were all in a killing mood, but fortunately the hunting season was over, so all Daniel could do was to cry, 'Click, click, you're dead,' much to the hilarity of the others.

We drove up to an isolated farm in a valley all of its own.

'We need eight goats,' Daniel reminded us as we went with the farmer towards a corrugated-iron hut at the back, from which Pancanto and the policeman later emerged carrying all eight goats in a couple of cloth sacks. Kicking and pathetically bleating, they were removed one at a time for Pancanto to thrust a knife in their throats while Daniel and the policeman held their legs. The blood was carefully drained into a pan, after which the goat was released and thrown half-dead on to a pile of rubbish, where it continued for the next ten minutes or so to give the occasional sad kick. Wasn't there a speedier and less painful manner of execution?

'It's very important,' explained the man with the single tooth, 'that as much blood as possible is removed before the goat dies.'

I gave him a puzzled look, and asked why.

'You mean you've never eaten a *tapa* of dried goat's blood?' he replied. 'They're quite delicious.'

By now Pancanto had hung the dead corpses from the branches of a tree, as if they were criminals whose punishment was intended to deter others. However, this gruesome warning had little impact on a nearby group of goats, who continued grazing obliviously as Pancanto slit the bellies of their former companions. An Alsatian dog with unnaturally blue pupils greedily lapped up the discarded white entrails. Pancanto, pausing from his task, gave me a big smile. He was a person whom I knew to be enormously kind and with whom I could share a black and ironic sense of humour. But he did not reveal perhaps his finer side when, for my benefit, he proceeded to cut out the goat's eyes and place them above his own, roaring with laughter as he did so. From that day onwards, whenever I went into the Choto, Daniel never failed to refer obliquely to my look of pallor and disgust at Pancanto's joke.

'When do you want to see some more goats being killed?' he would always ask, smiling and pointing to his eyes. 'We've got fifteen to do this Saturday. Or perhaps you'd like to see Pancanto kill a sheep. He's slaughtering a couple tomorrow.'

For a few hours after having witnessed my first and last goat slaughter I wondered whether I would ever be eating meat again. My education into country ways had indeed taken such a large step back that the very thought of El Choto, with its brash interior, oil-smothered food, and associations with goat, became momentarily unappealing. During crises such as these my city prejudices resurfaced, and I began dreaming of refined, exquisite cuisine served in exactly the sort of elegant, rural-style setting I had supposedly repudiated. The first time this happened I would never have imagined that even a fantasy such as this could be realized in Frailes.

I had managed to spend my entire first summer here, and a good few weeks of the winter, without being aware that the village harboured in its surroundings what I think of even now as one of Andalucía's greatest restaurants. Numerous times, on being driven to Frailes from Alcalá la Real, I had noticed an ordinary-looking roadside bar a few hundred metres away from Merce's and Caño's house. Known as the Rey de Copas, it was situated at the further end of the hamlet of Ribera Alta, another place you could pass by speedily in a car without having any idea of the charms that lay out of sight of the road. Miguel, when I questioned him about the bar, had told me it had a restaurant at the back, but had then screwed up his face and shaken his head. 'No, Maiquel, I wouldn't recommend you go there, the food is not authentic, there is nothing traditional about it.'

Keen as I then was to have only authentic experiences, I took heed of Miguel's advice, and gave no more thought to the place until over half a year later, when Merce suggested one day we should all go and have lunch there. I did not go in with high hopes, but came out after several hours as dazed as if I had just walked out of Aladdin's cave.

As a restaurant the Rey de Copas was as bizarrely conceived and commercially disastrous as Paqui's *pension*; but, as with the latter establishment, these very defects contributed to its uniqueness. It was a place whose contradictions, implausibility, and magical unexpectedness made it difficult to imagine as existing anywhere beyond the vicinity of Frailes. The sheer normality of its exterior, and the knowledge that you were in an out-of-the-way hamlet in an area not yet on any tourist map, contributed to the shock as you passed through the bar, frequented noisily by Pancanto and his kind, and entered a dining room that overwhelmed you with a sense of calm, spaciousness, and sophistication. Large round tables laid out with silver cutlery and candles, and draped in the finest white linen, were leisurely arranged over a ceramic tiled floor. Hispano-Moorish lanterns were suspended from a wooden-beam ceiling, while around you were antiques and pictures set against russet ochre walls. A log fire burnt in a solid stone hearth, and sunlight streamed in from windows overlooking a garden luxuriant with fruit trees and exotic plants. The mixture of urban elegance and rustic chic was a look that restaurateurs and hoteliers had been perfecting since the creation in the 1960s of the Colombe d'Or at St. Paul de Vence. What made the Rey de Copas so special was that it combined the aims of a luxury restaurant with the genuine homeliness, and endearing failings and idiosyncrasies, of an erratically run family establishment.

Demanding customers, with a preference for professionalism over eccentricity, would have been put off from the start by the cook's younger brother, José Luis, who worked as the restaurant's sole waiter. Tall, gauche, and with spiky blonde hair, he was as lacking in training as he was in enthusiasm for his job. As I got to know him outside the Rey de Copas, generally in the context of one of Frailes' late-night bars, he surprised me with his excitability when it came to playing at table football, or talking about sport, cars, and violent films. However, in the restaurant itself he was as sullen and monosyllabic as a sulky teenager. You could often be sitting for ages in an empty room before he came up to take your orders, which, like his opening of a bottle of wine, and the eventual bringing of the food, he did with a lack of grace and style that reminded me of Russian waiters from the communist period.

In a way too that recalled my experiences in communist Russia, the menu that José Luis ungraciously produced was largely filled with dishes that were either unavailable or made up from completely different ingredients to the ones stated. In the end my friends and I left the choice of food entirely in the hands of Juan the cook, a restless lover of experiment. Juan had opened his restaurant with the intention of recreating some of the dishes of the Hispano-Moorish period; and he claimed to have helped popularize in Spain such Moorish specialities as crisply fried cubes of aubergine coated in honey. Later he had defined his culinary aims in terms of keeping alive the gastronomic traditions of his native Jaén, while also reinterpreting these for modern times.

'A warm salad of chicken testicles flavoured with walnut oil,' José Luis would flatly announce, before plunking on the table one of a succession of similarly imaginative dishes which had the flair and designer look of *nouvelle cuisine*, but were also characterized by a hearty abundance more in keeping with traditional country cooking. Every time you thought you had come to the end of the meal, there would be José Luis in front of you again, saying something like, 'Lamb shanks on a bed of seaweed,' or, 'Pig trotters stuffed with almonds.' Juan's failure to take in basic practical considerations, such as a person's appetite, was integral to his culinary genius, as well as one of the reasons why his restaurant seemed destined to eventual closure.

The Rey de Copas had already severely reduced the once consid-erable wealth of Juan's handsome and domineering father Antonio, a local *señorito*, and passionate huntsman. Whereas Juan loved cooking for its own sake, and was more interested in recognition than in money, Antonio had founded the restaurant in the expectation of it being a sound financial investment. The problem was that he had never had a job before in his life, had little idea of the subtleties of business, and did not fully understand or appreciate Juan's style of cooking. Antonio's inability to see cooking as a creative activity was shared by his matronly wife Matilde, a down-to-earth and warm-hearted woman who was always shrugging her shoulders and com-menting on Juan's poor sense of time or urgency. The parents' lack of interest in food had been inherited by their youngest daughter María Ángeles who, of all the family members who regularly assisted in the restaurant, was the one whose sensibility most approximated to Juan's. Like Juan she was someone who aspired to a larger world beyond the comprehension of her parents. She read widely, was keen to travel, and was now enthusiastically studying for a degree in anthropology. The sadness of her predicament, like that of her brother, lay in the conflict between a desire to break away from her environment and an inability to do so. This was a conflict that mir-rored the fatal contradiction at the heart of the Rey de Copas itself, a place torn between opposing cultures, which succeeded in belonging properly neither to the one nor to the other.

Perhaps it was my own shifting sense of identity that made me develop such a strong sympathy for Juan, and led me to feel almost personally involved in his restaurant's destiny. A tall, and – when I first knew him – enormously fat man, Juan had the makings of a tragic personality. Despite his warm, open, and distinguished appear-ance, and the fact that he cut a most impressive figure in his white chef's outfit, he thought of himself as a physical aberration. Yet so genial did he appear, and so willing to talk with other people, that it took me time to realize the effort it cost him to go and meet his customers, and how much he suffered mentally on account of his weight. Juan's personal troubles, together with the problems of his restaurant, encouraged his natural inclinations towards travel. He was always looking for any excuse to go away, as if wanting constantly to escape from himself and his worries. While he still had the money, he would be endlessly disappearing, sometimes for several days, generally to the exasperation of his mother, who would be forced to tell prospective customers that she had no idea when her son would be back. He was prepared to travel for miles, even across the Spanish border, to indulge his love of antiques and of trying out different restaurants.

He was also ever anxious to perfect his own art, and frequently went to faraway gastronomic centres such as Barcelona to work for a few days for a chef he admired, or to sign up for courses such as 'avant-garde desserts'. And when he was not actually travelling, he enjoyed making plans for possible and often unlikely-sounding future trips. 'Maiquel, when shall we go and have lunch in Toledo? . . . When shall we drive to Úbeda to see that dresser I'm interested in? . . . When shall we spend a weekend in New York? . . .'

It was not surprising that Juan's restaurant was invariably empty. Too isolated to attract any passing trade, it catered almost entirely for his more refined acquaintances from Alcalá. Virtually no one, apart from El Sereno, Caño, and Merce, went there from Frailes itself, whose inhabitants were continually derided by Juan for their culinary conservatism. I had always rushed to the Fraileros' defence until I too cooked at the Rey de Copas, after promising to prepare some Italian recipes for a group of our friends from the village.

'Where's the meat?' was the response of one of them to my laboriously prepared home-made ravioli stuffed with ricotta and spinach.

'This is rabbit food,' said someone else, commenting on a salad of rocket and parmesan for which I had had to go all the way to Granada for the ingredients. After that I began envisaging Juan as a gastronomic saint hopelessly trying to convert the heathen.

In the meantime the need for customers at the Rey de Copas was becoming as desperate as Andalucía's need for rain. While sitting with me after one of his lunches Juan would sometimes put forward his latest new scheme for remedying this situation. I managed to talk him out of his idea for a medieval banquet, but he remained adamant about letting a Málaga-based company take over his restaurant for what seemed like a glorified Tupperware party. In return for a free meal prepared by Juan, all the diners had to do was to listen to a couple of salesmen trying to sell objects ranging from an electric frying-pan to a special mattress able to adapt itself so well to a person's body that a key placed underneath was supposedly unnoticeable. When the time came to host this major event, the restaurant was indeed as full as Juan had told me it would be. Not having to pay for what they had heard described as strange and exorbitantly priced food, a number of villagers had put in their first appearance at Juan's establishment. But the event proved a disaster in every respect, not least as a public relations exercise for the Rey de Copas. Juan's cooking, limited by the small budget provided by the company, was not revealed at its best, while the beauty of the interior was marred because the dining room had been rearranged to accommodate a giant mattress on which the largest person present at the lunch was obliged to lie down. 'Ouch!' this poor man shouted when his spine touched the key.

The schemes multiplied, as did the hours spent chatting with Juan, with whom I nearly always ended up talking about food in a pure, abstract way unrelated to the boring practicalities of having to make a living. Lunch at the Rey de Copas became the most time-consuming of my potential daily distractions, and generally left little time for the next important phase of my Frailes investigations: the exploration of the surrounding countryside. Juan, whom I soon realized was an even more awkward presence in nature than I was, had little interest in outdoor activities unless these involved planning some ridiculously complex picnic. He resisted all my efforts to lure him into the country, though he occasionally joined me for that obligatory intermediary stage in between lunch and the late afternoon walk: coffee in the Cueva. An avid lover of gossip, he sat with me at the darkest corner of the bar, listening to the latest village news imparted behind the counter by Villi, a wide-eyed, shyly smiling woman married to Merce's brother Pepín. Occasionally I was tempted to join the card players behind us, but I never gave in to this impulse. To become hooked on cards, as Merce assured me I would be, seemed a terminal state of indolence with which not even the long hours spent at the Rey de Copas could compare.

From the dark and smoky Cueva, where the sunlight never entered, I set off on long, ambitious walks that had been impractical during the heat of the summer. Needless to say, even without Juan it proved impossible to do any of these on my own. Ernesto, my companion at El Sereno's breakfast table, was keen to come along in the interests of trying to lose some of his weight. Caño too said he needed the exercise. Merce wanted to show me more of her favourite local beauty spots. Paqui, whose world rarely extended beyond the *Mesón*, acquired a sudden interest in nature. Caño's and Merce's two sons, Paqui's two daughters, and Pepín and Villi's only child Sergio, all saw the possibilities of new adventures. And El Sereno, of course, did not want to be left out of anything.

Our first group outing of the year was up to the so-called Cave of the Treasure, in the course of which I discovered that El Sereno's recklessness as a driver was matched by a comparable and potentially equally dangerous fearlessness as a walker. Undaunted by the presence in our group of children as young as eight he led the way by scrambling up over scree to the top of a sheer wooded slope.

'Slower! Slower!' protested Paqui and Merce as they fell increasingly behind while looking after a wailing child. Barely had we caught up with him and begun recovering our breath than he had disappeared into the cave, urging us to follow after him. A sweating Ernesto, shaking his head, sat down on a rock, and refused to go a step further. We all did the same, after which even El Sereno admitted that going deeper into the cave without a lantern just a couple of hours before nightfall was perhaps not such a good idea. In the end we curtailed our walk to pursue the safer activity of visiting the charming elderly inhabitants of the hamlet of El Rosales, who invited us to play bowls against a distractingly beautiful panorama where the bosky valley, setting sun, and rising crescent moon made me think I had escaped into a visionary landscape by Samuel Palmer.

This satisfying conclusion to the day encouraged further group walks over the following weeks: up to the bare summit of the Perón; down through waist-high wheat to the largest kermes oak of the Sierra Sur; across a windy plateau scattered with primeval stone huts swarming with giant spiders. El Sereno, unfailingly energetic and enthusiastic, insisted always on taking the lead, and was so convinced of his navigational expertise that he sometimes branched out on his own, saying that he would get to a particular place quicker than we would (which he always did). But gradually the novelty of the walks wore off on the children; Ernesto decided to go instead to an Alcalá gym; and Caño and Merce found themselves spending ever longer periods at the card table. By the beginning of April, the only regular walking companion I had left was El Sereno, faithful to the last.

The almost daily walks we began taking together highlighted an important aspect of a relationship which, while seeming at first like that of father and son, would appear eventually as the fortuitous concordance of two people united in fantasy and folly. Now it was the element of master and pupil which had come to the fore as we wandered sometimes for hours on end through ever remoter parts of the Sierra Sur. The story of our walks was reminiscent of the French Enlightenment tale of the *enfant sauvage*, except in reverse: instead of being the young savage who is taught by a doctor to take on the trappings of civilization, I was the product of a sophisticated urban environment learning to adapt to nature.

I could not have found a better teacher than El Sereno, under whose guidance I felt my prospects of surviving in the wild beginning significantly to improve. He revealed to me such unsuspected sources of instant nourishment as the white parts of uprooted reeds ('excellent for chewing'), almonds that were still green and moist, and minuscule red berries known as 'arse-blockers'. He showed me where to look for wild asparagus, and how to strip off the prickly leaves of a thistle, the stalks of which, he claimed, were wonderful when cooked. He introduced me to the pleasures of lying down in the middle of a field of barley, and tried to assure me that the dangers of nature were greatly exaggerated. At times I thought I was being prepared for the SAS as I was made to pole-vault over rivers or negotiate my way down sheer rocky slopes which people said afterwards we had been crazy to attempt. And there was at least one tip I learnt which would probably have had unfortunate results had I taken heed of it anywhere else but in the surroundings of Frailes.

'We have a saying,' said El Sereno, 'that anything grown in the countryside is grown for everyone.' Later that afternoon, as I was helping myself to a handful of almonds straight from the tree, I was caught in the act by the farmer whose property we were crossing. 'Wait there!' he shouted, before going off to look for a bag so that we could take with us as many almonds as we could manage.

If the farmer had not turned up at that particular moment, El

Sereno would almost certainly have gone off to search for him. For it was entirely characteristic of his personality that he would manage to find people with whom he could engage even in the middle of nowhere. Every time he saw a solitary man in the distance he had to make a detour to go and see him, and whenever we came across a farm he would immediately be knocking on the door or making one of those whistling sounds I had first heard him use with horses. Frequently, and without being asked, he would give someone his advice, whether on the planting of tomatoes, say, or the creation of a drainage system. Invariably these encounters would result in us being invited to have a look around the person's house, which helped me build up my knowledge of the area's traditional rural dwellings, with their pebble floors, plaster-covered wooden beams, and upper rooms partitioned into spaces reserved for the storage of wheat and other grains.

El Sereno, observing my typically urban middle-class dismay whenever an owner proudly showed me some modern 'improvement', himself developed into an ever more passionate conservationist. He began criticizing farmers for building new homes instead of restoring their old and neglected ones.

'Look over there,' he would say, pointing to a derelict structure. 'That's the sort of house that does our area proud, as my friend Maiquel, who's an English writer, will tell you. What you've built now could have been put up anywhere, it doesn't fit at all into the landscape, and its walls aren't thick enough to keep out the summer heat.'

And to those who argued about the cost and difficulties of restoration, he would answer back with an impressive dose of technical information he had picked up from an architect friend of mine who had come to see me from Murcia.

'You should know,' he told them excitedly, 'that there's this new system of roofing that allows you to place old tiles over a layer of insulating material. This is not only a more aesthetic and efficient alternative to building a modern roof, but it also works out a lot cheaper.'

Despite visiting farms in locations so remote and wild that you half-expected their residents to be relicts from the Middle Ages, not one of the places we went to at first had managed to retain a completely unaltered interior, or indeed was still without any basic modern facilities. Then one afternoon, searching for somewhere new to walk, we left the road to Cerezo Gordo, and deviated onto a track that climbed up to a cluster of ancient oaks. El Sereno, pointing out to me how the now hollow trunks survived purely by roots growing on the side, speculated whether these trees dated back to before the last millennium.

'Let's see what else we'll find if we keep driving,' he said, as we headed along the track towards the point where it disappeared over a ridge. On the other side the surface deteriorated, so we parked the car, and continued on foot along the upper slopes of a valley which led after a while to a hamlet of humble white farms. El Sereno, as usual, was soon talking to the inhabitants, giving them his opinions on roofing and drainage, and welcoming the opportunity to be shown around their homes. We were told almost immediately that this was a community without electricity. Though electrical pylons could be seen in the far distance, there was apparently no plan as yet to have the cables extended to this point. This was a place that politicians seemed to have forgotten about, thanks to its anomalous situation of belonging officially to the municipality of Valdepeñas de Jaén, while being far closer in distance to Frailes, itself a good hour away by car. A smiling farmer called Pedro revealed to us that a couple of journalists had promised to draw attention to the hamlet's plight in a short television feature, but so far nothing more from them had been heard.

'Without electricity,' he added without the slightest rancour, 'there's no future for us here, we won't be able to make a living any more.'

We went on our way, but not before asking Pedro where we would end up if we stayed to the now narrowing track. He mentioned a farm at least an hour's walk from here, where a man lived with his old and now decrepit mother.

'He's got the money, he could move with her down to Frailes, but she doesn't want to, she's been there all her life. They haven't even got a car.'

Then, shrugging his shoulders, he concluded that 'the quality of our lives out here is very poor.' El Sereno, who had been nodding all along, now shook his head in disagreement. He said he had been brought up in an isolated farm, and had loved the absence of traffic, the complete silence, and the sheer pleasure of being out in nature.

'You're right about that,' Pedro admitted. 'The solitary country life has its advantages, especially if you have a few animals to distract you.'

Having recently heard about the libidinous use to which a poor beast known as 'Domingo's donkey' had been put, I perhaps read too much into this last statement. Nonetheless Pedro helped feed my persistent lurid imaginings of what went on in remote rural communities by mentioning again the name of the man whose farm lay an hour ahead of us. I was convinced I had misheard him the first time, but clearly I had not. There really was somebody known as '*El Matasuegra*', the 'mother-in-law-killer'.

Of all the local nicknames I was gradually learning (and everyone here had one. this being the only way to distinguish between the countless Custodios, Mercedes, Manolos, Pacos, Pepes, and Antonios), '*El Matasuegra*' stood out even in such company as '*El Follao*' ('The Fucked'), '*El Escandoloso*' ('The Scandalous One'), '*El Tirapeos*' ('The Fart-thrower'), and the name unfortunately applied to one of Frailes's bakers, '*El Mucoso*' (the 'Snotty-nosed'). Nicknames of any sort, let alone these ones, were generally best not used in front of the person in question, even though they were freely bandied about by everyone else in the village, and had often been passed down from one generation to the next irrespective of how appropriate they still were, or whether their origins were remembered at all. As I walked with El Sereno further up the hill towards El Matasuegra's house, I asked him if anything was known about the story behind this particular name.

'Yes,' he replied, as we walked further up the mountain towards the man's house. 'The Matasuegra's father killed his mother-in-law with an axe. The man died soon afterwards in prison, after separating from his wife, who was much younger than he was. I think the Matasuegra was just a baby when all this happened.'

Our progress up the track was slow, with stops to open gates, talk to a passing shepherd, and collect thistle stalks, which I now learnt were more tender when found in the midst of thick clumps of grass. We walked between woods and a narrow stretch of cultivated fields that fell down to the rocky bed of a mountain stream. Colours and contours were sharpening as the late afternoon turned slowly to evening, giving to the view of the Sierra Nevada behind us a limpid blue cragginess. The house where the Matasuegra's grandmother had been killed stood in sparse isolation near the top of the bare slope onto which our track had emerged. It looked back to the distant peaks of Granada across one of those circular threshing floors that have been carved into the landscape as if for some archaic ritual, and are suitably known in Spain by the suggestive word '*era*'. El Sereno gave a shout to announce our arrival.

The old woman who emerged from the dark interior could have stepped out of the Middle Ages. Holding a bucket in one hand and a stick in the other, she hobbled around on legs that were like stumps swathed in filthy bandages. Her hair was covered by a dark shawl, and a stained brown apron was tied as if by rope to her worn black dress.

'My son's not at home,' she said. 'I don't know where he is, I shouldn't think he'll be back now until nightfall. Why don't you come and wait for him inside? Can I get you something to drink?'

El Sereno shook his head, saying that we didn't have the time, we should be going back before it got dark. But, as we stood on the threshold of her house, glimpsing across its pebble floor towards the glow from the fireplace, he stayed talking all the same. He was anxious to find out more about her, and she duly responded by telling us her woes.

She suffered, she said, from poor circulation; that was why her legs had swollen so much. She lifted her skirt slightly to show how she wore a pair of trousers underneath her knee-length socks. These gave her support, she claimed, and kept her warm; but her mobility was worsening every day. How old was she? 'Well over seventy,' she thought, but she wasn't sure, her memory was going. She could not remember her son's Christian name, she did not know how old he was either, 'perhaps over forty, it's time he got married'. In her bucket was a pair of his trousers which she was going to wash in the spring outside. When finally El Sereno made a move to leave, she began slowly to shuffle towards the water, moaning with every step she took.

'I've suffered,' she announced, as she waved us goodbye, 'from the moment I was born.'

As we walked in the twilight down the mountain, we encountered after a while a shadowy form working in the fields. This was, I gathered, the woman's son, the Matasuegra. El Sereno launched eagerly into another conversation, unconcerned now by the growing darkness. The Matasuegra proved no less willing to talk, and revealed a cheerful and almost urbane manner that barely tallied with his dramatic family history and obviously arduous domestic situation. With his thick curly brown hair, and lithe and sprightly manner, he also seemed remarkably youthful, and I could hardly believe it when he told us that he had just celebrated his fifty-second birthday. El Sereno, who by now had had a complete change of heart about the wonders of rural solitude, was soon telling him what to do with his life: he should buy a house in Frailes, get a sturdy vehicle, and find someone to look after him in preparation for the day when his mother would no longer be around. The Matasuegra, nodding his head in agreement, confided that he had not done 'what people say are the two best things in life – marry and get a driving licence'. There was, he then confessed, a woman he was interested in. She was a Colombian in her twenties, whom he had met through a cousin of his in Córdova. She had come to see him in his house, but had been put off by the 'four-hour walk to get there'. She had now found a job working as a maid in Fuengirola, but would happily come and marry him once he had sold the farm and moved into Frailes.

'So perhaps my life is going to change after all,' he smiled, as I anticipated the day when his farm, with its terrible story, would one day be tastefully transformed into a holiday home for the adventurous rural tourist.

So many of the afternoon walks I undertook with El Sereno would end like this – at night-time after having greatly furthered my knowledge of the natural and human life of the Sierra Sur. Once back in Frailes I would have plenty of time to reflect on all these new experiences after I had returned to my garden hut and to what was usually the most profitable part of my writing day. Working some-times into the early hours of the morning, I came to appreciate the pleasures of nocturnal solitude, and the inspiration of a world ruled by silence. I felt as if I were the master and sole inhabitant of my own planet, like the hero of Saint-Exupéry's children's fable, *The Little Prince*. Yet though there was no one now to disturb me in my work, and though not a soul stirred afterwards as I walked down the deserted hill towards the *Mesón*, I knew that Frailes by night was not as dead as I had first thought in the days after the wine festival. Even in a village as small as this, and at this time of continuing drought when few people supposedly had the heart or money to go out, there was always somewhere, I discovered, where one could find company and a drink almost until the dawn broke.

However much I was changing under the influence of a rural environment, I could not shake off so easily what I thought of as my profoundly urbanite desire to haunt late-night bars. The scope for fulfilling this in a small, out-of-the-way village in the province of Jaén had not at first seemed enormous, so I had resigned myself before my arrival to a routine of quieter and more sober nights than the ones to which I had been accustomed in centres such as Seville, Madrid and Barcelona. Perhaps, I had said to myself, I might even start behaving in a way that anyone but a Spaniard would consider as more appropriate to my age. What I had not taken into account, however, was that Frailes had no fewer than nine bars, and that it merely needed a group of faithful clients comprising little more than one per cent of the village population to enable at least three of these places to stay open regularly past three in the morning. This did not augur well for my attempts to achieve a healthier and more monastic lifestyle, especially as one of these late night venues was situated directly underneath my bedroom.

When Paqui had promised that the Discoteca Oh! would be functioning only at weekends, I had not imagined that her busiest night of the week would be on a Sunday, nor that she would soon be forced by declining finances to open the place whenever she felt like it. But this was a disco that differed from most other discos, or at least from any disco likely to be encountered outside of rural Spain. For a start this was not a place to which one generally came with the intention either of dancing or finding a partner. Those who wanted to do so would drive off on a Friday or Saturday night to Alcalá la Real, and would think of the Discoteca Oh! essentially as somewhere to go to on a Sunday to meet up with friends, play darts and table football, and generally while away what was left of the day following a protracted family lunch. During these Sunday reunions, which would invariably be drawn out well past midnight, the sort of people one might normally expect in a disco (teenagers and the unmarried young) would mingle with the stalwarts of the Frailes drinking scene – a group of mainly middle-aged and elderly men whose presence in the village's late-night bars was as dependable as the same dozen or so Spanish disco hits that Paqui would constantly be playing at a volume that often made conversation almost impossible.

A visit to the Discoteca Oh! regularly brought to an end my Frailes day. Whenever I saw a light on there, after descending late at night from El Sereno's garden, I would look inside to say hello to Paqui, intending always to stay just for a few minutes before finally making it to my bed. Almost always I would find her talking to someone while seated on top of the solitary portable gas heater that served so ineffectually to heat the entire room. And no less inevitably I too would be dragged into a barely audible conversation either with her or with one of those habitual drinkers who stood propped at the bar, where they managed to remain as oblivious to the deafening repetitive music as they were to the soundless television images that were projected all the time onto a giant canvas screen suspended in the darkness. No, I would tell them, I couldn't stay long, I needed to go to bed, I wanted to be up early the next morning, but the glass of whisky would be placed regardless on the counter in front of me, and then another, offered sometimes by someone with whom I might not even have been speaking.

My inability to tear myself away from this tenebrous environment could partly be explained in the same way as my tendency to be the last person to leave a party: I hated missing out on anything. But I also liked thinking that Merce's spirit had accompanied me into this alcoholic realm, and that my being here constituted one stage further in our journey together towards the heart of Frailes. I was getting to know more and more of the villagers, often under drunken circumstances likely to bring out more quickly the truth about their personalities. There were of course those boors whom I preferred to avoid, such as the tattooed, shaven-headed giant appropriately named Dionisio, who always eyed me aggressively before repeatedly slapping me on the shoulder, shouting out the names of British football players, and endlessly chanting the slogan '*Eng-er-land!*' Some of the other regulars, however, were totally compelling in their drunkenness, in particular the village street cleaner Bubi, who vented his considerable energies in solo snatches of dance so violent, impassioned, stylish, and idiosyncratic in their rhythms that you could almost have imagined for him some dazzling future as a performer. But what was so fascinating about Bubi was his alertness to all that was going on around him even when he was so drunk that he could barely speak. He projected the image of some existential philosopher who had seen through humanity, and had concluded, like Merce, that all ways of living were acceptable as long as they did not hurt anyone else.

There were moments in the Discoteca Oh! when I pictured the place as an irresistible glow to which all the strange creatures of the Frailes night would eventually be drawn. It was here, appropriately enough, that I finally met up with the two brothers who owned the mysterious House of the Armandos, where I had still to see as much as an open shutter.

'We've just got back from Granada with our mother,' explained Ezequiel, the older of the two, a heavily built man in his mid-fifties who, I discovered, loved telling jokes and prided himself on being the sole member of the local Atlético Madrid fan club.

'We've hardly been in Frailes recently,' added the younger brother, Fermín, whose appearance, more refined than that of Ezequiel, was more in keeping with the glamorous image I had formed of the two of them. With his moustache, cravat, and charming smile, like that of Omar Sharif, he could have been some aging matinée idol.

'Fermín,' Paqui interjected, 'speaks perfect English.'

'She is exaggerating,' he quietly protested. 'There might have been a time when I could defend myself as it were in your language, but that was many years ago.'

I would soon find out that it was part of Fermín's manner always to play down his own importance, to apologize almost for himself, and to try and blend as much as possible into the background. On the night of our first meeting it took some coaxing on my part to make him reveal that he had been an English teacher for many years, and had even been sent for a while on an exchange to Wolverhampton. 'I must confess,' he told me in his typically polite, aristocratic manner, 'that my experiences in *Los Midlands* were not altogether positive.'

Unlike Ezequiel, Fermín proved to be a regular visitor to the Discoteca Oh! The numerous times I sat next to him at the bar, however, were not sufficient for him to lose his natural discretion. He admitted that he had inherited his father's conservative views, and that he had been living a life of leisure now for some time, financed by the revenue from his estates. But he remained for me an enigma, and continued to be one even after I was invited to visit his house, which, inevitably perhaps, came as a disappointment after the weeks of mounting curiosity.

'There's nothing special about the place,' he said, guiding me around a building that had retained little of the past save for an iron-work and stained-glass conservatory where, surrounded by potted palms, his mother sat engaged in lacework. El Sereno had spoken about a library as majestic as that of Alexandria, though even this turned out to be interesting only in so far as it revealed the reading tastes of Fermín. I was amused to find he had an almost complete set of the writings of Gerald Brenan.

Talking with him once about Brenan when propped up at our usual places at the disco bar, I remarked on the curious position of a British middle-class intellectual in an Alpujarran village in the 1920s. As I said this, I became more aware than ever of Fermín's own incongruity in this world of hardened drunks who shared neither his political views, nor his privileged background, nor his broad cultural interests. Occasionally, when drink made him slightly more open than normal, he would confess that he did not know what he was doing wasting his time like this, and that there were surely better ways of diverting himself than having the same conversations every day with the same people. The person whose name he often quoted during these rare attacks of existential angst, the most inseparable and unusual of his nocturnal companions, was a man who was in every way his opposite, down to his having been born to one of Frailes's poorest families. That the two of them should be so often together in the Discoteca Oh! only strengthened my alcohol-induced impression that the place was nothing less than a microcosm of life itself.

Known to everyone by his nickname of '*Chica*' or 'Girl', the man had a congenital disease that made him appear sometimes like a village idiot. He had withered arms that hung lankly by his side, accentuating the droopiness of his weather-worn head, with its weak mouth, wide, expressionless eyes, and long straight hair at the back. When he opened his mouth, you assumed he was drunk, which he often was; but his disease had also left him with a speech defect that made each word he enunciated seem like a bursting bubble from a slowly boiling field of mud. When speeded up under the influence of drink, his speech became virtually incomprehensible other than to those who had spent long hours listening to his passionately uttered views.

Chica had an especial love of pop music. The first time I met him, late on a Sunday at the Discoteca Oh!, he became overexcited at the thought of knowing somebody 'from the land of the Beatles, Pink Floyd, the Stones . . .', and spent the next two hours rushing backwards and forwards from the bar to the sound box, where he appointed himself as the unofficial disc jockey for the night.

'And now, for the benefit of the English guest we have here tonight, I am going to play . . .' he drooled periodically, interrupting '*Un movimiento sexi*' or some other such Spanish hit. With his arms brought maniacally into action like those of a puppet, and with a capacious white linen shirt swirling above the giant buckle of a broad black leather belt (his clothes sense, like his musical tastes, was firmly rooted in the 1960s and 1970s), he animated Paqui's lugubrious disco, and made me envisage him, in some ideal future situation, as the stylish, handsome owner of a fashionable club. Not until we said goodbye did I realize that he did indeed have his own late night bar.

When Chica proposed on parting that we should meet up there some time, and then told me where it was, I thought at first he was joking. Even in this village of unlikely establishments, I could not believe that anyone would wish to have a bar on the steep and seemingly deserted alley that ran above the olive-oil factory. Yet, as I soon found out for myself, such a place not only existed (it was known, to the bafflement of the village's non-English speakers, as the 'Chica Boy') but also had the mirrored, veneered-wood look of an old-fashioned cocktail bar, such as you might have encountered in the middle of a city. Miles Davis was quietly playing in the background when I went there the first time, to find Chica illegally gambling with the bar's two clients. On my arrival he abandoned his cards, and got up to change the music. Making me listen to one tape after another of classic British pop, he occasionally joined in the singing himself, while tapping out the rhythms on the bar counter. Seeing Chica so happy was a heartening sight, but, as it turned out, I would have no more opportunity to do so at the Chica Boy. The place's declining commercial viability would force Chica to close the establishment down two weeks later. 'People don't understand music in this village,' he lamented.

Chica was one of those personalities whom I found difficult to picture outside the nether world of nocturnal bars. However, as time went on, and my friendship with him developed, I began seeing another side to his life and character. One night he invited me to come and have lunch at his parents' house, and told me to meet up beforehand at the Charro.

'He'll never turn up,' Caño and others kept warning me. 'He was probably pissed at the time, and won't remember a thing when he wakes up this morning.'

But Chica was waiting for me exactly at the appointed time, and we were soon making our way to his family home, a humble structure built around a cluttered courtyard with an outdoor staircase. His mother Josefa, a short, round woman with a broadly smiling face covered in warts, watched us approach from the upper balcony. She laughed raucously as she saw me studying the numerous kitsch objects – a wooden pixie holding a thermometer, a row of coat hooks made from goats' hooves, a cuckoo clock featuring Snow White and the Seven Dwarfs – that covered the outer walls. 'I love whimsy,' she declared. Later I heard from Chica that she had been worried all morning that a man like me would be made uncomfortable by their 'simple ways and pleasures'.

Instead I felt immediately at home in the Chica household, where I could appreciate the mixture of simplicity, spontaneous kindness, fantasy, experience of hardship, and love of drink that had gone into the making of Chica himself. He resembled in particular his genial father José, a slightly built man with a large head who mumbled at speed, and muttered, '*Correcto, correcto,*' whenever I made doubly sure I had heard correctly some of his extraordinary stories. While Josefa finished the cooking preparations he began telling me about his many years of working in a factory in Germany, where safety precautions had been minimal, and several of his colleagues had almost been killed. Talking in a way that soon became as difficult to understand as his son's, he rambled off in unexpected directions, so that suddenly I was transported from post-war Germany to Cuba at the time of the war of independence of 1898. José's father, a soldier in the Spanish army, had been arrested by the Cuban insurgents, and would have been executed at dawn had not a black woman fallen in love with him and arranged a terrifying escape which included battling with crocodiles and giant hairy spiders as he wandered for 'seven days and seven nights in the jungle'.

Chica, beaming and nodding like a child while José related this barely credible tale, then led me away to a cellar to show me a huge barrel of home-made wine 'pressed by our own feet'. Filtering off the layer of insects that floated on the surface, he filled a two-litre bottle with the murky liquid, and then picked up an ancient round of cheese ('1994 or 1993, I'm not quite sure') as well as one of their 'home-grown' melons, which he claimed could be stored in this dark cold room for over a year.

In search of a final additional ingredient for what he promised would be 'the best meal you've ever had', we went into his cell-like bedroom, where he sliced some meat off a large ham hanging almost directly above his pillow. Then we went back upstairs, where Josefa had placed on the table a great platter of the sautéed potatoes with onions and peppers that are known in Spain as '*papas a lo pobre*' (poor people's potatoes).

'How do you like your eggs?' she asked, to which I replied, 'As they come.'

'Oh, he's very refined!' she commented as she placed in front of me a terracotta bowl filled with hot oil and fried garlic. 'We eat our eggs like this,' she said, breaking up the cooked yolks in the oil and then stirring them vigorously to form a vomit-like mush. Half an hour later Chica was going back downstairs for some more wine as José and Josefa continued to feed me with food and stories.

By the time we had finished lunch Chica's married sister had made an appearance, together with her twelve-year-old Down's-syndrome son, who slobbered me with kisses. 'Though he can't speak, he's very intelligent,' said José, 'and very affectionate, as you can see.' Josefa meanwhile had taken out some old family photos, and was showing me snaps of a happy, youthful Chica, posing among the vineyards of southern France, where so many Fraileros had worked during the autumn months. 'Look how handsome he is,' she said adoringly.

Chica by now had had enough and was persuading me to come with him outside and search for wild asparagus. I found it difficult to keep up with him once we had left the village and begun darting through thorny bushes, up and down slithering slopes of pebbles and olive leaves, and over the rocky beds of streams, where Chica said he had seen snakes over two metres long during the summer months. The wine seemed to have given an additional lightness to his step, not to mention a boundless optimism.

'If we speed up a bit,' he urged, 'we might get as far as this ruined Moorish castle, it's about two hours away.'

'Moorish castle?' I asked incredulously.

'Yes,' he answered, 'I'm the only person who knows about it.'

Fortunately, he now remembered our original mission, and gave up the quest for chimeras to dedicate himself with no less zeal entirely to asparagus. 'Look there's some over there!' he shouted, rushing up the hill to collect some stalks, before rushing down again in an instant after sighting, sometimes at a distance of over twenty metres, a few more. But though he taught me how to scrutinize the ground below each olive tree, I failed to uncover a single stalk while he had gathered a whole basketful. I lacked not only Chica's years of practice but, more importantly, that sense of urgent necessity which had forced him since childhood to scour the countryside in search of sustenance. The collecting of asparagus was not just a diversion for him but a way of earning money now that the olive harvest was over and his bar had closed down. When we got back to the village at dusk, with Chica holding what he calculated was at least 5,000 pesetas' worth of asparagus, he wanted us to go right away to the Choto to celebrate. Placing the trophy on the bar counter for everyone to see, he stood there radiant with happiness.

I did not see Chica again for nearly two weeks, but I began to hear rumours. Bubi said that he had been offered a temporary job in Mallorca and was thinking of taking it. He had a small disability pension, and though he was able now to claim social security (like everyone in the village who only had seasonal work), he dismissed this as inadequate. When finally I encountered him again late one night at the Discoteca Oh! he was drunk and depressed.

'I'm going,' he muttered, 'first thing tomorrow. I don't want to leave here, I love my village, I love my family. It's a disgrace, people shouldn't be forced to find work far away from home, there should be work in the place you live. And all those so-called unemployed who get social security when they don't really need it, they've got expensive cars for Christ's sake, they don't know what it's like to be poor. There's so much corruption . . .' He persisted in this vein for a good while longer, then slumped his head on the counter, exhausted.

I remembered Merce telling me that of all the serious drinkers at the Discoteca, Chica was the only one who did not behave as he did out of choice. He cared about the opinions of others, and wanted more from life than to be merely an amiable curiosity who did exactly as he pleased. Seeing him in the near-empty Discoteca Oh! on the eve of his departure into exile brought home to me his vulnerability, and provided an image to latch on to whenever I became conscious of the tragic predicaments facing not only him but Frailes too.

'Maiquel,' he said as Paqui prepared to close for the night, 'I'm not well in the head.' He could barely open his mouth by now, and each word he uttered struggled to be released. 'I cannot,' he continued, before pausing, then starting again, until finally he stuttered, 'I cannot understand life.' Then the music was turned off, the lights went out, and a cold gust of wind came through the open door. Another day was over.

3

THE WEEKS AND then the months passed, and I became more in tune with the cyclical nature of country life, but the pleasantness of my own existence here could not disguise the fact that I was living in a village that seemed headed towards extinction. Novelty, a surge of hope, something completely out of the ordinary, was needed to challenge the fatalism of a world regulated, it seemed, by a sound which had never before intruded so much on my consciousness: the sound of bells announcing yet another death.

Two knells for a woman, three for a man, five for a nun, and six for a priest – that was the code from earlier centuries. Now there was a just a continuous ringing that I usually heard as I walked up early in the morning to El Sereno's house. Women stood outside their houses gossiping about what had happened.

'The mother of Custodio the cobbler died last night in her sleep . . .'; 'Dionisio's uncle went out into the fields, and dropped dead, just like that . . . I always thought he drank too much . . .'; 'Poor old Carmencita, she'd had that cancer for years . . .'; 'Litro was driving back from Alcalá at about three in the morning when the car swerved off the road . . .' Stories such as these, discussed over breakfast by El Sereno and Ernesto, on everyone's lips by late morning in the Charro, and relayed to me in full detail by Villi at the Cueva, continued to be mulled over until late afternoon when, all of a sudden, the card-playing stopped, and the village bars began to empty. The funerals were attended by most of the villagers, who, if not going to the actual Mass, either followed the foot procession through the streets of Frailes, or, at the very least, climbed up to the cemetery to offer their condolences to the family of the deceased.

This accumulation of deaths confirmed my growing suspicion that most people in Frailes were related, however distantly, to the same ten or so families. It also highlighted my fears for the village's future. The population, already little more than half what it had been at the end of the nineteenth century, continued to decline as its younger elements came to be greatly outnumbered by the elderly and retired. Benefit handouts, and the many agricultural grants now available, might have eradicated the extreme poverty that had led to such widespread emigration in earlier times; but it had not prevented the young from leaving, if only to neighbouring Alcalá. Jobs that satisfied the more demanding and materialistic tastes of the modern generation were few, and it was premature and unrealistic to expect salvation either from rural tourism or from the future local wine industry. As for a recent plan to revive the spa, this had not as yet got further than a promenade, half-completed and now abandoned, which stood in ridiculous isolation in the middle of a dry wasteland, drawing attention to the most pressing of all the village's current problems: another winter was almost over, and not a drop of rain had fallen.

Even the walnut tree in El Sereno's garden had started to die. As I stood under its cracked and desiccated branches, watching yet another funeral procession making its way up the cemetery hill, I could almost identify with Gibbon as he pondered the decline of a civilization. In these days of uncertainty, I thought it opportune to try and look more closely at Frailes's past, hoping perhaps to find patterns that might offer consolation for the present.

The facts I uncovered on the village's history remained frustratingly few, and I wondered how Santi had managed to make his soon to be published book on the subject no less than four hundred pages long. Known to the Moors as 'Alfralyas', Frailes had existed for centuries as a tiny and impoverished hamlet under the jurisdiction of Alcalá. Conflicting theories that its name was due either to the presence here of '*frailes*' (monks), or to the place's possible notoriety as a centre for '*fraudes*' (crimes) were merely attempts to lend substance to a community that for most of its history was of no importance whatsoever. Not until the nineteenth century did Frailes achieve any degree of prosperity, thanks to improved agricultural methods and the exploitation of its thermal waters. In 1835 the village made a definitive break with Alcalá, and by the 1890s its spa attracted not only wealthy Madrilenians but also Frailes's first known visitor of national importance, the writer Ángel Ganivet, a leading member of Spain's Generation of 1898. At this point of time Frailes's future as a thriving spa and market town might have seemed assured.

But, as I studied the village's history, I came to realize that there was something in the Frailes air, and perhaps even in the villagers themselves, that seemed to hold the place back just as it was on the point of achieving true success. A historian from Alcalá, writing in 1913, perceived the Fraileros as having 'lively personalities and quick imaginations', and an ability 'to grasp an idea instantly'; but he also complained how 'squalid ambition' and 'bad advice' had already led to the deterioration of their spa. Despite all the latter's potential for bringing to the community 'incalculable riches and benefits', the place had been reduced to 'a heap of uninhabited and half-ruined houses inexplicably left among yellow, sulphur-smelling streams that emerge from the ruins of the blocked-up pools and slowly cross the fields by way of the irrigation channel used by swineherds to give water to their pigs'.

The spa was briefly if brilliantly revived after being taken over by Alcalá's grandest family (one of whose descendants was José Luis, my guide around the 'House of the Doctor'). Made more attractive than ever before by the introduction of such facilities as lawn tennis courts and an outdoor cinema, it might have developed into one of Spain's most fashionable spas had the children of Alfonso XIII been able to come to Frailes, as Dean Ezequiel Mudarra had so passionately wished. But circumstances dictated otherwise. The king was forced to abdicate, Spain's Second Republic came into being, and then, in 1936, the civil war broke out, destroying the spa possibly for ever, and putting Frailes back to where it had started – small, poverty-stricken and obscure.

One of the consequences of living in a village dominated by the old was the extent to which the civil war and its aftermath loomed in the collective memory. This subject, of diminishing relevance to the majority of today's Spaniards, was still a highly controversial one in tight-knit, isolated communities such as Frailes, where the family and political history of every inhabitant was widely known. Stories from this period of atrocities and shifting political allegiances often turned up in conversations; but even someone so apparently unmindful of causing controversy as Santi hesitated before putting them into print.

There was certainly nothing to be read chronicling the war years that was nearly as vivid or revealing as what I could glean from talking, say, to the elderly card-players at the Cueva. Predictably, one of my most copious sources was El Sereno, who spoke about the past with his usual unfailing openness. I began finally to understand his antipathy towards the Catholic Church after hearing him retell the wartime experiences of his much-loved elder brother Fernando, who had been imprisoned in 1939 for having been a Republican deputy in his native village of Fuerte del Rey. While in prison in Jaén priests had tried hard to make him go to confession, which he had refused, unlike some of his fellow inmates whose supposedly confidential outpourings in the confessional had led to the arrests of many others, and even to their own death sentences. Fernando himself was eventually condemned to die, but was pardoned on the intervention of a young Nationalist whom he had saved earlier from being killed by Republicans.

'My brother suddenly understood that people of opposed political views could often be fighting for the same reasons,' commented El Sereno, who also admitted that barbarities were committed equally by both sides in Frailes, and that all the villagers, no matter what their politics, suffered afterwards in almost equal measure.

As I listened avidly to tales of these shadowy years, I discovered that the aspects of Frailes's history which appealed to me most were those so shrouded in secrecy as to acquire a gloss of myth and romance. Among the stories I was most drawn to were the ones connected with the post-war Republican resistance movement known as the *Maquis*. To Gerald Brenan, journeying across a devastated Andalucía in 1949, these fighters seem to have had the same romantic allure as bandits to foreign travellers in the nineteenth century. Like illustrious local bandits such as José-María (whose legendary status in nineteenth-century Europe almost equalled that of the Alhambra), the members of the *Maquis* took to hiding in Andalucía's plentiful caves, and – when not thought of as outright thugs – gained a reputation as glamorous, Robin Hood-like figures. Some of them had their deeds celebrated in popular songs and poems.

The wild, remote mountains of the Sierra Sur were perfect terrain for the *Maquis*, and indeed served as a centre of operations for two of their most notorious leaders, Tomás Villén ('*Cencerro*'), and Juan Saéz Palomino ('*Hojarrasquín*'). The former, a native of Castillo de Locubín (about twenty miles north-west of Frailes), was a communist whose first act of rebellion was the hardly chivalrous one of hitting out in a rage at his aunt, after she had conspired with the local priest in 1932 to deprive her nephew of property he believed had been left to him. The woman died, and Cencerro was thrown into prison, but, these being the liberal days of the Second Republic, was soon released on the intervention of a judge sympathetic to his political views. With the triumph of the Nationalists in 1939, however, the authorities threatened to reopen the case; and Cencerro, with his communist past, believed his chances of getting off lightly this time were small. He escaped into the mountains around Valdepeñas de Jaén, where he formed a small band of guerrillas who financed their activities with a series of armed robberies. They were often joined in these by the other famous *Maquis* leader, Hojarrasquín, who came from a hamlet near Alcalá and had displayed a brave and impetuous temperament while fighting during the war alongside such revolutionaries as the self-styled 'Pancho Villa'.

The guerrillas' most daring and famous escapade took place in the autumn of 1941, when they held up a coach that was driving along the spectacular mountain road between Jaén and Valdepeñas. Shouting, 'We are guerrillas of the Republic!' they told the women passengers to stay seated while they ordered the men outside and forced them to part with their money. According to a nineteen-year-old witness of the event, the attackers 'behaved correctly'. They gave water to a woman who was sick from fear, and returned money to a man who said he had collected it for a brother who was in a concentration camp.

Such courtesy, however, was not in any way held in their favour during the reprisals that followed. On the basis of an identification made by a right-wing passenger, Cencerro's associates and family were rounded up until eventually most of the guerrillas were captured and then executed. Only Cencerro himself, together with Hojarrasquín, managed to elude the *Guardia Civil* for the time being. The two men seem to have received considerable support from the inhabitants of Frailes, and were often seen openly in the village. At dawn on 28 December 1941 they were at an establishment called Las Constantinas, a brothel that had once existed on the river banks across from the Cueva.

The rest of the story I received directly from one of El Sereno's card-playing friends, a witty, distinguished-looking old man who had happened to be in the brothel at exactly the same time as the two legendary fighters. Alerted by the sound of gunfire, he had woken up to find the building surrounded by the *Guardia Civil*, who had been tipped off by a prostitute called María. The next moment he realized that the two outlaws had somehow succeeded in escaping from the brothel and were running off in different directions. 'They've done it again, I thought, somewhat admiringly.' But the police caught up almost immediately with Hojarrasquín, who, finding himself completely cornered, put a bullet in his head.

Cencerro was luckier, and indeed succeeded in holding out for almost six years longer, outliving most of the great *Maquis* leaders. Finally, on July 16, he was tracked down to a house in the middle of Valdepeñas where, for nearly twenty-four hours, he and his followers put up a suicidal last stand, during which they threw bombs at the police, and destroyed their own money so that no one else could lay hands on it. The impact of this siege on the inhabitants of Valdepeñas was still keenly felt, as I realized when I went one day with El Sereno to see the site where the bloody events had taken place.

'Is that where Cencerro was killed?' El Sereno asked a group of old men sitting chattering outside a completely rebuilt house at the junction of two streets. The men nodded, and then began recounting the event as if it had happened yesterday.

'The police eventually became so desperate,' one of them said, 'that they had to set fire to the building and reduce it to rubble. Almost everyone inside had been killed by then except for Cencerro and one of his mates. They survived for a while by locking themselves in the basement, but then died of their wounds and asphyxiation. I was standing where you see me today when they brought out the corpses.'

A historian from Alcalá later told me that the widows of both Cencerro and Hojarrasquín were still alive, but had always been reluctant to discuss their husbands' lives. In the end the only family member of the *Maquis* whom I met was Hojarrasquín's nephew, a youngish forty-year-old with an open, grinning face, whom I encountered by chance in the Discoteca Oh!, when he was in an advanced stage of drunkenness. After repeatedly telling an uninterested Paqui that his wife no longer slept with him ('Why on earth are you saying this?' she finally cried out in desperation), he turned to me to insist a good twenty times that olive oil could easily be put into a car's engine as a substitute for antifreeze. Only then did he introduce himself.

'Everyone calls me "Moustache", I've had one ever since I grew facial hair. As you're a writer, you might also be interested to know that my uncle was Hojarrasquín. I once cleared out a whole bar when I told someone this.' What he did not tell me, and which I found out the next morning over breakfast, was who his wife was.

'History has a habit of coming round in a circle,' observed El Sereno, after he had told me that the woman was the granddaughter of the *Guardia Civil* officer responsible for ensnaring both Hojarrasquín and Cencerro. The officer had even been awarded a silver trophy for his role in their deaths.

This 'hunter of men' (as the trophy described him) was the great scourge of the *Maquis*. I was informed of another of his vindictive deeds on one of my trips into the Sierra with El Sereno, who loved showing me the caves and remote farms that had sheltered the guerrillas. On this occasion, as we walked along a ridge-top path near La Hoya del Salobral, he pointed to a valley farm whose owner had grudgingly allowed a band of ten guerrillas to stay in his barn. Worried subsequently by rumours that the *Guardia Civil* knew, and were closing in on these men, the farmer advised them to sleep at night in a nearby cave. But fear got the better of him, and he reported their hiding-place to 'the hunter', who got there by daybreak and shot every one of them as they tried to escape. The farmer sold the property and moved on elsewhere, but his worry that the victims' families would one day get their revenge stayed with him over the years. In 1976, following Franco's death and the return of democracy to Spain, his anxieties reached breaking point. His dead body was found hanging from a walnut tree.

This tale of probable suicide dovetailed into another aspect of Frailes's history which had recently come to intrigue me, and would lead me back into that supernatural world I held responsible for having lured me to the village in the first place.

I had been talking with Merce's sister-in-law Villi in the Cueva when she started telling me of a radio programme in which the mayor and the parish priest Alberto had taken part. When I asked her what it had been about, she replied in a completely matter-of-fact tone, 'The triangle of suicides,' and seemed surprised by my bewilderment.

'You mean you don't know about it?'

I knew about the Bermuda Triangle, and even about the equally difficult to accept 'triangle of flamenco', which denoted the area of Andalucía where the finest flamenco reputedly and mysteriously originated; but I confessed I knew of no triangle in which the citizens of Frailes could possibly be involved. She then explained that it was the part of Spain, and possibly Europe, which had the highest incidences per capita of suicides, and specifically suicides by hanging. Also referred to as 'the triangle of the hanged ones', this was an area of the Sierra Sur delineated by the three townships of Alcalá, Castillo de Locubín, and Frailes. Out of a total population of around 35,000, 185 people were known to have killed themselves over the last year alone.

'Incredible but true,' said Villi, worried for a moment that I did not believe a word she was saying.

I would not have been the only one to have questioned the area's suicidal fame. A number of locals laughed when it was mentioned, and others became quite passionate in its refutation. Over a year and a half later, when the name of Frailes, no less plausibly, had spread far and wide, many villagers would take exception to a two-page article on the 'triangle of suicides' that appeared in the national newspaper *El Mundo*. They questioned the accuracy of the reporting, and were also incensed that their priest should have lent weight to the journalist's far-fetched views by telling her how three members of the same family had committed suicide within a month of his coming to the parish. I could see why publicizing Frailes as a village of suicides was not so desirable as far as rural tourism was concerned; and inevitably I had problems in squaring my view of the Fraileros as a remarkably balanced people with this image of a race of depressives. Nonetheless, as I got to know the village more intimately, I began wondering whether the place's reputation for suicides was so exaggerated after all. Two villagers had killed themselves within the short time of my being there; and so many people whom I knew from large, loving, and apparently happy families turned out to have had siblings who had died in this way. Some of the stories I was told were quite extraordinary, for instance the one about the middle-aged couple who were working together in the olive harvest: 'After they had lunch together in the fields the wife went off to have a pee. She came back five minutes later to find her husband of twenty years hanging by his own belt from one of the olive trees.'

If, as seemed likely, the area really did have such a high percentage of suicides, I was keen to know why. That the Finns were notoriously suicidal was not so surprising given their climate and lack of sunlight; that the Hungarians had also this reputation was slightly harder to understand, but nevertheless explicable in view of their being a nation of emotional extremes and heavy drinking. But I could find no reason whatsoever why the inhabitants of the Sierra Sur should be so keen to kill themselves, unless, of course, there were those among them who could no longer bear living in a society that was so outwardly cheerful, tolerant, easygoing, and supportive of others. Eventually I went to Alcalá to talk to a psychiatrist whom I was told had been interested in the phenomenon for a number of years.

'There are many myths about the "triangle of suicides",' said this dryly humorous and rather mocking individual. 'The most prevalent, as you probably know, is that the deaths are linked to the abundance of walnut trees in the area. These trees are said to secrete a special chemical that predisposes people to depressive impulses. I need hardly add that there is not an ounce of scientific truth in this. All that can be said is that the walnut tree has branches sturdy enough to support a heavy person's weight.'

So why were there supposedly so many suicides in the area?

'The most reasonable scientific explanation,' he replied, 'lies in heredity. The suicide gene is handed on from one generation to the next, as is the tradition of hanging oneself as opposed to using other methods such as pills.'

Merce had always convinced me that one of the miraculous features of Frailes was the absence of the physical and mental signs of inbreeding. Now, however, I was faced with the possibility that years of marrying into the same few families had left a legacy that I would never have expected.

Yet there seemed something more to this suicide phenomenon than mere genes. To investigate further into this and other Frailes matters I did what any local historian would have done. I visited the town of Jaén itself.

After weeks of barely leaving the village, I was not sure how I would react to being once again in a large and ugly town. I behaved, as it turned out, like some little travelled, wonder-struck villager discovering the glamour of the outside world. Previously I had thought of Jaén as a drab, provincial township redeemed by its position under a gauntly exposed Moorish citadel, and by the massive Renaissance cathedral below this. Now it seemed a place where a thriving intellectual life, evocative of the heady early years of Spain's democracy, lurked within the crammed, steep rows of post-1950 blocks.

This admittedly was an impression almost entirely derived from my meeting there with one of the province's most distinguished and prolific scholars, Manolo Urbano. Poet, critic, anthropologist, and the author of literally hundreds of books and articles covering every conceivable aspect of Jaén's cultural, gastronomic and folkloric heritage, Manolo lived on his own in a flat whose book-lined walls were also covered with paintings by his numerous artist friends. With his aquiline nose, crag-like outcrop of hair, and white beard tucked under his chin above an arty cravat, he had a look that was both intellectually imposing and reminiscent of some nineteenth-century Bohemian.

'Ask me any question you want,' he commanded in a deep husky voice suggestive of a lifetime of good living.

I kicked off, hesitatingly, with some general queries about Jaén history, which he answered with an impressive range of bibliographical references, and the occasional twinkle in his eye. Then, after he had poured out the first of many glasses of whisky, he stopped telling me about books I should read, and started instead to give away copies of his own prolific writings, which formed eventually a pile so high that he had to offer me a case as well so that I could carry them all.

It was not until after we had stumbled our way from his home to the library of the Institute of Jaén Studies that I finally broached the subject of suicide. By this stage of the day the tone of our conversation had lightened, assisted in part by the arrival on the scene of the library's mischievous young director, Salva, who had been asked by his friend Manolo to give me a tour of the building.

'We allow all scholars to use our resources,' Salva made clear from the start, 'on condition that they get here when the place opens at eight in the morning and stay here continuously until closing time at nine in the evening, without breaks for coffee, lunch, or alcoholic intake.'

Showing me afterwards the library's catalogue, he explained that 'we have tried here to bring together every single book or article that touches upon some aspect of Jaén's heritage, as well as works by every single author connected in some way with Jaén, however tenuous this person's link with the province, and however minor the writer. We even have two of your own books.'

Realizing that my status as a serious researcher could not get any lower, I decided at this point to risk a line of questioning that might have had both Manolo and Salva thinking of me as little different to a self-confessed UFO fanatic with a taste for the weird. After admitting to an interest in Jaén's esoteric phenomena, I asked if there was any explanation other than heredity as to why so many people reputedly hung themselves in the Sierra Sur.

Manolo, revealing only now that he himself was originally from 'within the triangle', appeared to speak more from the heart than from his anthropological brain when he replied by saying that the inhabitants of his native part of Jaén had a different conception of death to other people. To them there was no terror attached to death, indeed it was such an unremarkable occurrence that they could talk about somebody committing suicide in the same tone of voice as they might have used had the person become indisposed with a cold or gone off for a few days to Granada.

'What is curious, however,' he added, seeing me not fully convinced by his argument, 'is that Alcalá and Frailes should have been two of Andalucía's leading centres of Masonry and spiritualism. There is a theory that the local taste for suicide is connected with the spiritualist desire to communicate with the dead.'

Until that moment I had known nothing about Frailes's Masonic and spiritualist past. It was yet another revelation that strengthened my original impressions of a village of secretive depths, of a place that was somehow not quite of this world.

'If you're interested in those aspects of the Sierra Sur,' said Manolo, 'I suggest you get in touch with the former mayor of Alcalá, Paco Martín. And I'm sure you'll have some interesting insights if you spend time studying the Frailes cemetery.'

I chose first of all to see Paco Martín, whom I visited one morning at Alcalá, where he was now the director of a large secondary school. His original training, I had heard, was for the priesthood, but he had preferred instead to become a classics teacher, and had married in later life. As he stood outside his school waiting for me he looked less like a Spaniard than a stereotypical comic Frenchman, complete with beret, moustache, and a rosy, jocular expression. When he talked he appeared almost like an overexcited child, unstoppable in his enthusiasms, restless as a listener, short in his attention span, and utterly charming. He conveyed above all adoration for his native Alcalá, and had dedicated many if not most of his free moments researching the town's history.

To judge by the effusive greetings he received from everyone we passed as we set off walking towards the old centre, Paco's love for the town was matched by the affection in which he was held by its inhabitants; but he had not been, by his own reckoning, a successful mayor. 'I'm a historian,' he smiled, 'not a politician.'

Then suddenly he stood still for a moment in the street, and turned to face me. 'Tell me,' he said, 'what you want to see today.'

I had not in fact planned to see anything, I had merely wanted to find out about the area's links with Masonry and spiritualism. He did not wait for my reply, but simply consulted his watch. 'We'd better speed up, we've only got three hours or so before lunch.'

We were going up to the citadel, and we were going, in Paco's words, 'the long and picturesque' way. I was assured 'a treasure house of legends and the arcane'. We left the modern town, with its pretensions to be a grand city, and climbed through a district of cobbled streets and whitewashed old houses which many families – including Paco's own – had sold off or abandoned so as to move down to more easily accessible and socially prestigious apartment blocks. Many of the houses, Paco explained, had been bodegas until the 1960s, when the local wine industry began to die out.

The first of the 'secretive places' Paco said he would show me had not the esoteric dimension I was hoping for. We had entered an ordinary-looking house, and had descended, promisingly, several flights of steps, only to emerge into a room with giant vats of wine, and a group of old men smoking, drinking and playing cards.

'This is one of the only bodegas left, it's only open during the wine season. People bring their own tapas, just as they would have done in the Middle Ages. What do you think? Isn't it extraordinary! Would you have expected such a place?'

After a couple of glasses of the powerful *vino del terreno*, I wondered if my researches into darkest Alcalá would get any further than this. However, Paco, as if recalling the real purpose of our itinerary, then rushed me out into the street, where we were soon pausing outside a large ruinous building with a blocked-up central window. A tiny tabernacle, with an illuminated votive image, had been inserted in the middle of it. 'When you see a window like that,' Paco beamed, 'you can be certain that someone hung himself from its balcony.'

As befitted the author of probably the most detailed survey yet written of the folklore of the Sierra Sur, Paco laced historical explanations with folk tales and popular romances, and indeed mixed up fact and fiction to such an extent that he himself confessed that the tour on which he was taking me would end up 'in the style of Washington Irving'. With Paco as my guide, it was certainly easy to think of ourselves as travellers of the Romantic era climbing up to the then neglected and overgrown Alhambra, particularly in the later stages of our walk, once we had passed the last of the town's houses, and were negotiating a narrow, stony path running between walls choked with weeds and ivy. Paco had the gift, rare among local historians, of making ruins and their history come alive. As we meandered across the vast, rubbish-strewn, and only partially excavated citadel, he steered me through the real and legendary history of Alcalá, pointing out to me Palaeolithic tombs, secret passages through the rock, caves where witches had cast spells, stones from Roman temples, the foundations of an Islamic township, walls from which Moorish princesses had thrown themselves, medieval water cisterns, enigmatic, cabalistic-like inscriptions, storage urns peeping through the undergrowth, a ruined granary associated with Satanic rites, and the grand, eloquent shell of an abbey that had once been one of the best-endowed in Spain. By the end of our tour Paco had done all he could to convince me that this was a place steeped in an occult past. What I still lacked, however, was any real information on the two subjects that I had particularly hoped Paco would help me with.

But returning down the hill I was finally confronted with specific proof of Alcalá's strong Masonic links. I had hardly needed to search for this in forgotten corners of the old town. The evidence was to be found right on the main street, on the façade of a grand early nineteenth-century building that stood almost directly opposite the former palace of the Abbots of Alcalá. The ground-floor level had recently been transformed into a pizzeria and a shop selling mobile phones, but above this, inscribed over the main floor's central window, were the unmistakable mathematical tools symbolizing the Masons.

'But how could these have been allowed on public display? I thought the Masons were outlawed in Spain.'

Paco shrugged his shoulders, and told me of someone whom he was going to introduce me to in the town hall. 'Antonio Romero,' he said, 'has been studying for years the subject of Masonry in the Sierra Sur.'

Antonio Romero, an urbane and smartly-dressed civil servant, appeared the sort of person you could rely on for hard facts. Lacking the engaging whimsy of Paco, he approached his chosen field of history with the objectivity of a bureaucrat compiling a report. After confirming at the outset that Alcalá and Frailes had indeed been important Masonic centres, he then noted how odd it was that Alcalá should have had a Masonic lodge long before Jaén itself did. The lodge, occupying the building I had seen on the main street, had continued to function well into the twentieth-century while facing increasing opposition from the Church.

'Of course a distinction has to be made between the Masons who joined the order more for social reasons, and those who did so largely for spiritual and ideological ones. One of Alcalá's most distinguished citizens of the 1920s was a Mason, and there is even a street named after him. However, during this very same period, a doctor was thrown out of the town for belonging to the order. Then after 1939, as you know, Masonry was condemned by Franco, who often referred to the "Jewish-Masonic conspiracy".'

The view of Masonry as a subversive phenomenon was partly connected with the interest shown by so many of its members in spiritualism, a heretical belief in the eyes of traditional Catholics. Antonio took out from his desk a locally published magazine of 1889 that printed in full the text of a lecture given that year at the international spiritualist conference held in Paris.

'This was an extraordinarily difficult text to get hold of,' commented Antonio, who said that he had had to obtain it indirectly, almost secretly, from its owner, as was indeed true of so much of the documentation for his researches. After the abolition of Alcalá's Masonic lodge, many Masons had continued secretly to hold on to their spiritualist beliefs; and even today there were families reluctant to talk or publicly acknowledge this aspect of their past. Antonio mentioned a family in Frailes who had kept hidden over the years a reputed wealth of papers testifying to the fervent spiritualism of some of its earlier members. 'The family claims to have no knowledge of these, but I know for a fact that these papers exist.'

There were numerous issues to do with Masonry and spiritualism that remained for me unresolved, the most obvious of all being the reason why these two phenomena should have caught on in such a big way in communities so unimportant as Alcalá and Frailes.

'That is a question I have yet to answer,' Antonio admitted at the end of our meeting. I doubted whether I myself would be able to throw any more light on the subject. Nonetheless, obeying urges that were more sentimental than historical, I later took up Manolo Urbano's advice to look carefully at the cemetery of Frailes.

I had observed the place hundreds of times from El Sereno's garden, but had yet to go there, even though I now had a good excuse to do so. Then one day the mother of my drinking companion Bubi died, and I followed the funeral cortège up to the top of the cemetery hill. El Sereno was with me, and led me through the cemetery's main gate once we had paid our respects to Bubi and his brothers, who stood outside accepting the condolences of the villagers. The cemetery, situated on a steep slope with views towards a Frailes framed by cypresses, was intimate and welcoming, despite conditions that were hardly ideal for leisurely contemplation. A freezing wind was blowing, creating an appropriately dramatic sky of rapidly moving clouds that held at last the promise of rain. Shivering we walked quickly up to the top of the cemetery, where we came to a sheltered section lurking behind the large mausolea of the Mudarras and the Medinas, who even in death had tried outstripping each other in their architectural creations.

'Where we're now standing,' said El Sereno, 'was once separated from the rest of the cemetery by a wall. This was not taken down until the return of democracy in 1979.'

We were, he explained, in the part of the cemetery traditionally reserved for 'Protestants', a category that seemed mainly to comprise atheists, Jehovah's Witnesses, Masons, spiritualists, and suicide victims. 'They even brought Hojarrasquín here after he had shot himself.'

The tombs were remarkably simple, those of the poorest being merely white plaster slabs with names and dates handwritten in faded paint. I had to rely largely on El Sereno's memories to recognize the tombs of the 'heretics', the inscriptions themselves giving only the occasional hint as to the dead person's beliefs. Two of the inscriptions suggested lives dedicated to socialist causes, while another referred to the Masonic ideal of 'the perfecting of Man'; the longest of all appeared to be a paean to humanism, and made no mention whatsoever of an afterlife. But the most revealing feature of all was the sheer size of the area we were studying.

The distant drone of the parish priest at the start of the burial ceremony interrupted our tour, causing El Sereno and myself to slip quietly though a small gate in the cemetery's upper wall and into the field of olive trees that lay beyond. Experiencing a new burst of energy, as if in reaction to being released from a place of death, El Sereno gestured towards the summit of the hill, and insisted we keep on walking. We scrambled up through the olives, and through the odd scattering of almond and cherry trees, which sparkled now with a covering of white blossom. We were in land that belonged to El Sereno himself, and this extended right into an upper level of oaks, where we found a clearing from which there was an uninterrupted panorama from Alcalá to the Sierra Nevada. Around us were the ruins of a stone hut.

'This is the hut that I've promised one day to rebuild for Merce,' smiled El Sereno, as hopes for rain diminished under an expanding patch of clear evening sky. 'She wants a place for her tarot cards.'

Merce's interest in the occult was an aspect of her character that I had not at first taken very seriously. Though I veered curiously between scepticism and belief in my attitude towards the Santo Custodio, it was largely through superstitious fear that I lent any credence at all to such activities as tarot cards, palmistry and astrology. Nonetheless, for all my misgivings, I had always recognized in Merce a very special personality, and would not have been surprised to learn that she had healing and psychic powers. My great respect for her, combined with an expanding awareness of Frailes's esoteric past, and the knowledge that only miracles could now save the village, made me more sympathetic than I might otherwise have been when she confirmed for me that she saw herself in the same way that I had first perceived her in the Cueva – as a benign witch. She hoped to unleash forces that would steer her beloved village away from disaster and towards a future filled with dignity and recognition.

A first step towards this was to try and perfect the art of the tarot. Even before El Sereno had told me of her plans for the hut on his property, I knew of her intentions to hold tarot sessions in a candlelit Cueva. Later, on furthering her reading knowledge of the supernatural, she realized that she lacked two essential items that would make her a true diviner- a wooden box to keep the cards, and some silk on which to lay them out. These objects were not as easy to get hold of as one might have imagined; they needed, she believed, the intercession of people who gave out 'especially positive vibrations'. A few days after my visit to the cemetery she announced that El Sereno should be the person who was going to create the box, while I would be put in charge of acquiring the silk. In times to come I would think of my visit to the milliner's in Alcalá to purchase the necessary black and red material as a turning-point in my relationship towards Frailes. From being purely an observer I was on my way to becoming an active participant in its destiny.

The Saturday night when I handed over the silk at the Discoteca Oh! was when she told me of the local saying about rain.

'When someone sings badly it will rain,' she suddenly declared, turning towards me in the midst of a general discussion about the continuing drought.

I volunteered to help out, and was presented the perfect opportunity to do so the following day, after a long alcoholic lunch with friends of hers and Caño's at the Rey de Copas. On impulse we all drove on afterwards to the isolated *cortijo* of Puerta Alta. The morning's weather forecast had predicted possible short showers by midday; but by five in the afternoon, when our convoy of cars had unloaded us all at the estate, there was still not a cloud in the deep blue sky. The owner, Merce's millionaire cousin, was at home, and offered us from his bodega the last of the season's wine.

'Maiquel,' said Merce, 'it's time for you to sing.'

I was true to my word. Standing by the well in the courtyard, under the persistent cloudless sky, I began to bellow out an old Italian song I had picked up as a child from an Irish friend of my grandmother. The friend had been a pioneer in the rediscovery of medieval popular music, and the song had a shrill raucous quality that I had accentuated after years of performing the work as a party piece. For those accustomed only to my normal quiet voice, the experience of suddenly hearing me sing so loudly that all the many animals at Puerta Alta started to howl, came as a shock.

'Look!' shouted Merce's youngest son Alejandro, adding to the general astonishment. 'The sky has begun to darken.'

There was a definite smell of rain in the air after we left the estate at nightfall. I had never seen Merce quite so animated before, and she spent the bumpy journey laughing, crying, and shouting out her love for those present. The downpour came just after we had reached the safety of the Discoteca Oh!. It rained all night without stopping, and continued to do so the next day, until the gutters overflowed, and water gushed in great streams down the streets. As I hurried under an umbrella up to El Sereno's house, I passed a bewildered old man sheltering under a portal and trying to explain to his wife the miracle before their eyes. Three words stood out: 'The Englishman sang.'

4

IT RAINED PERSISTENTLY for weeks. It was the rainiest spring that anyone in Frailes could remember. But I was not there to witness it. Having performed my miracle I went to England, and did not come back again to the village until the middle of May, just when the sun emerged from hiding. The timing of my absence seemed calculated to heighten my new-found stature as a man of mysterious powers. I had left when the longed-for rain had finally arrived; and I had returned at the very moment when the effects of all this rain were brilliantly apparent.

The drive from Seville presented me with an Andalucía that appeared distilled through a dream. Beneath a sky as fresh as a new coat of paint sparkled multi-coloured constellations of spring flowers. The dusty greys and ochres of old had been succeeded by colours of unnatural brightness, with poppy fields redder than those of Monet, and grass and trees so green that your spirits were replenished merely by looking at them.

Joyous Andalucían folk tunes were playing loudly on the car radio, and my frequent exclamations of pleasure were met by contented smiles from the dapper driver, who sometimes swivelled his neck to offer me a full face view of his neatly trimmed moustache and gold-plated teeth. I was sitting in the front seat of his 'pirate taxi', which had the unwritten rights to the route between Frailes and Seville. The man himself, a short and wiry septuagenarian known to everyone in Frailes as 'Ferminillo' or 'Little Fermín', was different in every respect to Pancanto, his goat-killing counterpart on the Granada run. Nervously energetic, tirelessly hard-working, and with a voice that went up a pitch in moments of overexcitement, Ferminillo was someone whom at first I knew almost exclusively in the context of his taxi. In Frailes, where he lived half the week with his sister, he never frequented any of the bars, nor was he ever to be seen dallying talking in the streets. In Seville he had shared a flat for nearly forty years with a companion whose first and only visit to Frailes (back in the 1960s) had earned him the reputation as one of the most beautiful men ever to have come to the village. The rest of Ferminillo's life was largely a mystery to me, though I half-recalled having once been told that he had run a cinema, or perhaps even a chain of cinemas. Every so often I would try and engage him in conversation, but these attempts were usually defeated by the radio's distortedly high volume.

Despite an obvious incipient deafness, Ferminillo was someone who defied the ageing process in the same way that El Sereno did. As I journeyed with him from Seville on this life-affirming late spring day, I was conscious of how his uncanny youthfulness was in keeping with the astonishingly reinvigorated landscapes we were passing. The exceptional weather conditions, together with my cheerful mood, and the sense of relief that had come to characterize my returns to Frailes, were luckily almost sufficient to keep me diverted during a drive that was longer and more uncomfortable than usual. The problem of travelling with Ferminillo, as with any collective taxi, was that you could not chose the exact time you wanted to leave, nor could you predict when you would reach your destination. If you were fortunate enough to be the only passenger you had a chance of setting off at a reasonable time and undertaking the journey in just over two and a half hours.

Ferminillo was a skilful if aggressive driver who had little patience with other traffic. He was always coming up frighteningly close to the car in front, and was happy to overtake when on the point of reaching a bend. However, he was also a businessman who was prepared to protract the drive as much as possible in the interests of squeezing in yet another passenger, or delivering Frailes products that often involved massive detours. In the course of many journeys with him I would eventually feel that I knew the whereabouts of every single person of Frailes origin the length and breadth of eastern Andalucía.

On the day of my return from England Ferminillo excelled himself. Though he had picked me up long before dawn, we were still driving around the outskirts of Seville at eleven in the morning. There were now six of us crammed into the taxi, and the cargo of olive oil that had filled the boot had finally all been handed out. So when Ferminillo stopped the car one more time I imagined he had done so to remove, as he always did, the '*SP*' sign indicative of his vehicle's status as a '*Servicio Público*' (this helped him cut corners in the centre of a city, but prevented him from speeding too much once he was out in the country). But instead he got out to greet two further passengers, whom he led to the back of the car. It took me a few minutes to take in what he was doing. He was rearranging the boot so that the two of them could lie down in a space where people might normally have expected to travel either as corpses or kidnap victims.

Our arrival in Frailes early that afternoon was like an ecstatic release of pent-up tension. Extricating my stiff limbs from a car still redolent of the smell of one of the passenger's vomit, I breathed in the crisp, fresh air, and revived myself in the sight of a landscape setting that made me appreciate for the first time the full impact of Lorca's poem of bucolic longing, 'Green, how I love you green . . .' Soon El Sereno had come to meet me, and was rushing me off in his Suzuki down the main street, which now ran alongside an abundant stream babbling its way through limpid rock pools.

'There's something else that's going to surprise you,' he said as we headed out of the village, past the outlying Swiss-style chalet which had once struck me as so incongruous, but which now seemed integral to the Alpine-like transformation of the surrounding scenery.

After driving between crags glistening with lichen, and lush meadows that a singing Julie Andrews might happily have skipped over, we pulled to a halt at a viewpoint that overlooked what was normally a gaunt, blanched cliff rising from out of a valley of yellowing thistles and straw-like tufts of grass. Clambering to the top of an exposed rock that overhung the void, offering an even better view, we might have been nineteenth-century explorers discovering another of the world's wonders. From where we were standing we could see a torrent rushing wildly towards the edge of the cliff before leaping into space to form a waterfall a good fifty metres high. The faint colours of a rainbow shone phantom-like in the spray.

Surprises of a different kind awaited me once we were back later that afternoon in the village. 'I didn't know you were married,' chuckled El Sereno, taking out a file reserved for the growing number of newspaper cuttings chronicling the doings in the Sierra

Sur of the 'famous English writer Michael Jacobs'. Then he placed on the table in front of me an article from the *Diario de Jaén*. Its author, a brazenly persistent Alcalá-based journalist called Pepe Oneto, was a byword for inaccuracies, but I could find nothing wrong in the text except his customary misspellings and exaggerated perception of my position in the English literary world. Then I stared again at the accompanying photograph, which showed me with an arm placed on Merce's shoulders. 'Maiquel Jackobs and wife,' ran the accompanying caption.

'You're lucky that Caño is not a jealous husband,' joked El Sereno, who went on to imitate the bewilderment that the photo caused among certain, less informed, sectors of the village.

'It's not enough that this strange Englishman,' he parodied, barely able to contain his tears of laughter, 'turns up in Frailes as if from nowhere, and brings on the rain with his singing. On top of it all he is rumoured to have such sexual charisma that the women here are prepared at the drop of a hat to abandon their husbands. He's already succeeded in breaking up one of the village's happiest marriages.'

The following day in the Cueva I would hear from Villi a more credible if no less bizarre version of how some of the villagers responded to the photo. '"The strange thing about Maiquel's wife",' she smiled, repeating to me what someone had said to her, ' "is that she so closely resembles our Merce. Of course, if you look more closely at the photo you'll immediately realize she's a very different woman." '

It was also through Villi that I became aware of another and more extraordinary misunderstanding. 'You haven't finished yet your book on Frailes?' she asked in all seriousness. I said it was difficult to finish a book I had not even contemplated writing.

'That's strange,' she answered. 'People are saying that the book is excellent in every respect but one. You shouldn't have brought in the Santo Custodio.'

My 'wife', who was sitting next to me at the bar, then let out one of her distinctive laughs. 'They've confused him with Santi!' she shrieked. Santi's detailed history of Frailes, the fruit of years of fact-collecting, had apparently come out in my absence. I was flattered that there were people who believed that I was capable of researching, writing and publishing such a work in less than two months. But the realization that I was widely believed to have come to Frailes with the intention of writing about the village was perhaps responsible for instilling in me the idea for the present book. Local rumours, as well as some of the mistaken comments in the Jaén press, had, as I would soon find out, a curious way of anticipating the truth.

Already, as had been confidently predicted months before in the *Ideal de Jaén*, I had become part of the village's history. When I finally got hold of a copy of Santi's laboriously compiled list of dates, names and statistics (cautiously entitled *Frailes, A Vision of its History, 1860–1999*), I was amused to find myself featured no fewer than three times, once in the context of El Sereno's friends, another time with reference to the people who frequented the Bar La Cueva, and a third in the chapter devoted to 'Writers in Frailes'. This last chapter was the shortest in the book. From the time of Ángel Ganivet's seasons at the spa up to the year when Michael Jacobs started coming there 'in search of inspiration for his celebrated guides and travel books', the literary history of the village had been essentially a blank. Santi had been obliged to pad out his text with no fewer than thirty lines on a native Frailes author who had left the village at the age of two, and whose dozen or so privately published novels and volumes of verse included such poignant titles as *Dialogue with Solitude* and *Love Awoke Her*.

Had Santi delayed the publication of his book for a few more months, he might have managed a marginally longer chapter. As was the way with this village, no sooner had a text appeared on the hitherto almost non-existent subject of 'Writers in Frailes' than writers began to make a habit of coming there. The most salient aspect of my stay in the village during the late spring and early summer of the year 2000 was that it initiated a new phase in the cultural life of Frailes. This all started on the Sunday after my return with an invitation to Jaén to see an exhibition of paintings by an old friend of mine from Granada, Juan Antonio Díaz.

Juan Antonio, by profession an English lecturer at Granada university, was a one-man cultural renaissance whose talents roamed freely from boxing to cinema history, from abstract painting to literary criticism, from poetry to public relations. This bearded dandy with a reputation for parody, joke-telling, and fantastical digression, was also a forceful organizer who had managed to bring together for the closing of his Jaén exhibition an impressive representation of his intellectual friends. El Sereno, who had come with me from Frailes, together with Merce and Caño, was increasingly overwhelmed as I introduced him to these luminaries. This elite coterie, surely destined for at least a footnote in some future cultural history of Spain, numbered among its members my helpful source of anthropological and historical information, Manolo Urbano, doyen of the Jienense intelligentsia; Paco Fernández, a quietly spoken aesthete, artist and photographer, whom Frank Sinatra had once publicly declared to be his 'favourite photographer'; Ignacio Henares, an art critic of monumentally difficult prose who had the looks and reputed sexual prowess of a satyr, and Antonio Carvajal, a well known Granadan poet with a permanent ironic grin and the cultivated appearance of some literary eccentric from the past.

Our day together in Jaén soon proceeded to a famous old drinking institution called the Gorrión, which had remained virtually untouched over the years, down to peeling bullfight posters, smoke-tinted wallpaper shiny with grease, and a repellent mummified object that Manolo Urbano identified as a ham dating back to the First World War. Many drinks later I found myself joining in a general toast to anything Jienense. I was agreeing with El Sereno that Jaén's history as a simple agricultural town had resulted in inhabitants who were less arrogant and pretentious than those of Granada; and I was also made suddenly aware of how many of my Granadan friends were in fact originally from this province, including Juan Antonio himself. It would not be long, I sensed, before Juan Antonio moved on to the subject of his native mountain village of Cabra de Santo Cristo, which he always claimed was Spain's mythical epicentre. So I preempted him, and accorded the honour instead to Frailes, which prompted applause from Caño and Merce, and fond memories of the Rey de Copas from Manolo Urbano and Paco Fernández. By the end of the evening we had all decided to meet up the following week in Frailes for another agreeable day of food, drink and banter.

These were the origins of what Juan Antonio – in a homage to Bloomsbury – dubbed the 'Frailes Group'. We did not exactly represent the cutting edge of European culture, nor did we have youth on our side; but we formed a mutual support group ready to supply each other with catalogue introductions, photographs, prefaces, illustrations, and poetic eulogies. Our figurehead became El Sereno, who behaved like a euphoric, love-stricken teenager in the days following our trip to Jaén. His morning rounds to the town hall, the pharmacy, and the clinic were longer than ever now that he had to describe to everyone the glittering company of 'poets, writers, and artists of every kind' with whom he had had the privilege to spend his Sunday. This 'memorable occasion' had certainly extended his library's collection of signed publications, the latest examples of which he started showing to anyone he encountered in the streets. To witness how his brief resumé of each author changed significantly in just a few days was deeply revealing of his talents as a publicist and myth-maker. These talents were lavished above all on Antonio Carvajal, who started the week as 'one of Granada's leading poets', but was soon promoted to 'a poet said by many critics to be the greatest working in Spain today'. Eventually, after I had mentioned that one of his volumes was published in a bilingual American edition, Carvajal was apotheosed into 'the most outstanding Western poet of the present decade'.

In the meantime the journalist Pepe Oneto was doing his best to further the growing mythical reputation of Frailes itself.

'Under Maiquel Jacqob Frailes is becoming a lively centre of intellectual gatherings,' he wrote, in another of his articles for the *Diario de Jaén*, this one reproducing the same photo as before but with the caption 'Mikell Jacques *and friend*' ('our marriage was short but sweet,' commented Merce). It was true that select members of the Frailes Group had started becoming regular visitors to the village by the middle of June, but our conversations rarely attained a more elevated level than a discussion of the comparative merits of the pheasant patés of Frailes and Cabra de Santo Cristo. Our first reunion was at the Rey de Copas, and we met up on another occasion late at night at the Discoteca Oh!, where the drunks at the bar rubbed their eyes in disbelief at the entrance into their rustic world of such effete city types as an artist in a bright pink suit and a poet sporting an ebony cane and a panama hat.

Then the cook at the Rey de Copas, Juan Matías, proposed a group outing into the country. Juan was not the person he used to be. He had changed over the past few weeks as much as Frailes had done, though not thanks to any supernatural intervention. The unhappiness caused by his weight had become so extreme that he had taken the radical step of having a ring inserted in his stomach. Now he could swallow nothing but liquids, and was constantly being sick. But these drawbacks for a cook and food lover were compensated in his eyes by the loss already of fifty kilos and a corresponding growth in self-confidence. He made friends with everyone in the Frailes Group. He was up for all kinds of experiences.

We searched our minds for a place in the country that would satisfy the general high level of aesthetic sensibility. Juan opted for Merce's suggestion of a bucolic-sounding riverside spot tucked in a wooded mountainous valley leading from Cerezo Gordo to Puerta Alta. Then we discussed what we would eat when we got there. Juan's knowledge of picnics was still entirely theoretical, while mine had yet to be demonstrated in Frailes. The two of us were put in sole charge of the outing. We were being tested.

There was, of course, no question simply of making sandwiches, hard-boiling a few eggs, and throwing in some tomatoes, fruit, and cans of refreshment. Juan, despite the reduced state of his stomach, had standards of culinary excellence to maintain. There were, furthermore, expectations of a picnic common to most Spaniards, whether down-to-earth villagers or sybaritic city dwellers. A table, for instance, was required, as were seats, wineglasses, a full set of cutlery, ice-cold drinks, and, invariably, a rice dish cooked over a gas-fired 'paella ring'. Juan assumed responsibility for everything apart from the meat ingredients, for which I went off to Merce's and Caño's house to collect a chicken. A chuckling Caño handed me a shotgun, and advised me to point it at the necks of any of the fowls I saw running around in the garden. Merce came to my rescue by remembering a couple of baby turkeys whose drowned corpses she had picked up the day before from the swimming pool.

We all waited for Juan in the Cueva. His new and thinner self did not apparently extend to an improvement in punctuality, nor, as we were soon to discover, any increase in common sense. He turned up at around two in the afternoon, assuring us that everything we needed was at the back of his car.

'And the chairs? The table? The gas canister? The paella ring?' asked Caño over forty-five minutes later, after the five cars in our convoy had parked at the bottom of a rough track. I rushed to Juan's defence by saying that we were aiming for a genuine rustic experience. Sweating profusely under the full heat of the day, we unloaded the drowned baby turkeys, a giant paella pan, and three absurdly heavy wooden wine crates containing everything else that Juan had remembered. We walked fifty metres through trees down to a fast flowing river. That would have been the extent of our physical exercise for the day had we not had to spend the next hour collecting wood to make a fire. Juan, who by now had donned an elegant white apron bearing the insignia of the Rey de Copas, looked like a cordon bleu chef forced to undertake a survival course.

I helped him push together some boulders to form a trivet substitute on which the paella pan rested at a dangerous angle. He hunted for a kitchen knife in a crate filled with tins of sweet Navarre peppers, a sack of the finest Valencian rice, a bottle of reserve Manzanilla vinegar, and other gourmet items. He could not find one. The watermelon, which I had placed to cool in the river, together with the drinks, started bobbing downstream in the direction of Puerta Alta. There was no cutlery, nor any wine glasses, nor a chopping board, nor even any plates. We began to improvise. I searched for a flat piece of wood. I put to use a Swiss army knife which Caño had scornfully declared a '*mariconada*' ('a precious nonsense'). Some rice, half-cooked on one side, and burnt on the other, was ready to eat by around six o'clock in the evening. The few people who had any interest left in eating shared the same wooden spoon to dip into the pan. A salad was served in the plastic bag in which I had mixed it. A reserve Rioja was poured into glasses made from the sliced ends of plastic water bottles.

I thought the whole occasion an ingenious display of adaptation to the natural world on the part of Juan and myself. But this opinion was not widely shared, and least of all by Juan himself, who resolved never again to stray far from a well-equipped kitchen. His new ease with people was unaffected, however, as was the determination of the Frailes Group to meet up for future outdoor celebrations.

We chose unhesitatingly to eat from now on in El Sereno's garden, where we could sit in relative comfort around the upturned millstones. The walnut tree may have been sickly, or even dying, but its branches were still leafy enough to shade, during the heat of the day, our ever-expanding group. There were no more *mariconadas*. The food, prepared now by the whisky-swilling Pancanto, was always freshly killed lamb or goat, barbecued over charcoal, sautéed in garlic, or else stewed in a special creamy sauce made from the brains. The wine was a local red produced by an Alcalá vintner who had been made president of Frailes's future wine cooperative. Its remarkable quality lent support to a general feeling among us that great things were about to happen to the village.

Our gatherings, recorded by Santi in a series of articles he published under the title *Frailes: An Intimate Diary*, seemed symptomatic of the village's new lease of life. What was particularly encouraging was the way in which 'outsiders' who had never been to' Frailes before, or who knew the place only superficially, came away after a few hours in El Sereno's garden with a feeling of replenishment. Paco Fernández, who had once told Juan Antonio that he could never understand why I had fallen in love with 'the ugliest village in Jaén', was now even proposing making Frailes a colony for his artist students from Granada. All this, of course, made El Sereno more excited and youthful than ever.

'I haven't seen him like this for ages,' enthused Merce, who also confessed that there had been a time when she thought he had begun losing his memory and seeming at last his age. 'You and your friends have rejuvenated him. He's got more plans than ever for the future.'

The parties in El Sereno's garden, ever more ambitious, soon became confused with the activities of the summer festive season, when the spreading mood of good cheer found an outlet throughout the Sierra Sur in token religious celebrations involving fairgrounds, processions, dancing in public squares, cherry displays, burning of witches, endless free drinks and tapas. On June 13, the Fraileros honoured St Anthony by marching in candlelit procession to his little chapel in the upper village, traditional venue of virgins in search of husbands. The following week, for the Sacred Heart of Jesus, they adorned the streets with flowers and coloured sands, and then spent a night of *pasodobles* in the district around the Charro. But the main event before the August *feria* was the festival of St Peter on June 29, for which Paqui prepared by distributing posters for her disco in the bars of every single nearby town and village. It was the day on which her livelihood depended.

In the build-up to this great day a large Ferris wheel went up almost directly in front of the Discoteca Oh!, followed by nougat stalls, shooting ranges, a tent for bumper cars, improvised bars, a band stand. By midnight on the eve of St Peter's Day, most of Frailes, and a high proportion of the surrounding communities, were massed around the lower entrance to the village, parading up and down the street with their children, sitting eating at outdoor tables, crowding against the bar counters, or else dancing to pop music hits such as *Un movimiento sexi*, performed live by a troupe of platinum blondes in skimpy purple sequin dresses cut low at the back so as to reveal their underwear. Rising above the general commotion came the occasional raucous sounds of Cabildo's singing, while in the midst of all the chaos the bobbing head of Bubi assumed the crazed intense look that he usually put on at the point of breaking into his Apache-like stomp. The most ubiquitous person, however, was the emaciated village gypsy, Regalín, who, wearing a black waistcoat and white shirt as in some nineteenth-century print of 'typical' Andalucían life, restlessly wove his way in and out of the crowd as he raffled a giant ham carried high by one of his sons. Normally a quiet and discreet man, Regalín came triumphantly into his own during the summer festivals, relishing in particular that moment when he climbed onto the stage to pick out the winning card. The music stopped, the jiving, sequined beauties paused to adjust their dresses, and in the unearthly silence that followed, the voice of Regalín rang out like a wail of flamenco: '*The King of Hearts!*'

But the Day of St Peter belonged, above all, to Paqui. I had become so used to a sad and nearly empty Discoteca Oh! that I had never imagined being barely able to squeeze my way past the entrance at around four in the morning. To see the disco functioning as a disco should was a sight as satisfying as the water that now poured down Frailes's river. However, what amazed me more than anything was seeing the place crammed not just with young people dancing but with almost every other element in village society, from elderly couples with their families to babies miraculously asleep in their prams. A young woman trapped in her wheelchair by a wasting disease jerked her head slightly in time to the music. Paqui, in a black cocktail dress, alternated between snatches of ecstatic dance and throwing ice into glasses with a rhythmical fury. The shaven-headed Josélillo assisted her like a toy soldier gone mad ('I'm a certified lunatic, I've got papers to prove it,' he screamed over the music). While Antonio, the district nurse, stood in the centre of the floor, twisting his corpulent body with a sense of style as compelling as the gyrations of the muscular young village plumber Jesús, who appeared to control the whole sway of the crowd as he moved violently from side to side from behind the counter of the second bar, now finally brought into use for this day alone. Then I turned to the glass control box as if in search of the person on whom I could pin the miracle of the Discoteca Oh! And there he stood, in brown leather boots, a bandana beneath his headphones – the extraordinarily handsome man whom I had heard so much about. Taller than me, perhaps the tallest man in the room, he was Peter himself, the DJ from Alcalá's leading disco, the person who drew the crowds of girls, and introduced the touch of magic.

'That's Pedro from La Belle,' Paqui whispered right into my ear, as if introducing me to God Himself.

It was a week of climaxes. Following hard on the St Peter's Day festivities, an event occurred which seemed at the time like the closest Frailes would get to experiencing disruption to the cyclical regularity of everyday life. The occasion, prosaically, was the launch in Granada of a book I had done with Paco Fernández, who had taken the photographs, on the Moorish palace city of the Alhambra. The British publishers had not bothered to make copies of the work available on the day; but, to make up for this omission, some well-connected members of the Frailes Group had used their contacts to have at our disposal a magnificent early nineteenth-century villa on the Alhambra hill itself. For a hot Sunday morning in July the event was surprisingly well attended, with television and newspaper journalists, and a large representation of Granadan high society, who stood around in their elegant summer attire being served drinks by waiters in white jackets and black ties.

Coming straight from London, Madrid, or even Seville, Granada had always seemed to me like a village. Coming from Frailes, however, it appeared like the most intimidating and cosmopolitan of cities. The pretentious Gran Via de Colon, with its eclectic late nineteenth-century blocks, could have been Oxford Street or Fifth Avenue; the promenade along the river Genil recalled the banks of the Seine; the hill district of the Albaicín was like a whitewashed Hampstead with a strong whiff of the orient. It was strange to believe that you could reach all this from Frailes in less than an hour. The brusqueness of the transition, so exciting to young Fraileros in search of the bright lights, made it difficult at times to adjust to being in Granada. Having suddenly to face, on a Sunday morning, what the poet García Lorca famously called 'the worst bourgeoisie in the world', was for me a new variant on this experience. Fortunately I had not been left to do so on my own. El Sereno, naturally, had come, and so too had Merce, Caño, Santi, Paqui, Ernesto, Antonio the district nurse, Rafael the bank manager, and about thirty other Fraileros, including the mayor himself and his wife.

None of them truly understood the speech about the book given by the art critic Ignacio Henares, but then neither did I. The Hispanist Ian Gibson, another of the local celebrities invited to say a few words, had not read my text, but was brief and comprehensible. Antonio Carvajal recited a few of his poems; and a well-known pianist friend of theirs from Madrid, Guillermo González, played some *Alhambrista* music by Albéniz, Falla, and others.

As I hung around sheepishly with Paco Fernández on the stage, facing the crowded neo-Moorish hall, my attention became focused on Merce, who stuck out out amidst the sea of serious faces by standing smiling at the back, conducting the music with a peacock's feather. Afterwards she would be severely criticized for doing so by Antonio the mayor, who told her that this was no way to behave in 'elegant society', and that she had been disrespectful to the pianist. But Guillermo himself, far from minding, seems to have been subliminally inspired by her gesture, for when he met her properly for the first time, over a year later, he appeared to look on her as a muse of long standing. Merce's natural spontaneity, so beguiling in the context of that pretentious launch, may have had its effect on me too, for when my turn came to address the assembled crowd, I made a point of emphasizing my debt to Frailes and its people, and praising the village as the perfect place to escape from the 'stress' and 'crosses' of life.

About sixty of my listeners took heed of my advice, and ended up going that same day to Frailes to have lunch in El Sereno's garden, which was thereafter definitively established, in the eyes of the local press, as an earthly 'Parnassus'. The task of listing all the names of the great and mighty resulted in more misspellings than ever on the part of Pepe Oneto; and the fact that Ian Gibson was present (a figure almost comparable in fame, if not in looks, to 'Pedro from La Belle') made one young journalist forsake a plate of Pancanto's exquisite lamb so that she could tape-record an interview with him. The publicity for the village was enormous, and for over a week articles appeared in local and national papers that gave less attention to the actual launch than to the day's termination in Frailes.

Once again I profited from this moment of triumph to leave almost immediately for England. Santi, whose *Intimate Diary* had described the launch in exuberant detail, noted two days later that I had gone, and that 'picnics in Frailes would never be the same'. 'Life', he added, had 'returned to its usual monotony'.

On the night before my departure a small farewell party was held under the walnut tree. Antonio the district nurse sang songs to his own guitar accompaniment; Rafael and Ernesto played local folk tunes on their mandolins. This lyrical interlude, made more touching for me by my not knowing this time when I would be able to come back to Frailes, disintegrated soon into a general, unmelodic sing-song, during which some of those present looked anxiously at the beautiful starlit sky in the expectation that rain would soon be coming. We finished the night at the Discoteca Oh!, where Merce presented me as a parting gift a video that she hoped would always conjure up the village whenever I became nostalgic for it. Paqui offered to project it there and then on the disco's large background screen that normally no one ever looked at. So we sat with our whiskies under the rotating mirror ball and I tried as best as I could to keep my eyes open.

The video was a record of an event I never knew had happened – the appearance, over a decade before, of more than fifty Fraileros in a Seville television studio. They had gone there to take part in a popular programme on village life called *Tal que somos*, or 'This is how we are'. My friends sitting in the disco watching this video could be seen, greatly enlarged, as their younger selves on the screen before me, thus somehow adding to the growing confusion within my tired head between reality and its visual representation, between events as they really occurred and events as they came to be recorded. There was El Sereno seated like the village patriarch next to a Merce dressed just like the time when I first saw her, and talking about the Santo Custodio. And there were Ernesto and Rafael, with their mandolins, singing folkloric carols that would shortly win for their Frailes group a televised first prize for the finest Andalucían music of this kind.

The programme brought out the unity and comradeship of village life, as had the video of Merce's and Caño's wedding; and it also unwittingly affirmed the values of the small in the face of rapid glob-alization. But by five in the morning I was fast asleep on my seat, and having a dream that would prove prophetic. I was slouched in a crowded old cinema from the time of my childhood. The main film had not yet begun, and we were looking at one of those documen-tary shorts that went under the blanket title of *Look at Life*. The subject that night was a remote Andalucían village which for some reason had attracted the attention of the whole of Spain. The whirl of the projector could be heard in the background, but then the power failed, the recorded voices suddenly drooled to a halt, and we were plunged into darkness and silence.

Part Three

Cinema España

I

ALMOST FIVE MONTHS had passed since my last stay in Frailes. I had travelled in the meantime all over the American West and had seen natural wonders that made those of Europe seem tiny and insignificant. I had hiked between the massive granite cliffs of Yosemite, observed the Pacific fog bank roll out to sea from the redwood heights of Big Sur, canoed along empty volcanic lakes within sight of the solitary white pyramid of Mount Shasta. But, as I wrote in my postcards to Frailes, all these sublime moments made me miss all the more the less spectacular but no less memorable experiences I had had in the Sierra Sur: the sight of the horses galloping towards me at Puerta Alta; the apparition of the waterfall off the Valdepeñas road; and the time last summer when I was driving with El Sereno in a remote part of the Sierra when a family of ten wild boars rushed out across the track in front of us.

Back in the autumn in England the nostalgia for Frailes intensified. El Sereno, as if sensing this, signed a contract with Spain's national telephone company that allowed him to phone me every evening for an especially cheap rate (the news that he regularly called me in London had been reported by Pepe Oneto long before he had actually done so). Sitting in my Hackney study, with reggae music from my neighbours beating loud against the walls, I assimilated telephonically the minutiae of Frailes news and gossip: Merce was increasingly occupied with her tarot cards; another late-night bar had opened near the Guaneiro; the rains had returned, and there were more mushrooms than ever in the mountains. Occasionally, on leaving my house after one of these conversations, I would almost forget where I was, and begin greeting startled passersby with a hearty '¡Adios!', or be momentarily deluded into thinking, say, that the blue people carrier parked outside the Dove was Pancanto's, or that Ferminillo was driving down the Hackney Road in his grey-green Volkswagen. After almost fainting with excitement on seeing El Sereno's yellow Suzuki in Piccadilly, I knew my sanity was at risk if I stayed much longer in London. Less than a fortnight later, and with a speed I could only attribute to the intervention of the Santo Custodio himself, I had sorted out my personal and professional life as best as I could, and was able to tell El Sereno that I would be back in Frailes by the end of November. His list of activities we would do together on my return began now to extend into the unforeseeable future.

My first strong sensation on nearing 'home' was the sight of the snow on the Sierra Nevada. As Ferminillo drove me past Alcalá, I could concentrate on little else but the craggy, dazzling white strip that divided the rolling landscape of greens, ochres and browns from the relentless blue of the sky. In contrast to the winter before, when just a few streaks of snow had settled on the highest peaks, the mountains were covered now with a uniformly white mantle whose every crease and fold had become, under the piercing mid-morning sunlight, like the facets of a diamond.

The second impression, once I had got out at the *Mesón* and been met within minutes by the familiar Suzuki, was how old El Sereno seemed suddenly to have become. Would I mind, he asked, if I went with him to the hospital at Alcalá? His blood pressure, which had never before caused him any problems, had been worryingly high of late, and he was suffering chest pains. For all the pleasure he had in seeing me, he was unusually reserved and distracted as we drove off together to Alcalá so that he could have a cardiogram. I had always thought of him as a lone and fearless survivor of an old Spain that would never die; so it was disconcerting to see him as a worried old man in a vest waiting in a regulation grey-green hospital room to have his heart examined. When we got back to his Frailes doctor with the results, he relaxed more on being told that there was no sign of anything wrong with him. Antonio the district nurse, who had taken his blood pressure, then insisted on doing the same to me.

'Don't worry,' he said, looking at the results, and putting on a mock serious expression. 'You can continue eating and drinking to your heart's content.'

'I used to be like that,' sighed El Sereno, making me aware of another element in our relationship. He saw in me his younger self, through whom he hoped both to relive the past and to fulfil dreams that advancing age was putting further from his reach.

I embarked on this new stay in Frailes with the feeling that my friendship with El Sereno would have ever more unpredictable consequences, and that all the publicity the village had received in the summer was merely the prologue to greater events ahead. While waiting to see what would happen, I decided to drop any remaining pretence either of maintaining a rigid writing routine or of trying to isolate myself from village life. I was open now to all new experiences, and was keen to deepen my knowledge of a rural world to whose rhythms I was becoming increasingly accustomed.

I had returned in time for the most important season in the Frailes calendar. Its arrival was heralded by the ripening of the *kakis*, a bright red fruit of pudding-like texture that hung on trees like delicate Christmas baubles. Seeing these trees against the snows of the Sierra Nevada was a true sign that winter had come. And with the coming of the cold weather came the first of the pig slaughters.

The passing of the seasons could now be followed through the activities organized by Paqui for the Discoteca Oh!. Hitherto this was an establishment that seemed to have turned its back on the world outside; but falling clientele, and the continuing lack of guests at the *pension*, had obliged Paqui to organize not only weekly bingo nights, but also parties that celebrated the high points of the agricultural and festive year. On my first day back in Frailes I helped her put up posters throughout the village advertising a *Fiesta de la matanza* (literally a 'pig slaughter party') to be held on the last Sunday of November. When the day came, I sat at the bar counter with Paqui, scooping out with a spoon the pulp of *kakis* that had been cured in a tightly sealed container together with a glass of whisky. Those clients of the disco whose livers had been similarly preserved – notably, Cabildo, Bubi, Fermín and Chica (now back for the winter from Mallorca) – were soon joining us at the bar, followed by a crowd far larger than that of a normal Sunday night. By around midnight a good thirty people were squeezed up against the counter, holding bingo cards that had been given out with each drink ordered. Josélillo, standing in the control box, kept reading out the numbers until finally Bubi jumped off his seat, attacked the air with a violent succession of karate-like gestures, and screamed '*Bingo!*' A little live piglet, hidden up till now among the empty whisky bottles behind the counter, was held up high by Paqui as Bubi's prize. The unfortunate creature slipped out of her grasp, and, during its few moments of liberty, caused chaos and mirth by plunging squealing on to the dance floor, where it ran around hysterically among the flashing lights.

I had wanted idealistically to get the winning numbers so that I could save the piglet from certain death. My city sensibilities had yet to be shaken off after so short a time back in the country. Within a week or so they would be hardened by my first experiences of seeing large pigs killed, cut open, and gradually reduced to fillets, chops, and different kinds of charcuterie. Merce, a lover of animals, said she too hated the idea of any creature suffering, but that she accepted the *matanza* as an age-old reality of country life. For centuries families in isolated communities such as Frailes had managed to survive each year largely off the pigs they killed in the winter. In this age of the supermarket and ever stricter sanitary regulations the tradition was beginning generally to die out, though not in Frailes. The sacrifice of the pigs may no longer have been a necessity as before, but it was an excuse for a two-day working *fiesta* that brought together all the members of a typically extended Frailes family.

Fearing at first that I was going to be as traumatized by *matanzas* as I had been by the spectacle of Pancanto slaughtering the goats, I hoped that the domestic warmth exuding from these essentially family occasions would partly balance the elements of brutality. I was glad that the first one to which I had been invited was taking place in the basement of Merce's and Caño's welcoming stone house, and that it would be attended by a near full complement of the '*Pajaricos*' (the Little Birds), the endearing nickname given to Merce's much loved but now very dispersed family.

We all began gathering at dawn. It was the coldest day I had known in Frailes, and a layer of frost covered the olive trees. Huddling outside around a wood fire over which a cauldron of water had been placed, I watched the first rays of the sun touch the snows of the Sierra Nevada. The person in charge of the fire was Merce's father Pepe, a tall man with a shy smile and kind blue eyes. I had heard from Merce about his struggles to raise his family of nine children at a time when there was no unemployment benefit and little work to be had in the village once the olive harvest was over. Every autumn for over twenty years he had taken his wife and children to work with him as grape-pickers in the south of France, where the Spaniards were generally treated as second-class citizens by their French employers. The money gained in France and during the sub-sequent three months of harvesting olives all over Jaén, together with the pittance made from selling charcoal on rainy days, had been his main means of financial support. For food for his family he had depended heavily on what he caught hunting, and on the products of the annual *matanza*. 'We used always to kill six pigs,' he told me. 'Now it's only two.'

About thirty members of his family, including a good fifteen grandchildren, had assembled by the time Caño decided that it was time to go and kill the pigs, whose actual execution was to be carried out on the nearby farm where they had been raised. I got into the truck of a jovial and warm-hearted brother of Merce called Mige, who, before settling down to marriage and a hard-working life as a tractor driver in the Jaén town of Martos, had had a reputation as an enormously successful womanizer. He, Caño, Merce's serious eldest brother Paco, and myself were nominated for the awful-sounding job of holding the pig down while the professional slaughterman went about his business. I did not like the idea of being an accomplice to the murder, but Mige said I would soon forget my conscience after I had begun tasting the black pudding.

The loudly squealing animal was pulled by a hook in the neck into the yard, where we stood ready to place a strap around its belly and hoist it into the air with the aid of a rope and pulley. The effort of trying to restrain the beast as it tried to kick violently was a huge one, particularly when the slaughterman had sunk his knife into its dan-gling body. It gave out chillingly sharp squeals of pain and terror, and became so frightened that it shat abundantly and pissed all over Mige, much to the amusement of all the children present, who guffawed with laughter. The farmer's wife swept up the mess while Merce, doing a job traditionally reserved for women, placed her hand into the neck wound to direct the gushing blood into a bucket, from which wisps of steam rose into the freezing dawn air.

After the death of the second pig, which was already less shocking for me than that of the first, the trophies of the kill were carefully laid out at the back of a trailer and then driven back to the now boiling cauldron outside Caño's house. Each corpse was placed in turn in a flat-bottomed tin bath and covered in the hot water. Tucked in a

steaming bath on this cold day, the pigs radiated at last peace and contentment.

'We've got the worst part of the day over with,' said Mige, offering
me a glass of reviving aquavit. 'It's always terrible to have to kill an
animal.'

The next moment we all had scrapers in our hands and were
running them up and down the first pig's body, trying to get rid as
much as possible of its hair. The nails were pulled off with pliers, and
the corpse was then strung up with hooks attached to the virtually
unbreakable tendons on the front trotters. Having proved myself
inept with the scraper I was given a disposable razor to remove the
remaining hairs. While the other men vigorously bathed and scraped
the second pig, I and the children had the more satisfying task of
ensuring that the first one was as smooth as a Hellenistic sculpture.
The slaughterman, after coming eventually to inspect the handiwork,
gave a nod, and then proceeded to destroy our work of art by cleav-
ing the head in two with an axe, and ripping open the body in the
middle with a long knife. He cut off the hams, carefully removed the
entrails, and threw away the bladder, the only part of the pig that was
not going to be used ('I've known only the occasional stupid cat to
eat it,' he commented).

At this stage of the *matanza* the traditional tasks of the men were
effectively over. Their 'glory jobs' completed, they were now largely
free to devote much of the next thirty-six hours to gorging themselves on food and drink, leaving to the women the less showy and
infinitely more laborious duties of cleaning out the entrails, preparing the black pudding, salami, and chorizo sausage, and, of course,
providing the men with lunch and supper. I was determined to make
a stand against sexism in the *matanza*, and had the full support of
Merce, who immediately sat me down next to a sister-in-law and
elderly aunt, whose hands were fishing out entrails from a huge bowl
filled also with water and floating lemons. I was set to work right
away. Within minutes I was happily squeezing the entrails between
my fingers so as to rid them of their odorous contents.

The rest of the day was devoted mainly to the making of black
pudding or *morcilla*, for which a good two kilos of puréed onions had
been made the day before. The enjoyable part came with the mixing
of the onion mush with the spices and thick blood. Rolling up my
sleeves to well above the elbow, I immersed my hands into this gory

brew, and experienced in so doing a sensation of almost primeval bliss. Working in conjunction with the sister-in-law I used my hands like the blades of a Moulinex until finally I was told to bring the process to a halt by inscribing the surface with a cross and then blessing the whole by pressing my thumb into the centre of each segment while reciting the words 'In the name of the Father, the Son, and the Holy Ghost'. After barely a break we then used a manual sausage-maker to stuff the purple red mixture into foot-long lengths of entrails, which we then tied up tightly at the ends, so tightly in fact that some of my own blood and skin probably finished up in the completed *morcilla*.

By the next day, when it came to applying my now shredded fingers to the making of the salami and the chorizo, I had not only perfected my sausage skills, but had come to know the intimate histories of most of the women members of the *Pajarico* clan. So confident was I now, and so pleased to have played my part in the reinvention of the male role in a *matanza*, that the following week, when attending a slaughter organized by a charming teacher cousin of Paqui called Carmen, my automatic and unhesitant reaction was to don an apron and plunge my hands once more deep into a vat of blood. Before I began stirring, I allowed Paqui and two of her women relatives to dab my face and theirs with some of the liquid (a traditional touch, they assured me, if also one that looked good on camera). As I waited for someone to photograph this bloody scene, I took in the full beauty of the setting – a tiny old patio, complete with a large table made from an upturned mill stone, a walnut tree above, and a wall of rock down which gushed the water from a nearby spring. Carmen, pregnant with her first child, was looking on beatifically, while her widowed old father, sitting on a stool while poking some blazing logs with his walking stick, completed this perfect vignette of a homely, rural world straight from a Christmas card. Then suddenly the disco music started. Carmen's husband had driven up with his car, opened the door, and turned the radio on at full blast. I stirred the *morcilla* to the rhythms of the ubiquitous *Un movimiento sexi*.

At the beginning of December, just when the *matanza* season was in full swing, the village underwent its most dramatic annual transformation. On my daily climb to El Sereno's garden I found myself walking against a steady stream of people, trucks, vans, Land Rovers and trailers. Everyone, from teenagers to the very old, as well as women whom I reckoned must have spent the rest of the year hiding in their houses, appeared to be taking part in this exodus, leaving me with the sensation, the first day this happened, that they were escaping some natural catastrophe of which I, blindly continuing in the opposition direction, was foolishly unaware. Almost until nightfall the village remained deserted save for the very young, the infirm, and the twenty or so employees of Frailes's shops and public services. Entering the Charro at midday and then the Cueva after lunch only strengthened the feeling that the village had been struck down all of a sudden by a calamity such as the plague. Then, as daylight faded, the villagers started returning, the bars became more crowded than ever, and, from behind the *Caja Rural*, came a hideous rattling, accompanied by billowing clouds of smoke. A long queue of vehicles, piled high with olives, stretched right into the centre of what had always seemed to me like an industrial archaeological site of the 1950s. A conveyor belt of olives dripping with water soared now into the sky, before being sucked into the belly of a dark green monster of a building, from which a pulsating reddish glow could be glimpsed in the cracks of the corrugated iron casing. The olive oil cooperative had awakened at last from its nine-month hibernation.

Before coming to Frailes and seeing its olive harvest for myself, I had never been before in a place where I was quite so conscious of the dominance of a single product on its economy, culture, and way of life. Contrary to what I had first thought, however, the overriding importance accorded here to the olive was a relatively recent phenomenon. Though Jaén province is synonymous with olives in the eyes of most Spaniards, and indeed has inspired a mythology claiming centuries of intensive olive culture, the economy of this part of Andalucía was traditionally based on wheat. El Sereno was always reminding me that the landscapes of his youth in the *Campiña* were not today's infinite expanses of olive trees but rather endless, billowing, wheat fields. Pockets of olive cultivation had existed in the Sierra Sur, and throughout Jaén, since at least the time of the Greeks; but it was not until the middle of the twentieth century that government policies determined the agriculture of the province would be largely given over to the olive tree. The Spanish government, and later the European Community, offered farmers such financial incentives for concentrating on this crop that by the end of the century Jaén had come to produce no less than a tenth of the world's total supply of olive oil. Worryingly, the planting of these trees had by now started to spread beyond traditional agricultural areas and into the virgin slopes of mountainous zones such as the Sierra Sur. The damage being done to the local ecology had become noticeable even to me after little more than a year and a half of visiting these mountains. And a degree in higher economics was not necessary to appreciate what the consequences would be for Jaén should there be any sudden collapse in the world olive market.

The chances of this happening, however, seemed for the time being remote. The virtues of an olive-oil based Mediterranean diet were now so universally recognized that a massive demand for olive products had reached even Japan. A few days after the harvest had begun in Frailes an amused Villi showed me a photograph in the *Ideal de Jaén* in which a group of thirty or so Japanese men, dressed in jackets and ties, were collecting olives in a field near Martos. Growing publicity for the olive culture of Jaén in particular was naturally a boon for El Sereno and his tiny olive mill, which was already becoming known beyond Frailes and its surroundings. Articles on the mill began appearing in the local newspapers, and were contributing to the increased number of visitors who turned up without warning at his house.

El Sereno's rising status as a local celebrity received a further boost with the publication at this time of a book by his writer friend Juan Eslava Galán. Commissioned by the local government of Jaén, this lavishly illustrated work purported to be an 'olive route' through the province undertaken by a fictional Japanese man named Masaru (who can clearly be identified from the photos as a Chinese friend of the author's from Seville). Masaru, in the interests of finding out as much as possible about the wondrous olive, arrives just before Christmas at Frailes, and is given of course the warmest possible welcome by El Sereno, a photograph of whom, working in his mill, appears alongside the text, next to a reproduction of the *Serenolivo* label. Overpriced, slight in tone, and specialist in its focus, this was a book which I imagined would largely depend for its survival on the huge number of copies that the delighted El Sereno kept on ordering for himself. However, the work would prove so successful that Juan Eslava Galán was soon asked to write a follow-up volume covering the whole of Andalucía. Frailes would feature again, though with an additional illustration that helped further another developing myth:

taken on the day of the Alhambra launch, this new photograph showed the stalwarts of the Frailes Group assembled around a bowl of *remojón* in front of El Sereno's garden hut.

El Sereno was fast becoming a guru of the Olive Age, and I was lucky enough to be both his disciple and Boswell. Through his talks with the press and others he had honed his whole views on olive culture, and had settled on two topics in particular. One of these was the failure of Jaén to promote properly the quality of its oil, which had led to the iniquitous situation that Italian companies were getting the credit for oil that was bought in from here. An especially sad example of wasted opportunity was Frailes's own cooperative, which could easily have gained a reputation as the producer of one of Spain's finest oils had it bothered to publicize itself, or, at the very least, to sell the product to the outside market in more attractive and practically-sized containers than the current five-litre plastic bottles.

'Oil that is infinitely inferior,' he stressed, 'is better known simply because it is sold in the elegant designer bottles that the Italians are so good at making. And, what is more, if the bottle looks appealing, a litre of the stuff can be sold abroad for the same price we would pay here for five. We're complete innocents when it comes to marketing.'

But the theme that really got him going, and the one which was most likely to win for him widespread support, was the importance of having an oil that was ecologically sound. He was convinced that the combination of chemical curing and the collecting of olives from the ground was one day going to have fatal results.

'Who knows,' he said, 'what chemical waste we're picking up at the same time as the olives. I wouldn't be surprised if we end up one day having an olive catastrophe comparable to foot and mouth disease.'

El Sereno himself not only refused to use chemicals on his property, but also created his own oil exclusively from olives that had been picked directly from the tree. This was, he admitted, a quixotic practice in keeping with the laborious methods required for his minuscule annual production.

Wishing to extend my knowledge of olive cultivation from theory to practice, and feeling moreover slightly left out of all the harvesting activity around me, I decided to accompany El Sereno the day when he judged his olives ripe enough to be collected for their oil. Throwing four large plastic baskets into the Suzuki, we drove up to his fields above the cemetery, just as we had done in the spring when I had gone to help him pick cherries. Continuing leisurely on foot towards the upper reaches of his property, he looked carefully at each olive tree to choose which would be the most suitable to begin on. Within less than twenty minutes my hitherto limited fund of olive knowledge had expanded enormously. I knew now such terms as '*camá*' and '*alpechín*' (respectively the space between the trees, and the water that comes from the olive). I had learnt to distinguish between the many different types of olive, from the *picual* to the *cornicabra*. And I had discovered that one of the secrets of a good oil is to mix as many of these types as possible, and even include a few of the green, unripe olives that were generally used just for curing and eating. Such titbits of olive lore continued to accumulate once we had started filling the baskets.

'Some experts,' said El Sereno, 'believe that olives grown next to an almond tree provide better oil, while others swear that keeping the stones during the crushing process, as I do, is also beneficial.'

After a pleasant couple of hours of working in the mild sunlight, we called it a day and headed down to the Cueva for a refreshing late morning glass of beer. Altogether I could not have had a more relaxing or bucolic introduction to the labours of the olive fields. I was totally unprepared for the experience awaiting me that weekend.

The time had come for Paqui to repay her debt to her electrician cousin responsible for the complex wiring and lighting at the *Mesón*. Antonio Elvira, a short, blond-haired man in his late thirties, was in charge of an electrical workshop at a private institute at Alcalá; but, as with so many Fraileros, he had inherited olive fields that he tended during his free hours.

'Having olive trees,' he confided to me over a drink at the Discoteca Oh!, 'is a mixed blessing. They can take up most of your weekends, and not just at harvest time. They need care throughout the year. There's all the curing of the soil to do beforehand, the sweeping of the ground around them, and then all the pruning once the harvest is over, and the burning of the branches that have been broken or cut.' The actual harvesting, he added, was of course the worst part of all. 'Every time I go and collect my olives,' he said, 'every part of me hurts afterwards, down to my soul.' Clearly the more normal way of harvesting was rather more strenuous than El Sereno's; but I was none the less convinced he was exaggerating.

'Why don't you come along this Saturday?' he suggested. 'That's when Paqui will be helping out.'

Paqui knocked on my door at seven in the morning. Antonio was waiting outside in a van together with his mother, two long wooden poles, a mass of netting, a couple of rakes, and what looked like a machine-gun. Antonio's gangly younger brother Francisco, who was employed in a local sack-making factory, was going to join us once his morning shift was over. Altogether there would just be five of us working in the fields, which made me initially relieved: if I was going to reveal my incompetence, and stand out as an absurd anachronism, I preferred doing so in a small, intimate group such as this, rather than in a gathering numbering up to thirty people or more. I would soon realize the disadvantages of our limited working force: we would have to labour even harder if we were to fulfil Antonio's obsessive determination to complete all his remaining harvesting by nightfall. And we would miss out on the gossipy chit-chat and spirit of good cheer that were apparently prevalent in large groups, and so necessary to endure all the hard work.

I had set off with all the optimism in the world. With the sun rising in front of us, we drove up along a series of vertiginous tracks towards what Antonio described as among the highest olive slopes near the village. 'You might find them a bit steep,' he thought wise to add, to which I cheerily replied that I did not mind in the slightest. I relished the prospect of working at this dramatic angle within clear sight of the Sierra Nevada, whose snows were turning a vivid orange now that the sun was hitting them.

'We can't drive any higher than this,' announced Antonio, stopping the van just below the lowest of his olive trees. From here the plan was to walk with all the equipment to the very top of the slope, and then proceed slowly downwards. Entrusted with the netting I began determinedly marching up the slope only to find the terrain so gravelly that for each step taken I seemed to fall down two.

After suffering the ordeals of Tantalus I somehow managed to get to the top, some time after the others had done so. Paqui and her seventy-year-old aunt were already on their knees, collecting into a sack all the olives that had fallen to the ground. Antonio, meanwhile, was waiting impatiently for me to begin the laying-out of the nets. This was a finicky task involving much walking up and down around a tree, calculating the extent of the ground that needed to be covered, and then making sure that the lower part of the net was raised slightly so that the olives would not escape at the bottom. Then Antonio handed me one of the poles. I put it down for a moment to take out some sun cream. A few seconds later it had rolled almost all the way down to the van.

'The first lesson of the olive-picker,' chided an unamused Antonio, 'is always to lay his pole down sideways.'

Back again up the slope after retrieving the pole, and in a state by now of near collapse even before I had collected a single olive, I was given the briefest of tips on how to use the implement. All I had to do, instructed Antonio, was to strike the tree with the correct amount of force, making sure always to hit the branches from the side and never from above or below. A wrong move, or too heavy a blow, he warned, could cause irreparable damage to the tree. He was going to help me with the 'machine-gun', which turned out to be a mechanical vibrator that you held with a strap and pressed firmly against the larger branches.

'Let's get in there!' he shouted, turning on the engine, and instilling in me the fantasy that I was a soldier preparing to do battle with the olive.

'Take that!' I almost said, as I gave a mighty whack to this ancient symbol of peace, which responded with a shrapnel fire of black pellets that struck me all over my head and body before falling into the net below. This was, I masochistically admit, a pleasant sensation, and one that gave more satisfaction than my subsequent blows at the same branch in search of the recalcitrant olive survivors that hid away behind the leaves as if trying to escape from a massacre. Fifteen minutes later dying branches had been left in profusion on the ground, and the tree had been reduced to one of the gaunt skeletal shapes that you saw in photos of no man's land. 'I don't think you've entirely killed it,' Antonio decided.

'You can take up the rear,' he then shouted as he brought together the front corners of the net and charged without respite at the next tree, a good ten yards away along the disturbingly steep and slithery slope. I managed to keep up this pace for a further two trees, but then exhaustion, and a momentary distracted glance towards the Sierra Nevada, resulted in the inevitable. I dropped my corner of the net, and at least ten kilos of imprisoned olives made their bid for freedom.

'Why don't you go down to the van and bring the leather gourd containing the wine,' suggested Antonio, proposing a job more suitable to my capabilities.

A few hours later we all descended towards the van for lunch, which we ate under the shadow of a large gnarled tree. Paqui's aunt had prepared in an earthenware bowl the traditional olive-worker's repast – a *remojón* made just from oranges, salt cod, fig bread, and masses of oil. Antonio handed out recently made chorizo and *morcilla*, while Paqui used a penknife to cut up bread and cheese. The scene, with the four of us in clothes dirtied by soil and the black stains of olives, the women wearing headscarves, and the men in straw hats, summed up an Andalucían rural world that for many people, Fraileros included, was still wholly idyllic. All that was missing, I mused, was an element of the erotic.

Though sexual feelings, in my current physical state, were not exactly uppermost in my mind, I remembered from my literary researches that the olive harvest was traditionally renowned as an outlet for them. In a more repressive period of Spanish history this was indeed one of the few times of the year when men and women were able to mingle freely on a daily basis. The thousands of Andalucían folk songs known as *coplas aceituneras* (songs of the olive-workers) were dominated in their subject matter by the flirtations and romances of the olive season, many of which came to an end on the last day of the harvest, and many others consisted of little more than a stolen kiss while kneeling together on the ground, or a glimpse up a skirt from under a ladder. As I relaxed more while taking repeated swigs from the wine gourd, I started thinking of a young Frailera called Pepa. I had met her at the Cueva on the evening the harvest had begun, and I had bumped into her every morning as she walked down the hill on her way to the olive fields. Our exchanges were becoming longer and wittier every day. Now, as sleep slowly overtook me, she had become metamorphosed into the heroine of a *copla aceitunera*. Olive in complexion, and with a head shaped almost like a pointed *picual* olive, she squatted below a tree scooping the olives together with her bare arms. I thought I saw her for a moment smiling in my direction, but then the vision faded, and all I was aware of was Antonio tapping me on my shoulders and telling me that there were only four hours left to sunset.

My limbs were even stiffer than they had been before I had rested; but Antonio's brother Francisco had arrived to relieve me of my ineffectually executed duties as pole shaker and net carrier. I was now relegated to the woman's job of raking together the olives that had fallen from the as yet unshaken trees. This was my least demanding task so far, though I was still far from good at it. 'I think you've managed a ratio of five pebbles to every olive,' sighed Antonio, who unwisely decided at this point to give me a further chance to prove my manhood. He handed me over his 'machine-gun', which I almost immediately dropped, so taken aback was I by its weight. 'If you think that's heavy,' noted Antonio, 'you should try the advanced model, which shakes the whole tree.' With Antonio's and Francisco's help I strapped the implement to my body, and positioned it to an appropriate branch. Paqui and her aunt had stopped what they were doing to devote their full attention to what was going to happen next. I pulled the starter lead rather too tentatively. 'Harder!' shouted Antonio, 'Harder!' I tried again, and then again, until, after almost flooding the engine, I gave the lead a final sharp pull, and was thrown backwards to the ground in shock, as if I had fired an elephant gun.

'I think it's time for Maiquel to carry the olives back to the van,' said Antonio, looking despairingly at the lengthening shadows of the trees.

This last job, more suitable to a mule than a human being, was the worst of all. Treading repeatedly up and down a loose slope in the growing darkness, while carrying a forty-kilo sack of olives on a shoulder almost dislocated by the vibrator, was like an exercise to see how far human endurance could be pushed. Feeling at the end as if I had completed a six months' spell of hard labour in a Siberian prison camp, I thought back to a story I had heard from Ernesto a few days before. As a sixteen-year-old Ernesto had become so fed up one day with his studies that he informed his father that he would be giving up school forthwith. His father agreed, and took him that very day to work in the olive harvest, which left him after a few hours with bleeding hands, an aching body, and a determination never again to take a single day off from studying.

'My own father,' said Antonio when I told him this, 'was always saying when we were out harvesting, "There's either books, or there's this, that's all there is."'

Nightfall saw us back in the village patiently taking our place in the queue at the olive oil cooperative. When our turn came Antonio opened the back of his trailer and let the fruits of all our labours fall through a grate in the ground, below which they would be separated from the pebbles and then pulled up by conveyor belt to be weighed. Antonio went to the control cabin to be given the final result.

'We've collected 750 kilos,' said Antonio, which seemed to me an enormously impressive quantity. I anticipated an astonished reaction when I hobbled shortly afterwards into the Cueva and announced the figure to my card-playing friends. But they were more amused by my look of devastation than they were impressed by my capacities as an olive-picker.

'A group your size working for an entire day,' Caño calculated, 'should have collected at least 2,000 kilos.'

I sat at the bar exchanging experiences about olive-picking with my new friend Pepa, who was also fresh back from the fields.

'Now you'll understand, Maiquel, why I don't like my village as much as you do. For nine months of the year I can't get any work at all, and then I have three months of this.' Women, furthermore, were in some ways worse off than men. 'Though we at last now get paid as much as the men, there are still many men who resent this, thinking that ours is the easiest task. I can assure you that spending an entire day squatting and bending over is not much fun.' What seemed to me even harder to bear was the idea of having to keep up this back-breaking work every single day of the week, without even a break for Sunday. 'The only time we're let off is when it rains, but then of course we don't get paid.'

By the end of our conversation, she seemed quite prepared to ditch a day's pay for the sake of some rest. 'All I want now,' she said, 'is for it to rain.'

Her wish was soon granted. The crisp, clear days at the start of the winter were replaced by a long spell of unsettled weather, with strong winds, sudden storms, and long periods of drizzle that brought with them the prospect of having to prolong the olive harvest well into March. It was getting colder, or so it seemed to me at night in the *Mesón*, where I had taken to going to bed with two hot water bottles, a thermal vest, a knee-length nightshirt, and a thick pair of woollen hiking socks. The erratic heating and electrical system, for which Paqui and I had paid her cousin dearly, had never quite recovered since the day in early December when a drunken adolescent, leaving the disco to have a piss, caused an explosion by accidentally doing so inside the building's fuse box. The temperature of my room continued to plummet; and though this was not necessarily a gauge of the weather conditions outside, I was not altogether surprised to pull up the blinds one morning and discover that it was snowing.

The snow was too watery to settle in Frailes itself, but it appeared to have extensively covered the higher reaches of the Sierra Sur. El Sereno and I had a first-hand report of what it was like up there from a hunch-backed woman in her early eighties whom we met at the *Caja General* signing a document with her thumb print. She walked every week down to Frailes from her house near Los Rosales, and had not been put off from doing so that morning, when she said she had woken up to find a good half metre of snow on the ground. We offered to give her a lift back, as much for her sake, as for ours – we were desperate to see the snow for ourselves.

'It's been at least two years since the last snowfall,' commented El Sereno. 'But it's never snowed here in recent times as much as it did in the past. There was one winter in the sixties when Frailes was cut off from the outside world for a good two weeks.'

With the olive harvest temporarily halted for the day because of the weather, a festive atmosphere took hold of Frailes. Three other cars filled with our friends followed us up into the Sierra, where, having deposited the old woman, we all ended up having a snowball fight in front of the cave of the Santo Custodio. With the biting wind came a brief burst of sunshine that revealed a sight I had never seen before – olive fields under snow. Seen from high above, the raked circles of earth below each tree were transformed now into cakes on which a sugar-spattered candied decoration had been placed in the middle of the icing.

Everything about that day reinforced the feeling that Christmas was almost upon us. For lunch twelve of us crowded into El Sereno's garden hut for that quintessential Andalucían winter dish of bread-crumbs (*migas*) fried with garlic, pepper and bacon over a wood fire. We stood around the chimney breast dipping our forks into a giant frying pan, and then helped ourselves from a large tray to some home-made, paper-wrapped *polvorones* – almond and lard-based biscuits that are a ubiquitous feature of a Spanish Christmas. Afterwards Ernesto invited me to a carol rehearsal taking place in the basement of the pharmacy.

The assembled company belonged to a musical group founded by Ernesto's mother Doña Inmaculada. The songs I was going to hear, local folk carols known as *Villancicos*, were the ones that had earned for the group in 1992 the first prize in a competition organized by the Andalucían television channel Canal Sur. The make-up of the group had inevitably changed considerably since then, with at least five of the singers being from the village's current crop of teenagers, including a beautiful girl with wavy dark hair called Esther, who was the daughter of the local head of the *Guardia Civil*. But most of the key players from before had remained, notably Ernesto and the banker Rafael, Ernesto's doctor brother Pedro Jesús, Pedro Jesús's fiancée Belén, his future father-in-law Indalecio, and an eighty-four-year-old man whom I was meeting tonight for the first time, Luis Machuca.

Luis Machuca was introduced to me as the man who had done most to help Doña Inmaculada bring together the fast disappearing folk songs of the Sierra Sur. He had learnt these during his childhood and youth in an isolated *cortijo* near Cerezo Gordo, where singing and the telling of stories had once been the main forms of entertainment. Tall, with a soft-featured, open face, Luis exuded a saintly charisma, which reflected what I would later find out about his background. He had been a close friend of the Santo Custodio, whose sayings he had avidly recorded, and whose personality and common touch seemed partly to have rubbed off on him. Few other people I had known, even in Frailes, transmitted so instantly such a sense of serenity and kindness.

The commanding and stately Doña Inmaculada, a born musical leader, tapped her baton hard so that everyone stopped talking. Pedro Jesús finished tuning his guitar, and led the mandolins into action, after which the whole choir broke in loudly with the lyrics '*Let's go and sing!*', an exhortation that in turn sparked off a cacophony of exotic percussion instruments ranging from earthenware jugs sealed with drum skins to a bottle of anise struck with a spoon by Indalecio. One by one the soloists had their moments in the spotlight: first Esther, who had a surprisingly deep and powerful voice, then the more angelic-sounding Belén, and finally a voice that lacked the mellifluous tone of either but which instead was loud, shrill in its higher registers, and so penetratingly lucid that it went straight to the heart. It was the voice of Luis Machuca.

So carried away was I by the music that for a moment I forgot this was a rehearsal and that I was the only member of the audience. I burst into loud clapping. Afterwards, when everyone was clearing up and beginning to leave, I went to congratulate Luis, whose gently smiling face reflected the extent to which he too had enjoyed himself.

'He's a very foolhardy person,' said Doña Inmaculada in a mock chiding tone. 'He's had eight heart attacks, but he will never miss a rehearsal or performance.' After he left the room, she continued shaking her head, 'his wife died of a heart attack three years ago during the festivities of St Peter's Day. Even that hasn't stopped him. He could drop dead any minute, but he doesn't mind at all, he's got no fear of dying. He even says that he hopes to die when he's doing something he enjoys.'

Neither Doña Inmaculada nor Luis's family had succeeded in deterring him from wanting to perform with the group at midnight Mass this coming Christmas Eve; and he would probably join those among them, such as Ernesto and Pedro Jesús, who intended to drive up afterwards to the Santo Custodio's sanctuary at La Hoya del Salobral to continue singing and playing into the early hours of Christmas Day. But, more worryingly for Doña Inmaculada, there was nothing that would dissolve his determination to accompany the musicians on a potentially tiring outing planned for a few days from now, when *Villancico* groups from throughout Jaén would be descending on the provincial capital to demonstrate their skills.

The bus taking the group to this musical gathering set off after a late lunch on a day of renewed sunshine and pellucid skies. The musicians and their families took up the entire bus apart from two seats near the front, which had been left for El Sereno and myself, the group's unofficial fan club. Travelling for the first time with a bus load of Fraileros, and on an outing in which the village's cultural pride was at stake, strengthened my sense of having been adopted by the place, and of having truly become, as Paqui and others so often insisted, a Frailero myself. The atmosphere on board was like that of any lively coach outing – full of jokes, banter, and singing – but with the characteristically Spanish touch that everyone was shouting out conflicting instructions to the bus driver about how to get to our destination. Eventually arriving late at the centre of Jaén, we had to complete the journey on foot, and speed as quickly as possible along the pedestrian streets of the old town. My fears for Luis were growing, particularly on reaching the theatre where the event was taking place, and finding a complete confusion of people trying to get in. Audience and performers were finally separated, and El Sereno and I struggled for a seat in a tightly packed row in the dress circle.

A young girl dressed as the Virgin Mary sat at the front of the stage cradling her plastic Jesus, while each of the village groups, all in traditional costume, performed in turn behind her, two of them doing so while feigning to work in a *matanza*, others while holding rakes and poles as if they had just come from the olive groves. The standard of singing was uniformly high, though El Sereno regretted that the art of the *Villancico* was being undermined by the pernicious and ever spreading influence of the flamenco-derived *Sevillana*, the Spanish folk music best loved by foreigners. Then the lights went down, and the curtain was lifted to reveal the Frailes group dressed in the same costumes which Merce and her friends had surprised me with two summers ago on that now mythical visit to Custodio's garden. It was not just an excess of Frailero pride that made El Sereno and I aware immediately that this was music with an impact much more direct than anything we had heard before. The notion of Frailes as a 'virgin village' was reinforced by listening at last to *Villancicos* that were as pure as if they had come straight from one of the *cortijo* gatherings of Luis Machuca's youth. The audience, full of restless families, was soon so intensely involved in the music that, when Luis himself stepped forward to begin his solo, I feared that the built-up emotion in the theatre would be strong enough to induce in him a collapse. But he sang with his serene confidence, and his lips merely registered a contented smile when the absorbed silence in which he had been heard was broken by the loudest applause of the evening.

On the bus journey back, with the vision of a triumphant Frailes so fresh in my mind, schemes of mounting implausibility started coming to me. Thoughts about tape-recording and perhaps even videoing Luis Machuca merged into nebulous plans for some musical show, and then into fantasies about bringing the past back to life, and extracting for the world's benefit the purity of spirit that seemed contained in Luis's voice. A few days later I conceived a grand nostalgic project that would give shape to my unlikely dreams of placing Frailes on a stage of global dimensions.

This moment of inspiration came at a party held by Rafael the banker. The venue was a house he had just restored as a holiday home for the rural tourist. Rafael himself had been born and brought up in the building, and much of the charm of the place was due to the way in which standard elements of rustic chic such as traditional farm implements hanging on the walls were mitigated by genuine homely touches, for instance the embroidery commemorating Rafael's birth, the framed documents comprising his first financial transactions, photographs of his family eating *remojón* during the olive harvest, and a discreet altar containing an image of the Santo Custodio. For the party, which was intended as a mixture of a house-warming and a pre-Christmas celebration, he had invited some colleagues from Alcalá, and a handful of close friends, including his two inseparable companions from school days, Santi, and the man who had played such an important part in helping me first establish myself in Frailes, the cook Miguel Montes.

Though I had seen relatively little of Miguel since that first summer in the village, I had continued to think of him as a guardian figure, discreet, dignified, self-contained, and fearful of imposing, but always there if I needed him, and unfailingly reliable. During Rafael's party he spent most of his time in the kitchen, not only preparing the food but also hiding from the Alcalaínos, with whom he did not feel at ease. Santi and I went to join him there, and we began talking about their school escapades. Rafael, rushing in and out to collect wine and food, was delayed for ever longer periods by our company, and was soon drawn into the general conversation about the past. He laughed as he recalled how Santi and Miguel would come with him on their bicycles to serenade his future wife at night; and he evoked the excitement when Frailes's first television set was installed in the Cueva.

'Maiquel,' interrupted Miguel, 'life then in the village was so much more entertaining that it is today. Everyone now has their own televisions and videos, and, if they want to have some night life, all they have to do is get into their cars and drive off to Alcalá. In those days we weren't nearly so spoilt as people are today, the simplest things made us so incredibly happy. Oh, if only you had known Frailes when the cinema was still working!'

The mention of the village cinema was the great turning point in the conversation. For the rest of the night we talked about nothing else. I had been told before that Frailes had had one, but I had difficulty in picturing it as anything other than a large white sheet hanging in the back room of a bar, such as I had seen as a child in villages in Italy and Provence. But, as Miguel became progressively more carried away with what was clearly his pet obsession, I realized it had been a proper, purpose-built structure, with stalls and a dress circle, and even its own bar. It had been opened in the late 1940s, and had stayed functioning until the early 1970s, when, as with so many small cinemas throughout Europe, it could no longer compete with television and the rise of the video.

'So I imagine,' I said, 'it was then pulled down or turned into something else.'

'No!' answered Miguel emphatically. 'It's still exactly as it was, it's even got its original projector. I haven't been inside for years, few people have. But I know from its owner, Ferminillo, that nothing important has been touched. Next time you go with him in his taxi you should ask him about it, I'm sure he'd love to show you around. He and his father virtually built the place with their own hands.'

My mind was still racing with images of this hidden jewel while Miguel, Santi and Rafael breathlessly exchanged anecdotes.

'Do you remember,' asked Santi, 'how when we had no money at all we used to get in by climbing in from the river over the toilet wall?'

'And there was all hell to pay whenever Ferminillo caught you,' commented Miguel. 'He would drag you by your ears and kick you out by the front door.'

'I used to love it when the electricity broke down,' added Rafael, 'and Ferminillo had to turn on the emergency generator. The noise that thing made! You couldn't hear anything that was being said on the screen. And the quantities of black smoke made it impossible to see anything either.'

Both Rafael and Santi so enjoyed going to the cinema that they had taken on jobs there selling sweets, refreshments, and the sun-flower-seed husks known as *pipas*. Miguel's passion for the place had gone one stage further. After doing all manner of tasks for Ferminillo, from mending chairs to sweeping up afterwards, he was eventually allowed to become the latter's assistant projectionist.

'We used to show one or two films a week, perhaps three during the olive harvest, when people had more money to go out.'

I wanted to know what sort of films were particularly popular.

'Westerns were always a big hit. I think the film that launched the place was Errol Flynn's *Road to Santa Fe*. And just before they closed the cinema I remember there was this large poster in the bar announcing for future presentation a film called *The Sheriff Never Shot*. Well he never did. The poster hung around for weeks, and it's probably still there now. People kept on asking when they were going to show the film, and Ferminillo just shrugged his shoulders. Then the news went round that the Cinema España (that's what the place was called) was never going to open again.'

The brief pensive pause that followed was broken by the ceaselessly cheerful Rafael, who started recalling some of the famous Spanish films of the Franco years, such as Berlanga's *Welcome Mister Marshall*, the story of a village preparing for the arrival of the eponymous American general who masterminded the Marshall Plan.

'Then there were all those films with Sara Montiel,' interjected Santi, causing smiles all round.

'She was the sex goddess of her day,' Rafael explained. 'There was hardly a Spanish male of our generation who did not have some erotic fantasy about her.'

I said I had seen her on television just the day before launching her autobiography, *Life is a Pleasure*.

'Well, she's changed a bit since we fantasized about her,' said Rafael, 'but she still looks remarkably young for her age. What, she must be at least in her mid-seventies.'

'Her film *El último cuplé*,' butted in Miguel. 'Now that was probably the Cinema España's greatest hit.'

'We were far too young to be allowed to see it,' added Santi. 'It was a really controversial film for its day, probably the first truly sexy film to be passed by Franco's censors. Of course it would seem harmless to us now, but there are cultural commentators who think of it as the beginning of a softening in attitude on the part of the dictatorship. There were priests all over the country who wanted to have it banned. And there were many towns and villages that refused to show it.'

'It was shown in Frailes long before it went to Alcalá,' continued Miguel. 'People from all around the district crowded into the Cinema España to see it. Even though I was only about seven at the time, I can still picture the queues of cars coming into the village. The Alcalaínos were quite furious at not having got the film first.'

'I was always told,' laughed Santi, 'that the village birth rate doubled in the year after it came here.'

As the three men talked I was suddenly seized by an idea that seemed at the time so simple, obvious, and easy to realize. Even before seeing the cinema for myself, I was determined that the place should be reopened for just one magical night that would unleash floods of memories. We would show once again *El último cuplé*. Ferminillo would be around to eject gate-crashers by their ears. Miguel would be in the projection box; and Rafael and Santi would be walking up and down the aisles selling *pipas* and lemonade. And to crown it all, and to ensure that the Alcalinos would never again turn up their noses at the Fraileros, we would bring the villagers face to face with the star of their youthful dreams. We would invite Sara Montiel herself.

Out of this simple idea came repercussions greater than I would ever have imagined.

2

THE YEAR BEGAN on a note of drama. It was a winter's night in Scotland, and I was trapped upside down at night in an overturned car with a blizzard howling, and icy water from the stream below filling the vehicle slowly but steadily. It occurred to me then that I might never seen Frailes again, and that my body as it hung suspended by the safety belt had become like that of the pig I had helped to kill. The mobile phone in my hand should have been my lifeline, but a call to the emergency services had merely received an irritated response from the operator: 'There's nothing I can do, sir, unless you clearly state if you need the Police, the Fire Brigade, or the Ambulance service. I repeat . . .' Then the line was cut off.

My short return trip to Britain for the New Year had perhaps been a mistake. The more I stayed in Frailes the more unsafe the world seemed beyond the sphere of influence of the Santo Custodio. As I tried in my first surge of panic to free myself and my driver companion, I distracted myself with thoughts of the Sierra Sur, and of the protective spirit I was convinced resided there. And just at the point when I accepted there was nothing to be done I saw the familiar rounded face with the cropped fringe floating in my open wallet in the water. Then there was a knocking at the window, and a calm male voice was telling us quietly what to do. The stranger managed to open the door, and we crawled outside without a bruise. The man waited for the ambulance to come, then disappeared.

For some time afterwards I felt apprehensive in a car, even while being driven two weeks later by the experienced Ferminillo, with whom I was able at last to broach the subject of his cinema. I was his only passenger, and he appeared now in a mad rush to get to Frailes. It was seven o'clock in the evening, and the speed of his taxi seemed to rival that of the clouds racing against a night sky where a full moon could be fleetingly glimpsed, shining above a bare, mountainous landscape. Ferminillo, raising his voice above the screeching old tunes played on *Radiolé*, the local radio station, was shouting to me in a tone more nervous and excited than I had ever heard him use. He was talking about the indoor and outdoor cinemas he had once owned, in Granada, in Benidorm, in Valdepeñas de Jaén, and, of course, in Frailes itself. 'I lived for the cinema,' he shouted, overtaking simultaneously two trucks and a large, articulated lorry, 'but of course the cinema was different then to what it is today. Films now are just technique, there's no passion to them any more.' And as he turned the volume up on a tragic love song by Juanita Reina, the Sevillian Edith Piaf, he shouted in a voice louder than before, 'All technique, and not an ounce of passion!'

We did not even stop at the *Mesón* for me to leave my luggage. Ferminillo drove me instead in a rage towards the olive-oil factory, which was still shaking and fuming like an undefeated monster. The olive harvest had a good six more weeks to go, and the usual queue of trucks and trailers was lined on the steep street next to it. We overtook them all and swung to a halt on the pavement. The cinema, directly facing the factory, was a building to which I had barely given a glance before. Seen from above, from El Sereno's garden, it had seemed just a mass of broken roof tiles caving in on the untidy banks of the village stream. From the street it looked instead just like another of the village's ill-fated shops that had been forced to close down, such as the one further up the street with the sign 'Frozen Goods' permanently imprisoned within its metal shutters. All that immediately distinguished this from the village's many other failed enterprises was that it was the only one not to have kept its now redundant sign. Waiting on the pavement as Ferminillo took out his keys, I noticed for the first time the only obvious indication of its original function: cut into a rectangular marble niche was a small square opening that had been closed by a block of wood – a ticket office, I imagined.

Ferminillo pushed open the security gates to expose some elegant glass doors with mahogany frames. Together we stepped into the *Ambigú*, the evocative old Spanish word for a foyer bar, that ambiguous space where the reality of the outside world begins to dissolve into the unreality of the cinema experience. I waited in the semi-darkness, among coils of wire, metal ladders, and an abandoned fridge, while Ferminillo climbed upstairs to switch on the lights. The brash glare of a modern strip light illuminated an otherwise largely intact bar of art deco appearance. Apart from a few changes carried out in the last decade, when the place had apparently been briefly rented out as an electrical workshop, this was a post-war period piece, with pastel colours, a rounded formica counter, and a glass cabinet with bottles of Selzum *gaseosa* that I remembered from childhood visits to Franco's Spain. But it was not until I had followed Ferminillo through a door hung with the threadbare, tattered remains of a red velvet curtain that I knew that Miguel had not misled me.

The emotion that overwhelmed me on first entering that door was comparable to that felt, I imagine, by the tiny number of romantic travellers who climbed the Alhambra hill at the beginning of the 19th century, and contemplated the fragmentary remains of the Nasrid palaces when they were crumbling to the ground, overgrown, and inhabited by gypsies and vagrants. I experienced that night in the Cinema España a sense of awe and wonder that the streamlined Alhambra of today was incapable of inspiring in me. The building strengthened my growing conviction in the conquering powers of the small and humble; it confirmed my view of Frailes as a place where magic could be found behind the most ordinary surface.

A sign in old-fashioned Spanish commanding the audience to remove their hats ('Discover your Heads' were the actual words) mirrored my reverential response as I walked beneath a dress circle which, in a moment of disorientation, struck me as one of the raised choirs so characteristic of Spain's sixteenth-century churches. The feeling of being in a church lingered briefly as I was lured down the aisle towards a proscenium arch as impressively tall and as heavily adorned as one of those Spanish retable altars that soar up into the ceiling. A wooden lattice-work in gold, green, pink and red surrounded the arch, the inner sides of which had a series of red panels intended to give an effect of dramatic perspectival foreshortening. Diseased and disintegrating plaster walls in a lurid dark maroon enclosed the whole space, while above was a fake ceiling in stiffened, red-painted cloth with imitation panels whose gilded wood borders were half-falling off, and a precarious central roundel studded with pseudo-honeycomb cells. The whole look of the place, and the workmanship itself, had an endearingly personal stamp to it.

'Everything you see here was designed by my father, everything,' emphasized Ferminillo, his voice speeding up, and squeaking slightly as it got louder. 'He was an extraordinary man, there's no one like him today, no one. He had vision, he had energy, he could do everything, he ran the village band, he was a brilliant engineer, he even made his own car.'

As we stood in the dirt-encrusted auditorium, amidst discarded oil drums, washbasin stands, toilet bowls, and stacks of firewood, he pointed to a huge pile of wicker chairs and carved rows of wooden seating, all of which had been hand-made by his father.

'That too,' he added, indicating a metal stove with a giant rusting pipe shooting up to the very top of one of the side walls. 'That was his creation, it was fuelled by the crushed olive pulp we call *orujo*, it heated the cinema marvellously.'

I turned to the other wall to see what else I could find of his father's, but all that was there was a large 'No Smoking' sign darkened at the edges as if by smoke.

'No one paid any attention to that,' he said dismissively, corroborating what others would tell me about a typical winter's night here, when a rainstorm of *pipa* shells from above burst through the cloud formed by fumes from the heater, and smoke from hundreds of cigarettes, pipes and cigars.

Ferminillo returned quickly to the subject of his father, which would soon spur him on to a rambling but impassioned comparison between the values of the past and present.

'What I learnt from my father was the value of work, I learnt it from him when I was an eighteen-year-old, slaving away day and night to try and get the cinema finished for its opening night in 1949. Since then I've been working every moment of my life. Cards bore me, I don't go out drinking, I've got to be active all the time, I'm not lazy like today's youth. We live in a mediocre age, young people have it too easy, they spend too much time at home watching videos, they've got no talent. Why do you think film actors of the past were so much better, so much more passionate than those of today? It's because they knew what hardship was, they had to struggle to overcome it. Art thrives on hardship!'

With his whole body trembling now like an old projector, he strode with violent purpose towards the stage, prompting in me a vision of him as an actor on the point of declaiming a speech to the empty auditorium. But nimbly leaping up some collapsing steps, he merely walked across the stage's rotten floorboards to pull out a ladder that was resting against a heap of broken chairs and other rubbish. I watched him anxiously as he began climbing this ancient object whose rungs were either missing, cracked, or whittled away by woodworm and age. Tugging hard on a dangling rope he caused such commotion and clouds of dust that I feared that the whole building would fall down on top of us. A pole began creakily descending at an expressionistic angle. He gave another strong tug on the rope, and a large piece of plaster fell to the ground. The pole had now righted itself, and was jerkily bringing down with it a painted stage cloth featuring the red *trompe-l'oeil* curtains of a theatre. This cloth, when finally extended to its full width, was all that was needed to invest the general scene of decay with an unworldly new life. The curtains had been drawn apart, and, above the letters '*Industrias Bib-Rambla*', there floated a surreal collage in which a free-standing Roman-style arch framed two giant bars of chocolate, a cigar-shaped object marked '*Asia*', and the words, so appropriate to Ferminillo's performance with the rope, '*Worthy of a Triumphal Arch*'.

As if to acknowledge the applause of the audience, Ferminillo stepped out from behind the cloth, slapped his hands together to wipe off the dust, and stood proudly facing me at the centre of the stage. I went up to join him, and almost put my foot right through one of the fragile steps. He gestured to me to come behind the cloth, where he showed me the hole where you could watch the members of the audience take up their seats, and thus know when the performance should begin.

'The performance?' I queried, rather surprised. Ferminillo then explained that the Cinema España had served also as a theatre during the olive harvest, when the villagers had money to spare, and a great need to be entertained.

'We had variety shows, musicals, light dramas, and, above all, singing and dancing,' he said, urging me to study carefully the back of the stage cloth, which was densely scrawled with signatures, some by artists who had gone on afterwards to achieve national fame. 'We had "Las niñas de Marchena", Juanito Valderrama, El Osorio . . . Pepe Villeras . . .'

As his halting list continued, I was seized with a momentary vision. I saw the Cinema España as the type of provincial small theatre where my Italian mother had worked during her war years in Italy as a touring actress. I could conceive at last the small Sicilian theatre where my father had first set eyes on her in 1944 and fallen in love. And I wondered if part of this cinema's appeal to me was the opportunity it offered to confront the romantic legacy that tales of my parents' meeting had left me with. I blurted out to Ferminillo that my mother had been an actress, but he did not appear to register what I said, and simply smiled with his golden teeth, and hurried me down into the dark, dank space below the stage, where he showed me the toilets whose effluence had fallen directly into the stream outside, sometimes on to the feet of those unfortunate children who were trying to climb in.

Our tour was still far from over, and surprises would continue to mount. Returning to the *Ambigú*, we climbed from there past the dress circle – five tightly packed rows of benches – and then into what is known in Britain as 'the Gods' and in Frailes as 'the Chicken Coop'. Favoured once by children and the virtually penniless, this was now the most ruinous part of the whole building. Bare floor-boards and unvarnished wooden benches with gaping holes almost gave way beneath me as I tried to keep pace with the confidently marching Ferminillo, who assured me that I would only fall a few metres or so should the worst come to the worst. No sooner had we reached the relative safety of the other side than he darted down a dark staircase little wider than my shoulders to show me a poky space where, lost among spider webs, broken glass, and empty Selzum bottles, lay a large orange canister that he claimed was still three-quarters full with the gas he had once used to make *gaseosa*. Deeper down still was a long narrow room where another of his many tasks were carried out – painting the canvas posters that were hung across the street to announce the film on show. Behind a stack of slate boards chalked over with names of films and stars was a chaos of canvases, at the front of which was one crudely daubed with a half-length portrait of Sara Montiel in a low-cut green dress. '*El último cuplé*', read the faded letters.

Ferminillo, with his innate theatrical sense, left the climactic moment to the very end, when we had returned to the claustrophobic staircase and climbed to the highest point in the building, coming to a door marked 'No Entry'. Even those hardened, unromantic souls incapable of appreciating the beauty of a broken-down provincial cinema would have recognized at least the historical value of what lay behind this door. It was a projection booth such as one might have encountered aboard the *Marie Celeste*. Thirty years of dust had covered a room that looked as if it had been mysteriously abandoned during the showing of a film, and then left untouched. Everything was still there: the old reels and original cleaning chemicals; the peaked caps worn by Ferminillo and his father in the village band; the stack of music by the legendary 1950s singer Juanita Reina which had always been played at the start of the programme; even the compressed pile of completed censorship forms for every film that had ever been shown in the Cinema España. But, of course, the real interest for cinema buffs lay in the projector and surrounding equipment, which had all been constructed by Ferminillo's father, whom I began now to envisage as some crazed scientist straight out of an old Hollywood film. This whole part of the room resembled the type of laboratory where Frankenstein had created his monster, and acquired even more of this look after Ferminillo tried to rid me of my scepticism about everything being still in working order. For after turning on some switches, and forcefully pulling down a series of levers, he succeeded in causing a row of upturned coloured bulbs to start flickering nervously, which in turn sent the hands of an adjoining clock metre wildly turning, until finally sparks flew, lights flashed, and a fuse loudly exploded.

'That's modern electricity for you,' grumbled Ferminillo, opening the shutters so that light from the olive-oil factory would flood into the now darkened booth. 'Everything worked perfectly until a couple of years ago, when the Sevillana Company insisted that the building needed rewiring.'

He mended the fuse, and we returned to the *Ambigú* with my enthusiasm for the cinema as intact as ever, despite the technical failings.

'I'm just amazed,' I said. 'There can't be any other place like this in the whole of Spain.'

Ferminillo beamed with the satisfaction of someone who had finally been able to share a passion that he had kept to himself during the three decades of the cinema's closure. 'My brothers want me to sell the place, they can't understand why I want to keep it. But I'll never sell it, certainly not for the pittance I've so far been offered. I pay high taxes for the site. I've spent a fortune ensuring that rain will do no more damage to the structure. But I'd rather do that than give away for nothing a place that has been so important in my life.' He locked the doors, and closed the metal grilles, and then stood facing me in the street. 'My whole youth is buried here,' he announced in his shrill, emphatic way, 'my whole youth.'

Nervously, I judged this now the time to propose to him my idea of reopening the building for a showing of *El último cuplé* in the presence of Sara Montiel. My scheme, more quixotic than ever now that I had seen how much work needed to be done to make the place reasonably tidy and safe, was not at first properly understood by Ferminillo, who said that it was completely unfeasible in the building's present state.

'We'd have to reconstruct the place almost entirely, get rid of the proscenium arch, and install modern equipment and sound. Then perhaps the cinema could once again become a commercial proposition.'

The idea of a one night's artistic happening in a cinema that would be left almost exactly as it was, seemed beyond his immediate comprehension. I had overestimated his artistic instinct, and underestimated his commercial one. I attempted to explain myself again, and this time he just shrugged and muttered 'Perhaps.'

'If it's just for one night,' he added after further consideration, 'it might be a possibility, we'll see.' And the tone of voice in which he said this implied that I would probably never mention the matter again. He was not a believer in miracles.

The intercession of celestial powers was clearly going to be necessary for my scheme to have any chance of coming off. When I reached El Sereno's house later that night I realized I was not the only person in Frailes who had thought recently of invoking them.

'Go and have a look at the garden hut,' he urged with a teasing smile. He walked mischievously behind me as I headed towards a hut that now shimmered in the darkness with an unearthly reddish glow. I stepped inside to find my familiar writing room illuminated by the light of a dozen or so large red candles of the long-lasting kind generally placed in chapels. Four of them stood burning on top of the broken television set, on which now rested a blown-up framed image of the Santo Custodio, as well as a smaller photograph of the latter's successor, the Santo Manuel. The rest of the candles were distributed between some metal shelving and the chimney breast, and paid homage to more conventional devotional icons such as the Virgin of Mercedes, the Christ of the Cloth from nearby Moclín, the Virgin of Sorrows (patroness of the Calvary chapel above Frailes), and the heavily bearded San Fray Leopoldo, a saint much venerated in Granada.

This unlikely display of religiosity could be blamed on Merce, who had asked El Sereno to light a candle or two for her so that she could pass the Spanish state exams known as *Oposiciones*. This dreadful bureaucratic hurdle was one that all Spanish civic employees had at some stage to face, usually when they least expected it. Even if you had been doing the same job successfully for years, as Merce had done, you stood a very good chance of losing it if you were to fail this ridiculous test. At least two of my Andalucían friends had had nervous breakdowns while preparing for the *Oposiciones*, the consequence of hours locked indoors learning by heart entirely useless facts. Merce herself, when informed about the exams in the autumn, had tried at first to keep her mind off them by spending ever more of her time playing cards in the Cueva. She was also convinced that her enormous popularity in Frailes, not to mention the ever-watchful spirits in the village, would protect her. However, by the beginning of January, with the first part of the exams just a fortnight away, she had suggested to El Sereno, probably in that half-serious, half-jesting tone with which she and I conducted our conversations on the Santo Custodio, that a few lit candles might not come amiss.

El Sereno, a notorious cynic when it came to questions of religion and the supernatural, had responded to her suggestion in a way she could scarcely have imagined. As well as putting up the pseudo-altars to the Santos Custodio and Manuel, he had revealed a hitherto unknown talent as a parodist by writing a supplication on Merce's behalf to the Virgin of Sorrows.

'Most Blessed Virgin of Sorrows', it read, 'We Beseech you with all our Love and Devotion to Grant our dear friend Merce García such Inspiration in her Exams that those Correcting them will be left Speechless and have the Balls to Award her the maximum Mark of Ten out of Ten. And should you Heed Our Request we Sincerely Promise, Maiquel, Ernesto and I, to Climb up to the Calvary Chapel forthwith, and Recite there Three Our Fathers and Three Hail Maries.'

Merce, according to El Sereno, had been so pleased with this that she had promptly taken Loli the policewoman from the Town Hall to come and see it. Loli, then in the final stages of pregnancy, had subsequently asked El Sereno for something similar to help her experience the easiest possible birth and have the most perfect baby. He had responded with a supplication addressed to St Bartholomew, which he now read out to me in full, barely able to control his tears of laughter when he came to the part in which he promised the saint that if his wish should be conceded he would 'Make Love Three Times a Week should he Find a Suitable Woman, and, if not, then Have a Daily Wank'.

Merce had just had the news that she had passed the theoretical part of her *Oposiciones*; and Loli had given birth soon after Christmas to a strapping, healthy girl. Though the promised vows had yet to be fulfilled (as far as I knew), El Sereno had been encouraged by the success of his supplications to pen a third, this one being a plea to Fray Leopoldo to assist Merce in the second and last part of her exams, which were scheduled for the middle of February.

'Fray Leopoldo,' it began, 'Let me Be Completely Honest with You. I have Never for a Moment Believed in Heavenly Miracles. But now that Help is Needed for Someone who is like my own Flesh and Blood, I have no other Option than to become a Believer, and Beseech you from the Bottom of my Heart to . . .' The promise for conceding this particular favour was the most difficult one of all for El Sereno to carry out. His pledge, no less, was to be a devotee of Fray Leopoldo for the rest of his life.

Though conceived, by El Sereno at least, in a flippant and subversive spirit, the candle offerings, and their accompanying written texts, would seem in retrospect the harbingers of what Merce would call 'a Frailes gone mad'. The developing story of Merce's struggle with bureaucracy and the state would soon converge with the tale of my attempts to bring alive the Cinema España. Innocence would be pitted against corruption, ordinary people against politicians, Fraileros against Alcalaínos, and David against Goliath, in a saga heavily spiced with sexual fantasies, and implausible, near-inexplicable occurrences.

A sign that strange things were afoot in the village was the discovery I made at the end of my first night back, when I dropped briefly into the Discoteca Oh! and was told by Paqui that two young couples from Alicante had come to stay at the *pension*.

'They're not friends of yours? Nor family?' I asked incredulously. I had become so used to a *pension* where the high season was when I was there on my own, and the low season was when there was no one at all, that it took me some time to take in the fact that people with no connection either with Frailes or with me had turned up there just like that. I immediately rushed upstairs to see what these bizarre intruders were like. I found them in the sitting room looking totally miserable. The music from the disco was keeping them awake, and they were so cold in their rooms (the heating, inevitably, was not working) that they had come in here to play cards around the electrical brazier. Two of them appeared already to have succumbed to the flu. I asked how they had come to hear of Frailes, and one of them answered that he had picked up a leaflet in a restaurant in Alicante (which I later heard was run by one of Paqui's numerous cousins). I was worried now that they would leave the village with a terrible impression, and that they would be not only the first but also the last of Paqui's 'spontaneous' guests. Then I had the brainwave to propose they pay a visit first thing the next morning to El Sereno who, I was sure, would be only too happy to show them round. They took up my suggestion, and, by the time they left on the Sunday, laden with the usual gifts, were telling everyone that this was one of the best weekends in the country they had ever had. Soon after they had gone I walked into Paqui's kitchen to find it glowing with burning candles.

'What are the candles for?' I asked.

'For Merce,' she replied, 'for us, for the *Mesón*, for Frailes.'

My growing concern to spread the name of Frailes far and wide would find further fulfilment over the next few weeks as I undertook numerous short trips around the province of Jaén in the ubiquitous company of El Sereno, Santi, Merce and Caño. Viewing myself at times as a member of an ambassadorial delegation, I joined my friends in drumming up enthusiasm and support for the village that I thought might even come in handy when I seriously embarked on the Cinema España project. Influenced to a certain extent by the memories of El Sereno, which more than compensated for the absence of easily accessible information about the little-known places we were visiting, I began also to think of Jaén as a place more steeped in the atmosphere of the early and middle years of the twentieth century than most other parts of present-day Andalucía.

For instance, the sharp contrasts between rich and poor that had once been such a feature of the whole region were still chillingly apparent in the small town of Alcaudete, where a banker friend of El Sereno, after telling us of the pittance earned by the employees of the local *mantecado* biscuit factories, led us along a main street lined with majestic palaces of the 1920s and 1930s whose absentee owners still controlled over a third of the town's wealth. As for the civil war and its aftermath, I had been to no other place in the whole of Spain quite so evocative of this period as the whitewashed Cordovan-style town of Lopera, which stood among endless rolling fields once culti- vated not just with wheat but with vines. The town's chronicler took us straightaway to the one surviving bodega, an unaltered white building from the 1930s above whose massive oak barrels hung slogans typical of the Francoist past, such as 'Time is Gold', and 'Work honours Man'. Savouring, as if it were Proust's *madeleine*, a glass of fortified wine dating from the year the civil war ended, we continued our journey back into the past with a visit to an almost intact Nationalist bunker on the outskirts of the town. This helped set the scene for the most moving moment in our morning, when the chronicler walked us along a rough track shaded by olive trees to show us the exact spot where the young British poets John Cornford and Ralph Fox had been killed on 27 December 1936. They had been in a convoy trying to reach Lopera from Andújar, but had been trapped here in a Nationalist ambush in which nineteen Republicans died. Their driver, the only survivor, had told the story of the mas- sacre to the chronicler, who in turn had repeated it to the respective nephews of the poets. These men, who had cycled together all the way from England to Lopera just a few weeks before our visit, had promptly knelt on the ground, and scooped up a handful of earth to take back with them.

So much from Franço's Spain had remained in Jaén that I feared that, sooner or later, we would arrive at a cinema that disproved my hunch about the uniqueness of the Cinema España. Fortunately, we did not. We did, however, come across a number of other ruinous public structures from this period that aroused similar emotions, notably a giant flour factory from El Sereno's childhood village of Fuerte del Rey. The local mayor, as he kicked open a creaking door to reveal a dust-covered room filled with machines straight from Fritz Lang's *Metropolis*, told us of his plans to convert the place into a museum chronicling the wheat industry of Jaén. The project appealed to El Sereno, who now began having visions of the Cinema España as a museum explaining the history of the cinema to the children of Frailes. He nonetheless conceded that a mayor of the sensibility of Fuerte del Rey's would be needed to create such a place. This man, we both agreed, was exceptional among all the many local politicians we had met – dynamic, respectful of the past, and with the interests of his villagers so much at heart that he and his appointed councillors had famously renounced their salaries and given the money to the local poor and elderly.

But as a role model to inspire me in my romantic plans for the Cinema España, I needed someone less practical and sensible than the mayor of Fuerte del Rey. On another of our trips to the *Campiña* I found such a person in a recently deceased Jienese eccentric who had created here Jaén's most bizarre and affectionately regarded folly. 'You've never been before to the House of Stone?' asked a surprised El Sereno, as we arrived at Porcuna, a town I had once dismissed as ugly and uninteresting, but which I came to discover as a gold mine of curiosities. 'It's a building that shows what a man without education or money can achieve if he sets his heart on it.'

The house, built entirely in stone, down to the doors, tables, and even the topiary outside, was not exactly beautiful. But as an act of crazed will-power and obstinate persistence, it was certainly worthy of such one-man follies as the Watts Towers in Los Angeles, or the garden of the Facteur Cheval at Haute-Rives. A plaque on the exterior told how a certain Antonio Aguilera Ruedas, a quarry worker from Porcuna, created the building single-handed between 1931 and 1960. After spending the first year clearing the site of 2,865 cartloads of rubble with the aid of an ancient donkey which he had bought on the cheap, Aguilera Ruedas spent the two following years quarrying and carting the stone. Finally he began putting the thousands of pieces together, 'without proper financial means, or the hope of getting any, but with an incomparable health, abundant faith, a furious desire to work, and a strong touch of controlled madness'.

Inside the house I purchased a copy of the man's entertaining memoirs, *Stories of an Andalucían Madman*, which related his enormous satisfaction at being able to prove to his neighbours that his scheme was not just an act of madness that would never be brought to completion. On the booklet's last page appeared a short statement entitled, 'Definitive resumé: neither mad nor sane.'

'Neither Spain, nor "The House of Stone",' it continued, 'have been built on frivolity. Their foundations instead are those of love and sacrifice.'

Reading this and other passages out to Merce and Caño once we had left the building, I joked that the author could easily have been Ferminillo or his father. Then they told me in all seriousness that 'the House of Stone' had been an inspiration for their own stone house at Frailes, and that they had even used stones from the same quarry. 'People thought we too were mad until they saw the finished building,' said Merce.

Great honours for El Sereno would result from our next trip, which, thanks to his driving, would almost be our last. This time the two of us, together with Santi, were on a real official mission, for we had been sent by the town hall to make a courtesy call on the person invited to give the main speech at the forthcoming annual wine festival. This man, José María Suárez, lived in the far north of the province, in the unappealingly named, former mining town of Guarromán ('*guarro*' has the colloquial meaning of 'filthy pig'). A drily humorous *bon viveur* with a large moustache, Suárez was a part-time food writer who guided us around his town like a princely host, as was befitting someone who gloried in his title of Knight Commander of the Order of the Wooden Spoon, one of Spain's best known gastronomic societies.

A journalist from the *Ideal de Jaén* who had joined our party hinted that a new knight of the order was soon to be nominated. Over a long lunch José María finally announced to the press that this person was going to be none other than Manuel Ruíz López, better known as 'El Sereno', news of whose fame had now reached the northern borders of Andalucía. It was then decided to hold in Frailes itself, at the end of April, the ceremony in which El Sereno would be received into an order whose most recent members included such grand names of Spanish culture as the Nobel prize-winning novelist Camilo José Cela, the legendary bullfighter Curro Romero, and the Hollywood actor Antonio Banderas.

'What an honour for Frailes!' exclaimed Santi, as we left Guarromán later that afternoon, and headed quickly back home to announce the news to all and sundry. Normally on these return journeys, particularly after copious quantities of food and wine, I would fall into a deep sleep. But today there was little chance of sleeping. The unease I had felt in cars ever since my accident in the New Year was greater than ever, due to a combination of rainy conditions and El Sereno's insistence on replacing the tired Santi at the wheel. Once past Alcalá, where we dropped off Santi at his house, I consoled myself with the thought that we had reached the home stretch. Yet El Sereno was driving faster and more erratically than ever, and I was suddenly struck with the absolute conviction that something was going to happen, especially as we were approaching at a speed of nearly 120 kilometres an hour a notoriously dangerous curve where a white cross, permanently adorned with freshly cut flowers, marked the spot where at least two Fraileros had been killed and several others permanently injured. A few seconds after I had mentally imagined the event, the car shot off the road and leapt into the air at such an angle that I knew that I would once again be upside down, but this time after having fallen a good three metres and at a speed ten times greater than before. But El Sereno swerved violently on the wheel, the car righted itself, and we landed softly into mud.

'Thank goodness I've got quick reactions,' said El Sereno, as we got out of the undamaged car to decide how best we would leave the field. The joke about El Sereno's ability as a 'rally driver' would do the rounds at Frailes, but we thought it best not to tell the story to his sisters, to whom we explained our muddy state by saying that the town we had visited had lived up to its filthy name.

Soon after what El Sereno insisted on referring to as our 'incident', I purchased another image of the Santo Custodio, thinking by now that the first one had probably outworn its miraculous powers. In view of my two recent brushes with mortality, I decided also to give more urgent attention to how I was going to proceed with the Cinema España. I decided at last to explain my project to the person I believed would be the most sympathetic to impractical and ultimately pointless romantic gestures, Juan Matías of the Rey de Copas.

It was the perfect time to approach him. His weight was still diminishing, but not his natural restlessness, which was now making him more tempted than before to accept the offer of jobs elsewhere, and even to transplant his restaurant to Jaén, Granada, or places further afield still. For reasons not entirely selfish I wanted him to stay on in Frailes, where I was sure his persistence would one day be rewarded. I felt that getting him interested in the Cinema España would be a way of keeping him here. I got Ferminillo to open up the building for us at the soonest opportunity.

Juan was as spellbound as I had expected. More encouragingly, he believed like me that the only work needed was to get the projector operating, clear out the auditorium of everything but its seats, and make sure that bits of the ceiling did not collapse on the audience.

'I know how we'll raise the funds,' he said, interrupting my un-informed calculations about how much money would be necessary. 'We'll have a benefit lunch in my restaurant.'

I liked the idea; it had the potential of achieving two objectives at the same time: help resuscitate a dead institution, and perhaps save a dying one. The only way forward for the Rey de Copas, we both decided, was for the place to be seen frequented by the famous people and politicians we would invite for the lunch.

'When shall we have it?' Juan asked with his usual insistent tone.

Out of the top of my head I proposed the last Saturday in March. I suggested too that drinks should be served beforehand in the *Ambigú*.

'And what about the event with Sara Montiel?' Juan persisted. 'June 13,' I answered, 'St Anthony's Day, the day when the Cinema España opened in 1949.'

We agreed that the wine festival, due this year for the beginning of March, would be a good opportunity to raise interest in the fund-raising event. More 'celebrities' than ever were expected, which was one of the consequences of my symbiotic relationship with El Sereno, whose propensity to become 'wrapped up' in other people was further boosted by my own, and vice versa. I needed only to mention someone vaguely 'important' whom I knew, say, in Granada and Seville, than he was immediately on the phone to them, asking for their full names and addresses so that he could add them to a list of invitations now expanding out of all reasonable proportion. Every mayor from every village we had visited in Jaén seemed to be coming, together with such disparate personalities as a sherry baron from Jerez, a 'Lady' linked by marriage to the British aristocracy, the president of the Jaén regional government, and the founder of Granada's gastronomic society, who was arriving with a whole coach load of his fellow members. But the most striking feature of the list, and the one that would draw most of the attention of the local press, was the impressive number of writers. All of El Sereno's writer friends of old were turning up, together with the many ones whom he had met through me.

We had reached a phase when we started to think that anything was possible, that we had the power to invite to the village anyone we wanted to, and that everyone would be only too willing to come. It was at this moment, when our tiny world was beginning to seem the centre of the universe, that I had a phone call out of the blue from the Dutch writer Cees Nooteboom. I was a long-standing admirer of his work, and had been in contact with him before, but had only met once, at the end of a talk he had given in London. Now he was telling me that he had been commissioned to write a long travel piece for *El País* to celebrate twenty-five years of Spain's democracy. He wanted to come and see me in Frailes, and suggested a date that, by coincidence, was that of the village wine festival. When I reported this afterwards to El Sereno, I was able to say without exaggeration that Cees was one of Europe's leading writers. His magnificent short novel *The Following Story* had won the Aristeon, Europe's best-endowed literary prize, and his travelogue *Roads to Santiago* had been hailed as one of the greatest works on Spain in recent years. Mistakenly I also added that he was a writer tipped for the Nobel.

'The great Dutch writer Seis Noteboom, on the shortlist for this year's Nobel Prize for Literature, arrives today in Frailes to take part in the *Jornada del Vino*', wrote Pepe Oneto on 8 March 2001. Nooteboom's arrival coincided with the moment of maximum confusion. An estimated 3,000 people, engulfing my writing retreat in El Sereno's garden, were struggling for a piece of *morcilla* under conditions I had not seen before in Spain since I had last attended Holy Week in Seville. The sherry baron from Jerez and the president of the Jaén regional government had taken up and left; Lady E., after having made a taxi journey of over 300 kilometres to get to Frailes, had mysteriously disappeared; and the fifty or so members of Granada's gastronomic society were already in an advanced stage of inebriation.

I was standing to the side with the writers whom El Sereno had rounded up to safety when I saw the white-haired Nooteboom and his wife Simone about to be overwhelmed by the *morcilla*-seeking crowd. I rushed to grab them in time, and was able to bring them to the literary compound that had been set up to the side of El Sereno's house. Soon we were all being herded down the hill for the customary banquet within the basement of the Avenida.

Before too many bottles of Frailes's newly launched Matahermosa wine had been opened, I judged it time to distribute the hundreds of printed invitations for the cinema benefit lunch that an out-of-breath

Juan Matías had just presented me with. The invitations, printed in heavy ink with a 1950s typeface, had come out looking so lugubrious that some of the surprised-looking people to whom I handed them thought I was giving out obituary notices. Soon I would have a surprise myself. The meal was barely over when Juan Eslava Galán rose suddenly from the table, together with eight other writers and their wives. It appeared that Alcalá's *concejala de cultura* (cultural officer), a cold, elegant blonde called Ana Cortecero, had succeeded in luring them away from Frailes on the flimsy excuse of a 'special tour' of Alcalá's citadel.

'The Alcalaínos always have to be the protagonists,' commented a briefly crest-fallen El Sereno, seeing the fruits of all his labours snatched away from him by the enemy. 'When they saw what a group of celebrities we had gathered they could not contain their jealousy.' I told him not to worry, we would soon be having our revenge. In any case, I added, we had held on to Cees Nooteboom, the only one of the writers with a truly international reputation.

Cees had indeed been so taken by Frailes that, after surviving the drunken marathon of the wine festival, he chose to stay on in the village for a few more days. He, and his shy, warm-hearted wife Simone, whom Merce instantly singled out as a person with a 'very special sensibility', were among the first foreigners I knew who appeared to appreciate what drew me to this outwardly ordinary place. El Sereno, with the assistance of Merce and Caño, made sure that they saw as many as possible of our favourite sites in the Sierra Sur. One day was dedicated almost entirely to the estate of Puerta Alta, which we entered from its highest point, just as we had the first time I had ever been there. Simone, an excellent photographer, recorded the views of the Sierra Nevada with her camera.

While all this was going on El Sereno started uncharacteristically to walk away from us. Merce advised me not to follow him. He had told her that he wanted to descend on foot to the farm buildings far below us, and was proposing to do so by a route that she thought would be dangerous for anyone without his extraordinary agility. There was something he had set his mind on doing before he died, he had announced to her, and he felt that today might be his last opportunity. He wished to climb over the natural stone bridge where we had once seen the eagle swooping.

To be reminded again of El Sereno's mortality was as disconcerting as it had been the time I had seen him in the cardiac unit of Alcalá hospital. I was worried too that his mystical-seeming quest to walk on the stone bridge had something of a death wish about it. I could not let him do it on his own, and, making light of Merce's warnings, scrambled down the steep slope in shoes that were hardly appropriate to mountaineering. It took a good ten minutes to catch him up, and, when I did so, he seemed almost to accelerate his pace as he made his way over rocks and bracken towards the precipice below. An imperial eagle, perhaps the same one I had observed before, leapt threateningly into the void, displaying a wingspan that El Sereno calculated as being at least two metres.

We were nearing the bridge, and the dangers of what we were doing became more apparent as the thick, spiky undergrowth made it difficult to know where we were placing our feet. Though the sun had shone uninterruptedly over the past day, recent extensive rains had made some of the covered rock slippery. El Sereno went first, with a degree of caution unusual for him.

'When were you more frightened?' he asked. 'When we were doing the rally-driving or now?'

I muttered that I was not sure, but I was in no mood for answering, for we were now a third of the way across the bridge, and I was only too conscious of being on a ledge little wider than my body, with a terrifying drop on either side of us. Once El Sereno had reached the middle he stopped crawling and stood up, and encouraged me to do the same. I resolutely kept my position while he remained standing waving excitedly like a child to attract the attention of the tiny specks below whom we identified as Merce, Caño, Cees, and Simone. Simone took a photo of the two us, which pleased El Sereno immensely, as he wanted to have this historic moment recorded. Later, in his telling of the tale, there was not just one eagle but three, the wing spans of which kept growing until they reached 'four metres at least'.

The sense of invincibility that moments such as these encouraged made all the more shocking the news we received the day after Cees and Simone's departure: Merce had failed the practical part of her *oposiciones*. It was almost impossible for us to accept that the woman who had spent ten years serving her community so successfully and enthusiastically should effectively be told by the bureaucrats of Jaén that she was not doing her job properly. Yet we had suspected for the past few weeks that something was wrong. Caño and I had accompanied her to Jaén for the practical exam, which took the form of a spoken defence of a paper she had written. My influential Jienense friend Manolo Urbano had offered beforehand to say a few words on her behalf to the examining board, but Merce did not want to resort to corruption, and preferred to be judged on her own merits. In the end she had come out of the exam feeling she had done as best as she could. A few days later, however, she was informed by telegram that everyone who had taken the exam that day had to redo it the following week, 'for reasons that have occurred'. These reasons, she heard from a colleague, were supposedly that the board had not had the full quota of examiners to be legally valid. Understandably she faced her examiners the second time in a fighting spirit, demanding a proper explanation. 'Relax,' one of them had said reassuringly. 'We are your friends,' a phrase she would remember two weeks later when she received the notice of her failure.

Merce's tendency to speak straight from the heart rather than from the mind was a quality liable to create enemies for her within the political world. She was coming now to accept that there was someone, perhaps even from Frailes, but more likely from Alcalá, who was out to pull her down from her pedestal, to send her far away from her beloved village.

The dent to Merce's confidence began to affect us all, and did much to erode our arrogant belief that everything in Frailes had become possible. My plans for the Cinema España, for instance, started seeming silly, irrelevant, and less likely to come off. The fund-raising lunch, now less than a fortnight away, was considered by Caño a waste of time that would be of possible benefit only to Juan Matías and would involve a lot of hours sitting around with politicians and pretentious Alcalaínos. He doubted whether he would attend the lunch himself. Only Merce, despite her current mood, remained unfailingly supportive; but the consolation this gave me was soon offset by the pessimistic pronouncements of my architect friend from Murcia, Quique Andrés.

Quique had returned to Frailes to give me his professional advice on the structural stability of the Cinema España. Ferminillo, ever more amazed and pleased by the interest his building was causing, was only too happy to show him around. This time we were joined by El Sereno, who, like the vast majority of Fraileros, had not been back inside the place since its closure thirty years ago. While he and

Ferminillo reminisced about the cinema's heyday, Quique cast his large, quizzical blue eyes over such details as the collapsing false ceiling, the huge gaps and cracks in the plaster-coated walls, the damp patches, and the floorboards that continued to break as we walked over them. His look was not the uncritical one of romantics such as Juan, Merce and myself.

'If you're going to have a public function here,' he said in a tone that commanded the immediate respect of El Sereno, 'then you're going to have to have a document signed for insurance purposes.'

An unfazed Ferminillo did not think of this as a problem. The building, he said emphatically, was perfectly safe, and he had already put in a lot of money recently to ensure that the roof would not collapse. 'Most architects would happily testify to the building's safety,' he concluded in his high-pitched tetchy voice. 'Well I wouldn't,' smiled Quique.

'I can see why you like the building,' Quique told me afterwards when I was alone with him and El Sereno, 'but there's no way that you can do anything with it at the moment. It doesn't comply with a single modern security regulation. You and Ferminillo could be thrown into prison if anything happened. A piece of falling plaster could seriously injure somebody, the place could easily catch fire, and there isn't even a proper toilet.'

El Sereno nodded in agreement. 'We'd be risking people's lives,' he said. 'We'd be better off showing the film in the school playground, where we always hold a cinema festival in the summer.'

I defended myself with diminishing conviction, agreeing that we would be ill-advised to have people sitting in the 'Chicken Coop'. I said we would hire one of those portable toilet cabins if necessary. I emphasized that it was going to be a private function limited perhaps to as few as 200 people, well perhaps only 100, well okay then, we'll say fifty.

'It's still too much of a risk,' said Quique.

I had forgotten that there was a world outside Frailes where life was becoming increasingly restricted by such boring factors as security regulations, insurance liabilities, and toilet facilities; and I was very surprised that El Sereno was siding with Quique in putting practical considerations before romantic dreams. Later I went to report all this to Ferminillo, who had emerged as almost more fervent a supporter of the cinema project than myself.

'As soon as you get an architect today involved in anything,' he said hysterically, 'you're lost. They know all about rules and regulations, and how to do fancy designs, but when it comes to knowing what holds up a wall or ceiling, they don't know what they're talking about. They're ignorant, they're spineless, they've no vision. And they're complete amateurs if you compare them to people like my father.'

Cheered though I was by having Ferminillo on my side, I had suddenly developed under Quique's influence a sense of social responsibility, not to mention a fear of prison. Ferminillo ridiculed my worries.

'Nothing dangerous is going to happen,' he shouted, 'absolutely nothing! You could even cram one hundred people into the Chicken Coop and still nothing would happen.'

I said I was sure he was right, but that it might perhaps be a good idea to have, say, a fire-extinguisher at hand. Or perhaps provide the audience with construction helmets. In any case, I added, when it came to the fund-raising event, we were going to have to limit the number of visitors to the cinema to no more than fifty. To allow more people than that inside the building would surely be foolish until we had undertaken the very minimum of safety precautions. At the very least we would have to remove all the dangling pieces of wood from the ceiling, and the worst of the collapsing plaster. Quite apart from anything, I stressed, it would be utterly impossible to seat more than fifty people in Juan's restaurant. But Ferminillo was far too agitated to take in properly what I was saying. 'Nothing is going to happen,' he kept on screaming, 'nothing!'

Secretly I began hoping that no one was going to respond to the benefit lunch invitations. I was worried that I had put expectations into Ferminillo's head that were going to be disappointed; and I wanted to put a stop to the project before it started affecting the feeling of profound peace I had known ever since coming to Frailes. But, during these days of maximum uncertainty, something else unexpected occurred that heightened my suspicion I was being directed by forces wholly beyond my control. I received a phone call from an actress friend from England.

My friend said she had just had lunch in London with a rising young star in the film world, John Shahnazarian, to whom she had spoken about Frailes's 'amazing cinema'. I had told her about the place, and about my plans for it, at her birthday party early in January, before I had even been inside the building. She had loved in particular the idea of bringing into the abandoned cinema an ancient sex star whose mummified appearance would match that of the building itself. This image, which had come to me during the later stages of the party, had now been relayed to John, whose first reaction was 'Wow!'. John, she continued telling me, was 'this crazy, wonderful American' who had acted in Hollywood films such as Spielberg's *Saving Private Ryan*, and had gone on to direct a 'brilliant short film' with Rod Steiger.

'When I told John about Frailes, and the Cinema España, and Sara Montiel, he just flipped. He said he'd really love to come and make a film about it. I wouldn't put it past him if he flew out next week to see you.'

Then, a few days later, my mobile rang, and there was an American voice on the line saying, 'Hi, Mike, this is John, how are you doing?' I was standing in the garden of the Rey de Copas, where the flowers seemed always in bloom. And soon I was answering questions about *El último cuplé*, a film I had never seen before, or knew anything about other than the passions that it had once inspired.

'Well, you know,' I said in answer to one of John's questions, 'it's one of those typical popular Spanish films of the fifties, but a lot more risqué. It's got all those classic ingredients – tragic songs, bullfighting, death, and a femme fatale whose sexuality is so blatant that she excites uncontrollable erotic urges in every man she meets. It was shown in Frailes long before it reached other parts of Andalucía. People poured into the village from every single corner of the region.'

'Wow, that sounds great, Mike. Tell me some more about this Ferminillo dude. He built the whole cinema with his bare hands?'

The unreality of our whole exchange was encouraging me to exaggerate, as was my desire to tell John exactly the sort of things I imagined he wanted me to say. Yet when it came to describing both Frailes and the Cinema España, I could hardly improve on facts that, in the telling, must have appeared improbable enough. In condensing over the phone to someone I had never met before disparate phenomena ranging from the Santo Custodio to the miraculously untouched projection booth, I became fully aware of the uniqueness of Frailes, and I saw clearly for first time that the cinema was the epitome of all that was strange and magical about the village itself.

'Wow, Mike,' said a voice now that seemed faint and distant as I lost myself in my thoughts. 'We've got to make this movie, we've got to make it.'

From the time of this call, the pace of developments took me wholly by surprise. My realization that there might be some curious link between the Cinema España and the Santo Custodio had apparently unblocked the obstructions caused by reason, caution, and practical common sense. Two days later John was once more on the phone, this time to speak the words I thought were only heard in fantasies: 'The producers love the project, they're on board.'

Then a young woman called Ella von Schreitter got back to me on the phone and said, in a voice that was all sweetness and honey, 'Michael, that's such a lovely project you've got going.' She, John, and another producer called Nicolai, were all coming to Frailes for the weekend of the benefit lunch, and she wondered if I could find them somewhere to stay in the village. I did not offer them the rooms above the disco, but mentioned instead Rafael's tastefully decorated *Casa rural*.

'Oh, that would be fantastic,' cooed Ella. 'I can't wait to be there. And the village sounds a dream.'

There were just ten days left before they planned to arrive, and for most of this time I had contractually committed myself to leading a tour of thirty retired British people around Moorish Spain. Arrangements for the benefit lunch could not have been more chaotic, and we had not even decided how much we were going to charge those who came. The 'sensible' village archivist Mari Tere, who turned out to be none other than Ferminillo's niece, tried to persuade Juan to establish a price per head of 2,000 pesetas, which Juan considered so ridiculously cheap that he would not cover his costs, let alone raise money for the cinema. He was thinking of a price at least three times greater.

'No one in Frailes would be prepared to pay that amount,' argued Mari Tere, to which Juan replied that we were not aiming to attract Fraileros. We wanted people with money, politicians, celebrities, the sort of people, he said, whose presence would lend weight both to our project and to his restaurant.

'But who have you got so far?' asked an exasperated Mari Tere. The truth was that no one had so far committed themselves to coming, apart from John and his two colleagues, and the elusive Lady

E., whom only I had caught a brief glimpse of at the wine festival. On the invitations we had so widely distributed Juan had forgotten to put a telephone number so that people could contact us and reserve a place for the event. Hundreds of people might be descending on Frailes for that day, or virtually no one at all.

I reckoned that the second possibility was the greater of the two, and immediately got into contact with a friend from Granada with expertise in public relations, Juan Antonio Díaz.

'We need at least forty people coming to Frailes on Saturday week,' I shouted desperately on my mobile.

'I'll do my best,' he said, just at the moment when I saw Ferminillo's car pull up next to me in a fury on the street.

'What's happening,' Ferminillo screamed from behind the open window. 'Where are all the posters?'

'What posters?'

'The posters for the fund-raising event, of course, what else? They should have been papered by now all over the village. I want to have hundreds of people visiting my cinema on that day. The place deserves it, it's a hidden jewel, there's no other place like it in the whole of Spain.'

Telling Ferminillo about the impending arrival in Frailes of a young 'Hollywood' director had perhaps been unwise. The news had gone to his head, he had lost all touch with reality. I told him to calm down, and that we had got matters completely under control. Safety considerations, I reminded him, and the size of Juan's restaurant, had obliged us to maintain what I described as a 'highly selective guest list'. But he was not listening, he had taken his foot off the brake, and was driving off. I looked at my watch. I was due in Granada to meet my group of British tourists in less than two hours' time and I would not be back in Frailes until the morning the event was due to take place. So I had no other choice now than to leave all that remained to be done in the hands of the crazed Ferminillo and the childishly irresponsible Juan Matías. Then I thought of a third alternative: I prayed to the Santo Custodio.

On the last Saturday of March, on the day the spectre of disaster loomed, I took an early morning train from Ronda to Granada. I felt strangely relaxed. Talking later to El Sereno on my mobile, in between disappearing into tunnels, I was assured that all that was humanly possible had been done, and that the rest was up to fate.

John Shahnazarian, Ella von Schreitter, and Nicolai had arrived the night before, and El Sereno, needless to say, had keenly assumed the role of their guardian and cicerone.

'What are they like?' I asked.

'Very friendly and polite,' he replied, adding that he, Ferminillo and Rafael were about to show them inside the cinema.

Then I rang up Merce, who told me that El Sereno was loving every minute of their company, even though the only one of them who spoke Spanish was Ella.

'She's sweet, affectionate, young and beautiful . . . Well, you can imagine what El Sereno's like with her.'

Unfortunately, I could. I only hoped that she had been sufficiently won over by his genuine charms and courtesy not to take too seriously a display of unreconstructed Spanish machismo of roughly the same era of *El último cuplé*.

'She's already had one noticeable effect on him,' Merce added. 'He won't have anyone say a word any more about the dangers of the Cinema España. He's completely on your side.'

During my week's absence from Frailes something had happened that I thought augured well for my plans to revive the dead. The Lady Diana had reopened. Officially its name had been changed to the Angelillo (the little angel) after the name of the new boyish-looking owner, Ángel Custodio. But the large letters 'Lady Diana' had remained, thus consolidating the mystifying Frailes tradition of having establishments with a dual identity. The bar's most endearing feature was its large outdoor terrace, under the awning of which I sat over a late breakfast as I waited for the arrival of El Sereno and the new village guests. It was one of those mornings that filled you with the joy of life. The sun shone under a cloudless sky so clear and bright that everything seemed to sparkle with a fresh coat of gloss paint. The recent termination of this year's long and successful olive harvest was apparent in the return of a relaxed weekend atmosphere. Groups of men and women, instead of rushing off as before into the fields, now had time to spare, to stroll leisurely up and down the street, to chat around the fountain by the bus stop, to relish the prospect of a long family lunch. Into this peaceful rural world entered an apparition that could have come straight from Mars.

I saw him slip out of Rafael's car, followed by a tall thin man with a shock of curly light brown hair. Of the two of them there was not the slightest doubt which one was John Shahnazarian, the American film director. Massive but all muscles, he strode confidently towards me, his arched arms swinging as if activated by an electrical current. He wore a T-shirt and combat trousers, and had a shaved head that sparkled in the sun like a giant, bronzed olive. Only his eyes, concealed at first behind shaped designer glasses, contradicted the overall brutality of his appearance. Pale and blue, they suggested hidden reserves of kindness and sensitivity.

John was not a person with small talk. Once he had grabbed my hand firmly in his, he tried to express in words the emotions that had been shaking through his body.

'It's absolutely fantastic, man, it's absolutely fan-fucking-tastic. When I went into that cinema, it was just like wow! I just couldn't fucking believe it, man. And that projection booth, it's amazing, absolutely amazing, just like that Ferminillo dude. He's a human fucking ball of energy.'

Nicolai, a quieter man with the manner of someone educated at a liberal British public school, voiced his enthusiasm in a rather different manner. 'Yes,' he said, 'I was quite impressed. I think John will do a great film about the place.'

I asked where Ella was.

'She's gone off with that old dude,' John replied. 'What's his name? El Sereno? He's fucking amazing for his age. He wanted to show her some olive mill or something in his house. I think he's got the hots for her. She asked us to send out a search party if she wasn't back in ten minutes.'

John and Nicolai ordered their first beers of the day. '*Grande, grande*,' John said to the friendly Ángel Custodio, who brought back litre-sized glasses which I had never seen before in Spain except on the coast. We got straight to business. John said they were wanting to make a demonstration tape this weekend that Ella would take to Cannes on Monday. They had a digital video camera which they would be using to film the fund-raising event, 'get a feel of the village', and interview as many people as possible about their memories of the cinema.

'So Mike, what's the story from your end?' John continued, as he lifted up the little that remained of his '*grande*'. In the light of Quique's warnings about the perilous state of the cinema, I had given up all expectations about having the place ready for June 13.

Mumbling vaguely about the unforeseen work that had to be done, I proposed delaying the Sara Montiel event until the autumn.

'That's too late man, too late,' John said, shaking his head. 'We've got to stick to what we originally agreed upon.'

El Sereno's Suzuki finally arrived, bringing with it a slightly red-faced Ella, a petite woman in her late twenties with tightly curled orange hair, fine features, and large blue eyes. Her accent was very English, but her appearance was difficult to place. I found out later that she was the result of an affair between a Uruguayan labourer and a renegade Viennese aristocrat who now lived in Paris. El Sereno, who had drawn his chair up right next to hers, tapped her on the arm and encouraged her to show us all the bottle of *Serenolivo* she had just been given. On it he had appended a personalized typed inscription, which I was obliged to translate in impromptu verse: 'If you want to enjoy a sex life satisfactory and complete/then make sure to have *Serenolivo* whenever you eat.'

Before El Sereno was able to expand on this idea, I heard a voice behind me shout 'Michael!' and turned round to see Lady E. She had brought with her two English friends, who lived for most of the year in a luxury colony near the Murcian coast, but hardly spoke a word of Spanish. El Sereno and Rafael joined another table to ours, so that the new arrivals could sit down. The resulting unhomogeneous group created a cacophony of English sounds such as had never before been heard in Frailes.

As I watched Rafael and El Sereno happily listening to conversations of which they did not understand a word, I noticed how pleased they both seemed by the presence of foreigners in their village, and how they displayed a tolerance towards them that was in marked contrast to the developing tensions within our English-speaking group ('That English couple are going to be the death of me,' John would later confide). Awkwardly finding myself between the two worlds, I breathed more easily on seeing the smiling faces of Merce and Paqui, followed closely by a convoy of three cars with Granadan number plates. My public relations expert Juan Antonio had arrived, together with all the people whom he had been able to gather from the original 'Frailes Group', as well as some acquaintances he had bumped into that morning in his local newspaper kiosk. An atmosphere of controlled anarchy, so typical of a Spanish *fiesta*, was mounting, and made us take in our stride the subsequent appearance of those whom we now considered the pantomime 'baddies' – the Alcalá *concejala de cultura* Ana Cortecero and her colleagues from the cultural department of Alcalá's town hall.

The Jienese intellectual Manolo Urbano, acting as a messenger from Ferminillo, clapped his hands, and announced in his deep, booming voice that we were all anxiously awaited at the cinema. We finished our drinks, and paraded down the village street, forming a procession so unlikely in its make-up that we must have appeared to passers-by like a band of freaks that had been let out for the day. My heart was beating. A small crowd had assembled outside the cinema, in which I could make out the mayor, members of the local press, the head of the Andalucían tourist board (whom Paqui's politically scheming sister had succeeded in dragging over from Seville for the occasion), and the newly elected president of the Frailes wine cooperative, the bald-headed Marcelino from Alcalá. I saw then that the window of the ticket office had been unblocked, and that a pair of eyes were staring out from behind it. I was trying to peer further inside when a small fat man in suit, waistcoat and tie came up to give me an embrace.

It was Paqui's cousin, Luis Aceituno, a man who last December had suffered the massive heart attack I thought had been destined for the singer Luis Machuca. Luis Aceituno was like an apparition from the dead, sweating and grey-skinned, but with an expression of intense joy. A passionate and sentimental Frailero whose job had obliged him to settle in Seville, I had gone to see him a couple of days ago, during a break from my tour. Though in constant pain he was still determined to be in his beloved Frailes for what he and the press were calling the cinema's 'reopening', but his doctors had told him that on no account should he do so. I had had the strong feeling, such as I had had before in the presence of the dying, that I would never see him again. But here he was; he had defied death, and the sight of him before me now was like a symbol of the crazed act of momentary resurrection I envisaged for the building behind us.

Together we made our way into the *Ambigú*, where at least thirty people were talking excitedly in a room astonishingly improved merely by the clearing away of the minor later additions, and the placing of a bowl of flowers. But what gave to the scene the quality of some strange dream of the past was seeing Juan Matías's brother José Luis in white shirt, bow tie, and black jacket, weaving his way among the crowd bearing aloft an exquisite silver platter supporting champagne and canapés.

All my well-intentioned ideas about keeping strict control on the movements of a select crowd had by now been made a mockery of, as people continued streaming into the building, and heading off inside in all directions, even going up into the collapsing Chicken Coop, which we had entirely forgotten to rope off. After several glasses of champagne I was past caring about safety, and was being carried away instead by a mood of nostalgia that took hold of the assembled drinkers like an outbreak of hysteria. Repeated cries of 'Wow, wow!', 'Fantastic, man!', and 'Let's shoot!', pierced occasionally through the growing commotion.

But louder than anything was the shriek of Merce as she suddenly noticed who was sitting inside the old ticket booth. 'It's Carmela,' she shouted, gesturing to me to come over, 'Ferminillo's sister, she hasn't been out of the house in years, she's never seen in public.' Merce informed me hurriedly about Carmela's nun-like existence, and her renowned beauty as a young woman, and then insisted I go and meet her. Even at close quarters Carmela's face had an uncannily youthful bloom, with barely a wrinkle, and not a trace of make-up. 'I'm the same age as Sara Montiel,' she proudly declared, 'almost to the very day.' Then she smiled as Merce said something that enhanced the poignancy of the whole occasion: 'She's sitting where she always sat since the age of fifteen. She was the one who always sold us our tickets.'

We would soon all be drifting over to the Rey de Copas, or so I had imagined. My original idea was that people would have a drink in the *Ambigú*, admire the auditorium for a few moments, and then head off for lunch. But no one appeared keen to leave the cinema, especially as there were rumours, which I could barely believe, that Ferminillo was about to show us a short film. I was still unbelieving even after word had spread rapidly among us that we were all to gather in the auditorium.

However, when the exciting chattering around me was suddenly silenced by the distorted echoing music of Juanita Reina, I began to accept that some miracle or magic was about to be performed. A great cheer arose from the crowd as Ferminillo skipped confidently on to the stage and hoisted up the stage cloth. Then he went away, turned off the house lights, and reappeared again, this time to walk with his effeminate step the whole length of the stage, pulling out as he did so a long piece of torn and dirty off-white curtain that could have been a winding shroud. José Luis and his silver tray made a final loop around the auditorium's stacks of wood and chairs before the music screeched to a halt, and a death-like hush descended on the crowd.

Sparks seemed to fly from the distantly high projection booth, followed by the loud whirr of a projector. A series of scratches and meaningless numbers ran nervously past on the filthy improvised screen, to be replaced by blurred colour images of a Spanish coastal resort from around the mid-1960s. We were looking at one of those short documentary round-ups that had always preceded the showing of the main film during the Franco era. A loud recorded voice praised the beauties of Benidorm before the scene changed to the house of a now forgotten young novelist, then to a fairground, then to the typing pool of an office, then to an industrial exhibition displaying, among other objects, a clumsy mechanical model illustrating the workings of the heart. The images in themselves no longer mattered, and the laughter of the first minute had given way to a tight knot in the throat. To see a film projected against the ruins of an abandoned auditorium was a moment of the purest theatricality. It was also the most eloquent visual expression I had ever known of the past being brought back miraculously to life.

In those seconds between the lights going up and the cheerfully exaggerated applause and joke shouts of 'Bravo!' that came afterwards, I noticed handkerchiefs being brought out, eyes rubbed, and a distraught Luis Aceituno leaning against his wife. We filed out half-stunned into the open air, where Santi and Pepe Oneto had us all posed against the cinema's façade for photographs that would illustrate articles entitled, respectively, 'The Cinema España Opens its Doors Again after Thirty Years', and 'The Dream of English Writer Maiquels Jacquo Becomes a Reality'.

Arm in arm with Merce and Paqui I walked down the village street, enjoying a brief taste of celebrity as cars kept on stopping to offer us a lift, and a handful of passers-by, to whom the news of the miracle of the Cinema España had already filtered through, gave us a loud cheer. We were light-headed and full of an irrational optimism. Our fears for the survival of the village had all gone, as had, in these fleeting moments of triumph, Merce's growing worries about being forced to work far away from her family and friends. We believed once again that we were capable of achieving anything; and we laughed as we imagined our voices and faces, and the streets of small, insignificant Frailes, soon filling a studio screen in faraway Cannes.

We walked the whole three kilometres to the Rey de Copas, preferring in our selfishness to get there last of all, and to leave to the others the chaos we knew would certainly ensue when a crowd far larger than predicted tried to cram into the normally deserted dining room. A large round of applause greeted our late appearance in a room so packed with tables and chairs that the overworked José Luis, after surviving all the obstacles of the Cinema España, had gone on a temporary strike and retreated to the kitchen to shout at his brother. After being pulled from one table to the next we managed to fit in three extra places on the small table taken up by John, Nicolai, Ella, and El Sereno. I calculated that with a bit of luck lunch might be over by nightfall.

There were twenty of us in the garden by the time we had struggled through an experimental rice dish made from chicken's crests and cod tripe. With John asking the questions, and myself translating, the conversation was now almost entirely about Sara Montiel, whose central role in the youthful dreams of those present was accepted by everyone except the art historian Ignacio Henares (who draw attention to himself by perversely denying her importance). But John was not interested in dissenting voices, or indeed in subtleties of opinion. What he wanted was raw passion. When the archivist Mari Tere imitated with heart-felt conviction the dying Montiel as she sang the last *Cuplé*, John made her do a repeat performance for the camera. But what he was really hoping for from our conversation in the garden was talk about sex. And the person best capable of providing that was El Sereno.

'I saw Sara once in person when she entered a bar where I was sitting in Granada, and I was frankly disappointed,' he began unpromisingly. 'She was not the idol on the screen. Her skin was pasty, and she seemed stocky and funnily proportioned.'

But then he started talking about her impact in the cinema, and John's ears began pricking up. I had always suspected El Sereno of being a potential media star, and he did not disappoint me. He had spent much of his life living off his wits, behaving in a manner he knew would please other people; and now he was doing the same for

John, guessing uncannily what the director was looking for, and performing accordingly with a completely spontaneous talent. After a lifetime of serving others, the time had finally come to be the protagonist himself.

'When you saw couples coming out of the cinema after seeing *El último cuplé*,' he said excitedly, warming up at last to the theme of sexual passion, 'there was no point in asking them what the film had been like. If you did so the only answer you were likely to get would be something vague like "very interesting" or "the singing was nice". But they wouldn't have been able to tell you much else, they had only been half-watching. You could tell that from the state of them. The women had red faces, and the men had great bulges in their trousers. As for the men who had gone in on their own, you saw them rushing out from the cinema and heading straight down to the stream, where they would masturbate behind the first available bush. Most of the single men could not wait that long. The night I saw the film myself, the whole auditorium seemed to be shaking with furiously moving arms.'

I saw the climax coming, for I had heard the story several times before, and had observed the increasing exaggerations. What had been a 'trickle of semen' dribbling down the central aisle, had expanded into a 'stream', and then into a 'river'. Now, for the benefit of the camera, 'the whole auditorium was awash with rivers of semen'. John jumped up from his seat, put his arm around El Sereno, and said, 'Wow, man, that was fucking brilliant. *Fantastico*, man, *fantastico*.'

Once we had eaten the last of the puddings, and drunk our fill of liquor and *cava*, it was already a respectable hour for those who had survived the lunch to move on to the Discoteca Oh!. Ella, thinking of the tiring days ahead of her, sensibly retired to bed, but Nicolai and John were in a mood to celebrate. The near-empty disco turned out to be not quite the sort of place they had in mind, but they sat down resignedly on their own in the gaping centre of this dark, cold space, and began drinking bottles of beer at an alarming rate. It was when they had got into the whiskies that El Sereno and I started worrying. John was now standing at the bar, and had got involved in a drunken exchange of gestures with the tough Dionisio. The two of them were slapping each other's backs and generally indulging in what seemed like an amicable bout of male bonding when John asked me the Spanish word for knife. Holding Dionisio by the wrist he shouted out in pidgin Spanish, '*Tu, yo, hermanos de sangre*' (You, me, blood brothers).

Remembering a villager once telling me that he did not mind what people I brought to Frailes as long as they were not 'hooligans', I thought this a good moment to take John and Nicolai back to their house, preferably in as discreet a fashion as possible. With his persuasive charm, El Sereno managed without too much fuss to get them outside the disco, where his Suzuki was waiting. But then John, followed shortly by Nicolai, climbed onto the car roof and threw himself flat across it. When first he and then his friend refused to budge, there was nothing we could do but to drive off and hope they would hold on tightly.

'I can quite understand their behaviour,' said the ever tolerant El Sereno. Loud banging sounds were now coming from above, and the roof was sagging dangerously under their weight. 'They're young, they have different traditions to ours, they've had an exciting day.' Fortunately we got past the headquarters of the *Guardia Civil* without anyone noticing us, for by now John's head was peering at us upside down through the front window, with a grimacing expression. He and Nicolai finally rolled down to the ground, got up, and started walking of their own accord along the street, singing and swearing. Hooliganism had reached Frailes.

We turned up at their house the next morning an hour later than they had requested, hoping that this would give them more time to shake off their hangovers. But the door was opened by Ella, who said that her two colleagues were still sound asleep.

'That's all right, we'll just take you,' smiled El Sereno, who was looking at her in a way that made his expression of yesterday seem innocently paternal. She was barefoot and wearing nothing but a towel around her slender body.

'You shouldn't dress like that,' he continued, holding her arm. 'Look at the effect you're having on Maiquel. He's gone green with desire, he looks as if he's going to throw up the whole of yesterday's lunch.'

I had in recent weeks become almost immune to the salacious comments El Sereno addressed to all the new women he met, few of whom were upset by them, either because they thought he was joking, or else because they saw them as an inevitable if not always desirable aspect of a man wishing to appear perpetually young. Ella too was fundamentally unconcerned by his advances. But as I watched his behaviour towards her, I saw further proof of a new development in his sexual fantasies. These were not only becoming more intense, but they were also being attributed to me. Our symbiotic relationship had reached the stage at which he, aware of the limitations of his age, was hoping that his now unrealizable desires would be carried out by the person whom he now considered as his younger self.

Long before being implied in this two-man Don Juan team of formidable combined years, if not powers, I had been intrigued by El Sereno's sexual past. His life, I was discovering, had been filled with inconsequential encounters more intense perhaps in the memory than they had been in actuality. He told me he had had three 'official' girl friends, but the idea of losing his freedom had never appealed to him. According to Merce, with whom I often talked about El Sereno, none of these girl friends had lasted more than a few months. El Sereno had been a very desirable and handsome man, as I could tell from the old photographs he had now taken to showing me; but he was obviously impossible as a partner.

'One of his girl friends,' said Merce, 'was a neighbour of my parents. My mother remembers her as an extraordinary beauty who was genuinely in love with him. But then he went off with someone else . . . He's always been like that. He's totally obsessed with some woman for a few days or weeks, then he completely forgets her after he's met another one. Perhaps his life would have been different had he not always had his sisters looking after him.'

In telling me about a side to El Sereno's character that many people might have found reprehensible, Merce had not intended to be critical of our friend. She accepted, as I did, that the qualities that made him such a hopeless partner were also integral to his uniqueness. They were the same qualities that made him so eternally young, so restless in his enthusiasms, so excited by novelty, so fascinated generally by new people. They were also his act of rebellion against a world in which sexual and romantic choices had been traditionally limited. The normal pattern for people who spent their lives in an isolated village such as Frailes was to marry young, and with someone known since childhood. Those who did not, or had scandalous affairs, homosexual tendencies, or illegitimate children, generally ended up moving to a city or large town. The single men who stayed on in the village tended to live with their parents until the latter had died, becoming solitary regulars in places such as the Discoteca Oh!, and finding sexual gratification in occasional visits to a *puti-club* or brothel. One of the best known of these near Frailes was a corrugated iron shack marked in pink neon lighting with the word '*Atrévete*' ('Be a dare!').

El Sereno's amorous desires were now heating up to such an extent that I wondered what the poor Ella had in store for her. Happily, by the time she had dressed and the 'boys' were in a fit state, the day was half over, and there was no time for anything but the completion of the demonstration tape that was to be taken to Cannes the next morning. We ended up doing a workmanlike tour of the places I instinctively knew would appeal to John, such as the cave of the Santo Custodio, the Bar La Cueva, and, of course, Puerta Alta, which I had intended as the place where Sara Montiel would stay.

As we stood among all the dogs, peacocks and turkeys that surrounded the estate's main building, El Sereno placed his hand on Ella's shoulder, and directed her eyes to the natural bridge that he and I had walked over three weeks before.

'You see that bridge,' he told her. 'Maiquel and I are the only humans ever known to have crossed it. The people who were watching us from below thought we were mad, but then applauded us wildly when they saw us fend off an attack by giant eagles.'

Even John, restless by now to move on, seemed stirred by this tale of exceptional bravery.

The last stop of the day was the only place that John himself chose to visit – the village cemetery. I could see by now how his mind was working. He had got sex on film, now he wanted death. This was Spain, after all, land of sun and shade, and of extreme passions. Leaving him and Nicolai staring with awe at a tarantula crawling into the crack of a marble tomb slab, I rejoined Ella and El Sereno. They were standing next to a very simple mausoleum at the cemetery's entrance.

'You know the person who's going to be buried here?' he was saying to her. 'He's called Manuel Ruíz López.' Ella looked perplexed. 'He's standing next to you. He's better known as El Sereno.'

Responding in the way El Sereno had probably anticipated, she assumed an expression of sadness and tender concern, and stroked his arm. 'Oh, don't talk about dying,' she pleaded.

Delighted by such loving attention, El Sereno went on talking. 'I don't believe in tombs or in an after life,' he said, 'but society expects us to have some sort of memorial.' He read out the inscription on the tomb of a younger sister, and then showed the niches that had been reserved for his two elder ones, and for himself.

'I don't like all this,' he continued 'I'm not frightened about death, but I don't like it.' Then he held the bare flesh of her arm in his hand, and said in a voice more touching than lecherous, 'This is what I like. I like you.'

He smiled shyly, and looked into her blue eyes. And I noticed goose pimples form above her delicate veins, and a flush go to her face. 'I love life,' he added, condensing into three words the whole philosophy of his existence.

3

ASTER WEEK WAS already upon us, and no fewer than 300 vintage Citroëns from all over Spain were due to reach Frailes by Good Friday. Every available room and house to rent, and even the whole of Paqui's *pension*, had been taken over for the occasion. No one quite understood why the village had been chosen this year for a national gathering of Citroën owners. Some people saw it as part of the continuing cycle of madness into which the village had been drawn.

The parish priest, seeing the quiet rhythms of village life so brutally disrupted, and fearful of matters getting completely beyond the Church's control, decided to retaliate with a revival of the traditional annual passion play. While the Citroëns noisily assembled on the cemetery hill, the death and resurrection of Christ were inaudibly performed on the slopes opposite, in a theatrical version dating back to the mists of Frailes's history, and last put on here over forty years ago. Peter was played by an elderly man whose father, in earlier days, had performed the same role with such enthusiasm that he had insisted on being buried in the costume, key and all. Christ meanwhile was acted by the tall and powerfully built El Escandoloso, currently implicated in a genuine scandal involving the beautiful married woman who ran the Guaneiro. Thinking about the personal histories of the cast distracted me from the religious message of the spectacle. So too did El Sereno's memories of the event in the 1950s, when several of those taking part had been fervent anarchists involved in the burning of religious images.

The activities of the Holy Week kept me diverted while waiting impatiently for news from Cannes. We just had two more months before the planned event on June 13, but there seemed little point in getting the cinema ready until I had heard from Ella. Eventually she phoned me. John's confidence about finding a co-producer for his documentary had been unduly optimistic. There had been, she said, 'a lot of interest in the project', but as yet nothing had been signed. Before wasting any more time, it was essential that we made sure Sara Montiel was willing to come to Frailes. Without her definite agreement, a deal was unlikely; and without a documentary, and the consequent international publicity it would give her, there was little probability of her having any interest in visiting an obscure Jaén village. I had seriously underestimated the importance of Sara Montiel when I had first thought of inviting her here. She was, I now realized, the Spanish-speaking world's equivalent of Sophia Loren, Gina Lollobrigida, and Marlene Dietrich all rolled into one. On her last public appearance in Andalucía, Santi informed me, the traffic in central Granada had been paralyzed for several hours.

Ella had managed to secure her phone number, and promised to give her a ring. A few days later she got back to me with the news that she had spoken directly to the star herself. Sara had not instantly discounted the possibility of coming to Frailes, but said she was going to be very busy over the next two months, with a show about her life on the point of opening in Barcelona, and celebrations in her honour to be hosted in Madrid, New York, and Buenos Aires. She needed, in any case, to see a proposal in writing. Ella, putting on her sweetest voice, persuaded me to do this.

Recent tasks I had undertaken out of love for Frailes, such as a publicity leaflet for the Rey de Copas, had helped me master the art of heartfelt, over-the-top prose, and I put these newly acquired skills to full effect in my letter to Sara Montiel. Frailes, I wrote, though a humble community, was a place where devotion to her was so intense and widespread that a homage there would be more genuine and touching than anything that a large city, with all its facilities and glamour, could offer. It would, I emphasized, be a homage straight from the heart of the Spanish people.

That Frailes was capable of honouring someone in so memorable a fashion would not seem such a wild claim the following week, when El Sereno was finally received into the gastronomic order of the Wooden Spoon. The ceremony of the knighting was one that this exclusively male institution had always conducted in smart restaurants, before a select gathering of other members of the order. But El

Sereno insisted on breaking with this tradition, so that over 100 people of both sexes could eat the simple but exquisite food of Miguel Montes in the relaxing and seductive setting of his garden. The knights, arriving in their casual clothes, donned their red cloaks and assembled in a row outside my writing hut, in front of which the knight commander, José María Suárez from Guarromán, read out some words from a pseudo-medieval parchment. The kneeling El Sereno, touched by the tip of José María's sword, rose to his feet to have a cloak placed on his shoulders, and a wooden spoon pinned to it.

'This is the most important moment of my life,' he declared, prompting a tear or two from his sisters, who would that day be seen eating in public for the first time anyone could remember. Then cloaks were removed, and everyone sat down at round tables laid with silverware and draped in damask linen. Under the shade of the walnut tree, we ate plates of goat stew, and drank Matahermosa until the sun had set. The occasion, with all its absurd potential, was an unforgettable mixture of simple rural munificence and an almost unworldly beauty.

But such was the new pace of Frailes life that scarcely had there been time to reflect on what had happened than the next celebration had begun, the festive pilgrimage held nominally in honour of the Virgin of La Cabeza.

The Santo Custodio, everyone knew but few openly admitted, was the token excuse for what outwardly appeared a drunken brawl in which devotion of any kind seemed largely limited to a few moments of dutiful admiration of the parading float of the Virgin, followed by a short climb to join the queue that had formed outside Custodio's cave. The sounds of prayer and religious song could barely be heard above a general fairground commotion in which shouts from the vendors at side stalls, the screams of children playing on a giant, inflatable castle, the boom from a tent where a disco had been set up, and the general chatter and laughter from the improvised bars, were all in discordant competition with each other. Stalwarts from the Discoteca Oh! formed a raucous singing group under the bar erected in front of the Brotherhood House of the Frailes devotees of the Virgin de la Cabeza. Half the village came and went, and then the evening set in, and the crowds slowly dispersed. As we drove home ourselves, we passed a legless Bubi staggering downhill with his toy guitar.

A week later, Cees Nooteboom's article on how Spain had changed in the last twenty-five years appeared in a special colour supplement of *El País* commemorating the quarter of a century of the newspaper's existence. As El Sereno would announce to the world in his greatly exaggerated style, 'There's just a couple of paragraphs about Madrid and Barcelona, and three entire pages devoted to Frailes!' He himself was featured prominently of course, and described as living with his two unmarried sisters in a domestic arrangement that had all the makings of a Balzac story. I too got a long mention as El Sereno's inseparable English friend who lived above a disco, worked in a 'type of monk's cell', and spent the time in between these two places greeting so many people in the streets that Nooteboom was surprised I got any writing done. A description that particularly caught the attention of Caño and Merce was Frailes's 'archaic hospitality', which thereafter became our catchphrase whenever we invited someone from outside the village to a drink or meal.

For a long time afterwards, Fraileros living in other parts of Spain who had seen Nooteboom's article would be ringing through to El Sereno and others to express their joy that their humble native village had appeared in a major newspaper article. Discussing all this with Merce, I insisted that we should make use of the publicity Frailes was receiving to draw attention to the plight of the village's social worker. Action was needed quickly, for already Merce had had confirmation that she was being kicked out of her beloved Frailes and transferred to a town in the far north of Jaén, about two and a half hours away by car. Merce's complaints about irregularities in her *Oposiciones* had so far been met with silence; and she had had further evidence that she had some mysterious opponent who was determined to get rid of her.

With the help of El Sereno, I got a local journalist we knew to write an article on her case for the *Ideal de Jaén*. Then, sitting next to Merce in her town hall office, I began penning a letter in her defence to *El País*. I admitted that though as a foreigner I had no right to intervene in the Spanish bureaucratic system I felt a moral obligation as both a human being and a 'lover of the village of Frailes' to comment on the absurdity and cruelty of getting rid of a greatly adored and successful social worker and packing her off to a faraway place where separation from her family was likely to create social problems for herself. And if she really was deemed incompetent in her job, why, I argued, should another community be punished with so bad a worker?

The following afternoon I received a call while sitting at the counter of La Cueva. It was Ella von Schreitter, telling me that Sara Montiel had agreed to come to Frailes on St Anthony's Day, as we had originally planned. I was almost trembling with shock, and keen to announce the news to all and sundry. But no one in the bar except Merce believed me; the others carried on playing their cards regardless. I went off the next day to the Seville *Feria*, where I wrongly anticipated a more responsive audience among those exiles from Frailes who took an active part in their adopted city's week-long party.

'Sara Montiel?' one of them said in a tone of the most complete scepticism. 'You'd find it easier to move mountains than to get her to Frailes. She might say she'll come, but she's an artist, and artists are all the same. Temperamental and unreliable. And she more than anyone. They say she's the worst sort of primadonna.'

On balance, I considered it best to take El Sereno's advice not to talk any more about her possible visit, but merely to play down all rumours that she might be coming. I would only lose respect and credibility should she change her mind, or if something else unforeseen occurred. However, matters went beyond my control. On my return from Seville I discovered that an announcement about her impending arrival in Frailes had already been published in the editorial pages of the *Ideal de Jaén*. Under a photograph of a youthful Sara Montiel, smoking one of the cigars that were her trademark, were a few lines to the effect that, thanks to me, the unimaginable was about to happen, and that the Fraileros would soon meet the film star whom they had only envisaged seeing in their dreams.

Every new day in Frailes now brought with it the expectation of some strange new visit. The sight one morning outside my door of the head of the local *Guardia Civil* was a momentarily disturbing apparition, until I realized that this gentle, friendly man, had come because he had heard reports that a television crew from the prestigious programme *Informe Semanal* might be coming to Frailes, presumably, he thought, to do a programme about a water dispute with Alcalá.

'This is a quiet village,' he explained, 'and I have to pass on to my superiors any rumours about abnormal activities.'

I said I would keep him abreast of any developments of this kind, though I decided this was not the time to worry him about the crowds likely to turn up for Sara Montiel.

All these rumours surrounding the Cinema España and Sara's visit there had at least one desired effect: they helped free memories of the past. Most of the villagers who now stopped me in the street, or came to visit me in El Sereno's garden, did so because they wanted to talk about what life in Frailes had once been like. One woman remembered how she longed for rainy days, when her father could devote himself to selling charcoal, and there was money available for them to go to the cinema. Another recalled how her wedding party had been held there: it was normal, she explained, for the cinema's seating to be taken up at the end of a film or spectacle, and the auditorium given over to dancing. Everyone who had known the cinema in its heyday was curious to see the place again, and show to their children where some of the happiest hours of their youth had been spent. I tried hard to curb their excitement, but there was little I could do in the face of relentless press speculation. Such now was the talk about Frailes in the media that a live radio programme was organized one morning in the village school. El Sereno took part, and so too did the priest and the mayor, both of whom said they refused to accept that Sara was coming until they actually saw her. But the language of doubt and caution was one that the children themselves did not understand.

'On June 13,' sweetly declared the eight-year-old girl who had been chosen as the newscaster, 'a very important event is going to take place in Frailes. The actress Sara Montiel is coming to visit us. This is the most exciting thing to have happened to this village in all its history.'

My bags by now were all prepared for an emergency departure from Frailes in case of Sara's non-appearance. A daily series of frantic calls from Ella indicated that matters at her end were going from bad to worse. The most unexpected of the many problems was that it looked as if it was going to be impossible for us to get hold of a copy of *El último cuplé*. The rights to this and many other classics of Spanish cinema of the 1950s and 1960s had been reputedly bought for a pittance by a business associate of the flamboyant and controversial mayor of Marbella, Gil y Gil. This in itself would not have been a problem had not the rights to *El último cuplé* also been claimed by a dubious-sounding outfit registered in Tanzania. Until the dispute between the two parties was resolved – and it had already been going on for many years – no one in Spain was going to be allowed access to the original celluloid version of one of Spain's best-known films.

Meanwhile, little interest was shown in what was being done with the Cinema España. That was exclusively my problem, and I would probably have met with an impatient reaction from John and Ella had I described in detail the dilemmas, fears and irritations that the building was causing me. I had thought it better not to embark on the preparation of the cinema until the film deal was signed and sealed; but now that Sara Montiel was in principle 'on board', and there were merely four weeks left before her supposed visit, I told Ferminillo that we needed to get started soon on our restoration campaign.

'Get the cinema ready by June 13?' he responded. 'That's totally impossible. You'll have to tell Sara to come later.'

When I said that stars of her calibre usually had an inflexible schedule, and that if we were to postpone her visit she would almost certainly pull out, he put forward another objection. 'And where's the money going to come from?'

This was indeed a worry. There was clearly not going be a penny available from the film people; and the donations promised by others had so far not materialized. 'From the proceeds of the benefit lunch,' I lied, knowing full well that all the money that had been made had disappeared into helping Juan's ailing restaurant.

Ferminillo pressed for details, which I was unable to supply him with. In the end I had to assure him that if the worst came to the worst I would take on all the costs myself. This satisfied him for the few moments it took before he had come up with another, and far more disconcerting question. 'And how much shall we charge the people who come to the film?'

I said firmly that unless the event was going to be a private, non-profit-making function we stood no chance of getting the film free, let alone of showing it in a ruinous building. As I wearily repeated my case, I peered further into the depths of Ferminillo's meanness. In a village of such extraordinary generosity as Frailes, this was a quality of his that was both surprising and notorious. He had the reputation of the local Scrooge, and had managed to hoard up more money than almost anyone else in the village. What, everyone wanted to know, did a man with no heirs and few expenses need with all that money?

Faced with Ferminillo's tight-fistedness and intransigence, I welcomed more than ever the unflagging support for the cinema project I was now getting from El Sereno. He had seen how such an event could heap the village in glory; and he had never quite shaken off his vision of Ella von Schreitter in her towel. His determination to forge ahead 'for Frailes and for Ella' was strengthened by his publicly declared wish not 'to leave Maiquel alone in his madness'. In explaining why he was devoting so much of his energy to helping me out with the cinema, he also resorted to another of his old Spanish sayings: 'The luck of one madman,' he said, 'is to find another.'

Wondering how we would begin making the cinema presentable before June 13, El Sereno thought first of all of getting the town hall involved, and employing the youths from the village's unemployment training scheme. However, the cinema was private property; and Antonio the mayor, who still did not believe that Sara would be coming, did not want to divert municipal funds and resources into a building that could be publicly used only with Ferminillo's permission.

'Antonio's of course entirely right,' said El Sereno, who then convinced me that the town hall's refusal to help was in fact a blessing in disguise. 'If we had accepted assistance from the authorities we'd only have been compromising ourselves,' he said in a fighting tone of voice. 'We want to show people what can be achieved through private initiative. And we'll pay for everything out of our own pockets if necessary.'

For days we drove around the village putting together a workforce of builders, carpenters, cleaners, and others who would be prepared to help out. We were offered ladders, and the free use of a lorry by a friend of ours known to everyone as 'Custodio the Builder', an entirely selfless and famously hard-working man who had learnt his trade largely under El Sereno's guidance.

All would have gone as well as we could have hoped for had it not been for another of Ferminillo's infuriating character traits: his complete refusal to let anyone work inside the cinema if he was not there himself. He was like an egotistical child who did not want anyone else to play with his toy. I pointed out repeatedly that a team of responsible workers could hardly damage further a building that had been falling down for years; but every time I tried to argue my point, he went almost mad with rage.

'This building is my whole life!' he screamed, waving his arms around like a hysterical chipmunk. 'I'm not having people wandering in and out as if this was a public toilet!' Given that he was spending more than half his week in Seville, I told him that we might as well stop pretending that the work would be completed in time for Sara's visit. 'So be it then,' he said.

What I had not taken into account was the continuing capacity for back-breaking work of Ferminillo himself. The same stubbornness and obsessive zeal that made it difficult for anyone to challenge his views would soon lead him to devote what free hours he had to labour away on the building with a Herculean determination. Memories of how he had worked day and night as a teenager to get the cinema ready for its opening on 13 June 1949 must obviously have come to haunt him. He was turned eventually into a man possessed, who would sometimes be seen emerging from the cinema at five in the morning only to return there four hours later. Whenever I saw a light on in the building in the middle of the night I knew he would be there dressed in his blue overalls, lying on top of the scaffolding with a miner's hat on his head as he single-handedly repaired the ceiling. If the building was going to be ready in time, then the credit would be almost entirely due to this maniacal septuagenarian.

Seeing Ferminillo like this made me confident again that we would achieve our aims. When we were at last able to put back the seating, this feeling was boosted by what seemed like a sign from heaven. The benches that Ferminillo's father had designed and built himself proved to be in a far better condition than we had imagined, but there were still too few of them to fill the auditorium. Ferminillo remembered selling some of them off in the late 1970s, but he did not know where they had got to now. El Sereno, making enquiries around the village, heard that they were somewhere in La Hoya del Salobral. We rushed off there in his Suzuki, and spoke to almost everyone in the hamlet until finally an old woman told us that they were in one of the Brotherhood Houses of the Virgin of La Cabeza. Her husband, who had the key, was working in the fields, but she said we would be able to see them if we put our faces to the window. The strange man in white who sold all the trinkets of the Santo Custodio was standing directly behind us as we gazed in astonishment at a row of ten perfectly preserved benches from the Cinema España. The building they were in was at the very foot of the steps leading up to the Santo Custodio's cave. It was as if the saintly faith healer had lent his blessing to our project.

However, the reassurance this gave me was still not sufficient to curb all my worries. With only two weeks to go, Ferminillo working away like a madman, and still no positive news from Ella, I knew that the consequence for me of any pull-out by the film people was likely now to be little less than public castration at the cinema's door. I tried to distract myself with activities unconnected with the whole project. The obsession with the Cinema España had taken over my Frailes existence to such an extent that it was necessary to be reminded occasionally of the healing beauty of the natural surroundings.

El Sereno and I, together with a soulful Almerían friend, went off one afternoon to explore a hermitage near Valdepeñas called Chircales. Surrounded by springs, oaks and cypresses, at the upper end of an otherwise empty valley, the place had the picturesque look from afar of some rambling Tuscan farmhouse. From nearby you could see the vestiges of its architecture being reclaimed by nature. Water gushing from a moss-choked stream poured into the broken basin of an eighteenth-century fountain. A giant palm broke through the paving stones of a small courtyard where a humble church sheltered a miraculous sixteenth-century Crucifixion, taken in procession every year to Valdepeñas. Christ's apparition to a shepherd in an adjoining cave, dripping now with candles and ex-votos, was the official reason for the hermitage's existence. But what made our outing so special to us was what we found behind a rusted gate, to which the words 'Entry Forbidden' had been half-heartedly attached.

Pushing the gate open, we walked into a bosky garden that had been laid out at the beginning of the last century in a style of vaguely Moorish inspiration. Box hedges, secretive alleys, fountains, pergolas, and a long swimming pool, evocative of summer parties of the 1920s, were among the components of this private domain; but the hedges were uncut, the grass had gone wild, the ceramic tiles were cracked, and all the water that was left now hurried past in a single, uncontrolled torrent. Higher up, where all civilizing touches had succumbed completely to brambles, bushes, goats, and collapsed barbed-wire fences, there were caves built into the cliffs where Moors fleeing from the Christians in the sixteenth century had once lived in hiding. El Sereno, who had acquired by now some of my love for romantic decay, held our Almerían friend tightly above her bare midriff, and declared the garden, with its Moorish echoes, to be 'our Alhambra'.

The Almerían had a love of walking. She persuaded us at the weekend to undertake the most ambitious of our explorations of the Sierra. Merce and Caño, adopting the respective roles of guardian angel and voice of common sense, thought it best for our safety to come with us. Our starting-point was the solitary ruins of 'the Factory of Light', an early twentieth-century electrical plant whose old-fashioned name had a hint of the miraculous, and conveyed for me some mythical hybrid between Frailes's cinema and the olive-oil factory.

'You've got the title of your book,' said Merce, as we trod delicately over nettles and mounds of collapsed masonry to look inside the exposed interior, where a wooden waterwheel, lying on its side, appeared like a marvel from the ancient past. A track, parallel to the rushing stream below, headed deeper into a steep-sided valley where oaks and meadowland battled with erosion and newly planted pines. Far ahead of us was what seemed to be the entrance to a canyon, guarded by an outcrop of rock that soared above the greenery like a rearing dragon. As we walked spellbound towards this, we were drawn further into the valley than any of us had been before.

We headed on to a narrow forest path that climbed and climbed, beyond the trees, between bushes of thyme and lavender, and across sheer slopes of rock falling at a dizzying angle straight down to the ever more diminutive stream. The fast approaching dragon turned orange in the changing light. The greens intensified. The rock pinnacles multiplied. The path reached its highest point and turned to face a canyon more dramatic than anything we had expected. It was full of monsters and giant forms: a leaping horse; a growling Cerberus; a pair of entwined lovers. The shapes changed from orange to red. A bloodshot full moon appeared in the evening sky. We were a good hour away from the forestry hut where we had intended spending the night. The terrain would become dangerous in the dark. But not even Caño or Merce could tear themselves away from the spectacle in front of us. They embraced each other tightly as the rays of the moon penetrated the canyon's secret crevices. The Almerían placed herself between El Sereno and me, and slipped her arms between ours. An unearthly white glow, as if coming from the

Factory of Light, transformed the mountainous countryside into a landscape from a dream.

For a whole weekend nothing else in life seemed to matter, except the pursuit of beauty, happiness, and romantic adventures. But Monday came, the Almerían left, and I received a tired call from Ella, who was due at Frailes with the film crew in less than a day. She had hopes of sorting out the copyright problem relating to *El último cuplé*, but nothing was yet on paper, and she and the crew would have to delay their arrival until at least the night of June 10.

Meanwhile, a crew from Canal Sur Television had made arrangements through the town hall to do a documentary on the Cinema España, and was due to arrive the next day. I hoped this might provide Ferminillo with some consolation in the increasingly likely case of all his efforts coming to nothing.

On the afternoon of the expected arrival of a four-person team from Canal Sur, I went to the cinema to see how Ferminillo was doing. He claimed he had no idea that a television company was coming, and was furious that they had not got in touch with him. He was at any rate on the point of going off to Seville, and was not prepared to change his plans on account of 'some ill-mannered arty types'.

'I have managed to spend seventy years without being filmed,' he shouted, 'and I can't see any reason for making a two-minute appearance now!'

I admired his attitude, while also knowing that as soon as the film crew had lavished his cinema with praise, he would be all charm and smiles, and ready to accommodate their every wish. The crew turned up about fifteen minutes later, and that was indeed exactly what happened.

Ferminillo had every reason to be proud of what he had achieved in little more than three weeks. The ceiling had been made stable; the seating was all in place; a new screen had gone up behind the stage cloth; and the maroon plaster walls were papered with original Sara Montiel film posters that the over-diligent cleaners had almost thrown away. New life and glitter had been given to the place without causing it to lose any of its emotive atmosphere of times gone by. The unreal, indefinable world it belonged to became apparent under the glare of the coloured spotlights which the excited television crew started putting up around the building. The lights were all in place in time for the cameraman to capture a moment of spontaneous poetry, when a group of young children, who had succeeded in entering the building unnoticed by Ferminillo, walked slowly with wide-staring eyes towards the stage cloth, as if witnessing a supernatural apparition.

Ferminillo, overwhelmed by so many admiring glances, later revealed his mastery of the theatrical surprise once again. Taking us all to a corner of the auditorium that was covered by a large cloth, he lifted this up like a magician pulling a handkerchief from a top hat, revealing some green slats of wood that formed the letters CINEMA ESPAÑA. This was the cinema's original sign, and he had come across it a few days before while clearing away some empty cases of *gaseosa*.

Now that there was a television camera around, Ferminillo thought this an ideal opportunity to hang these letters on the cinema's façade. A small crowd assembled to watch him do this; and the cameraman caught us all on film applauding as the final 'A' was screwed into the white wall. Ferminillo's niece Mari Tere was playing to the camera, while his sister Carmela, reappearing into public view for the first time since the benefit lunch, was looking more uncannily youthful than ever. Among the faces was one I did not know at all: fair-skinned and freckly, its owner's status as a foreigner was confirmed by sandals and a rucksack. He came up and said in English, 'I presume you're Michael Jacobs. I saw your article about Frailes in the *Times Literary Supplement*, and thought I would see the village for myself.'

The article had been published over a year before, and no one else had visited Frailes as a result of it.

'I'm a fellow scribbler,' the man continued, 'and I'm looking for a bolt-hole in which to write.'

He had already installed himself in the *Mesón*, though he was staying 'this time' for one night only. I invited him to join us for drinks at the Rey de Copas, where, before falling asleep, he ensured that his visit to Frailes had at least one positive consequence. For it was this man who told me about Sara Montiel's interest in the psychic and the supernatural. The next morning I found a note in my bedroom in which he gave some useful advice. 'Remember', the note said, 'if the conversation flags with Sara, talk about UFOs.'

Late on the afternoon of Friday, June 9, while El Sereno and I were in La Hoya del Salobral, lifting cinema benches into the lorry of Custodio the Builder, the longed-for call came from Ella. A deal had been reached with the Spanish producers. A film crew much larger than anticipated would be arriving in Frailes by tomorrow night. For the first two nights accommodation for ten people only would be required, and additional rooms in which all the equipment could be carefully guarded. Equally urgent was for me to find an interpreter prepared to work free of charge for the whole week of the filming, starting first thing on the Sunday morning.

'Hi, Mike,' said John, joining in the call at this moment. 'Let me run over the shooting schedule with you, so you can get locations sorted out, and people on hand for their interviews.'

I relayed these messages afterwards to El Sereno, who said he would not be having his blood pressure checked again in the foreseeable future.

As I sat in the lorry, between him and Custodio the Builder who had freely offered his help without any personal gain in mind, I was able briefly to see life in perspective and laugh to myself at the fundamental absurdity of this vain and hectic world that would soon be coming to Frailes. But these moments of peaceful, sane reflection would prove to be the last for some time to come. As soon as we were back in the village, El Sereno and I set about our multitude of tasks. He wrote down a list of all that we had to do; but soon abandoned it after we found ourselves endlessly diverted from the job in hand by additional requests from John and Ella, by thoughts about tasks we had forgotten to include, and by increasing phone calls from journalists. El Sereno, seeing how much time I was spending on the mobile, had bought one himself; but, like so many of the pieces of new technology he loved to acquire, he did not learn how to use it properly, and gave it to me to look after. In the build-up to Sara Montiel's supposed visit, I began using the two phones simultaneously, sometimes keeping one person on hold while dealing with another request, and once even giving a live radio interview on one line while another journalist waited on the other.

We were still not entirely convinced that Sara would soon be here, nor were the village authorities. Now that the big day approached, the idea of the great actress in Frailes seemed more ridiculous than ever. People drew my attention to Berlanga's film *Welcome Mister Marshall*, in which a whole village, after weeks of getting the local band rehearsed, preparing floral tributes, and arranging the most festive of welcomes for their distinguished American guest, is told by the red-faced mayor that Mister Marshall would not be visiting them after all. The mayor of Frailes, perhaps remembering the film, was refusing to make any arrangements in case Sara did not come. Though El Sereno and I had not wanted his collaboration, nor any other politician's, in our chimerical project, it was disturbing to know that we were entirely on our own in deciding how the village would receive the most famous visitor in its history.

Our powers of improvisation would clearly be tested to their limits; but there were certain basic steps that had been taken to prevent total chaos from descending on the village. We went straight-away on the Saturday morning to see the priest, to make absolutely sure that the procession organized at Frailes every June 13 in honour of St Anthony would not overlap with Sara's arrival at the cinema. Then we drove around the village in search of the head of the *Guardia Civil*, to ask him about the possibility of laying on a couple of police to block off the area around the cinema, and to stop people from crossing the protective cordon. He said he would see what he could do, but warned me that he would need permission from his superiors at Alcalá. I kept quiet about John's idea of having a fleet of armed police on motorcycles blaring away on their horns as they led Sara's car through the village streets ('That'll look fucking great on film, man').

By late on the Saturday night miracles had begun to happen. After numerous frantic phone calls I had lured to Frailes a person I was sure would make the best possible interpreter for John: Fiona was a young friend from Seville who was intelligent, kind, sensitive, half-English, half-Spanish, and, more to the point, willing to work for nothing. But the greatest miracle was that John, Ella and their disparate team had all arrived, albeit several hours later than they said they would. Seeing them all together in the Discoteca Oh! by three o'clock in the morning was like having a patchwork of my life before me. Two of the Sevillian crew, like Fiona herself, were people I knew from my late friend Esperanza's circle at the Seville *Feria*, while the stills photographer, John's mother-in-law, was an Anglo-Irish woman who, I discovered, had been brought into this world by my gynae-cologist great-uncle from Dublin. Among the others was a Sevillian production assistant called Sonsoles, whose character, like that of Ella, would soon turn out to have the underlying ruthlessness necessary to the profession. There was also a Londoner of Afro-Caribbean origin, whom El Sereno reckoned to be the first black person in Frailes since the 1950s, when, implausibly enough, the village had a black Cuban policeman with a taste for salsa music.

Nothing in Frailes's history, however, could have prepared the villagers for the sight confronting them late on the Sunday morning, when the film people gathered for breakfast at a bar near the Cueva. Something more potentially disturbing than hooliganism had now reached the village, I felt, but I could not define at first quite what this was. The motley crew, as they paced in and out of the bar, gave the superficial impression of a hyperactive circus troupe that had suddenly come to town. But the fact that they were all talking into mobile phones in a mixture of Spanish and English contradicted this. The image that most stuck in my mind was that of an invading army. John appeared to be shouting instructions in an irritated tone. Ella had a clipboard out, and was nodding and taking notes. Sonsoles, her phone apparently attached to an exposed bra strap, was gesturing with Latin abandon. The elderly villagers who spent their days sitting by the roadside had the cowed look of people whose community had been taken over by the enemy.

The morning was showery and grey, as if the beauty of the Sierra Sur did not want to reveal itself to these aliens. Low-lying clouds made visibility poor; but nothing was going to deter John from his plan of spending the rest of the day shooting at Puerta Alta. I suggested we had lunch beforehand at La Hoya del Salobral, which would give time perhaps for the clouds to clear. 'Lunch?' exclaimed John, horrified. 'Fuck that!'

'We can't have lunch now,' firmly intervened Ella. 'We've got to get down to shooting.'

Fiona from Seville, wondering by now what she had let herself in for, had the look of a shy pupil arriving at a tough new school. She decided to ally herself to El Sereno and myself, even if this meant travelling to the Puerta Alta in the Suzuki.

I imagined the weather conditions would at least put a stop to John's mad scheme of filming El Sereno and myself having a conversation while seated on top of Puerta Alta's natural arch. The idea had initially appealed to El Sereno, but he now had to admit that the rain would make the climb even more slippery and dangerous, not so much for himself, but for the others. Fiona confessed to having a great fear of heights.

'Let's get moving!' John shouted, clapping his hands. The additional danger of the rain seemed to have made him more determined than ever to start climbing. El Sereno took the lead, and I followed directly behind him, carrying, as instructed, two folding chairs. 'What does he want those for?' he asked. I could now tell him that John wanted them on top of the arch for us to sit on.

'But it's stupid having chairs up there,' El Sereno argued. 'It would be much safer for us to sit directly on the rock.'

I tried explaining that John was probably attracted to the surrealism of the image. Then I added that if John was keen on illustrating the saying that the luck of a madman was to find another, then he could not have found a better way of doing so.

We attempted to set up the chairs on the arch, but this proved impossible. Most of the crew, including an ashen-faced Fiona, watched nervously from afar as the chairs slipped every time we tried sitting on them. One of the cameramen lost his footing while trying to pass us, but fortunately caught hold of a tough bunch of thyme. John meanwhile was standing up fearlessly and yelling to the sound man to come closer to the narrow rock seat where El Sereno and I had eventually been forced to position ourselves. A completely unforeseen problem presented itself when the sun burst suddenly through the clouds and shone with all its mid-afternoon fury on our unprotected heads and skin. Knowing by now the slowness of the filming process, and seeing how the sky was becoming completely clear, I reckoned we had a tough time ahead of us.

'Let's get rolling,' John ordered. Ella snapped the clapperboard, and the first scene rolled of *Rewind: El último cuplé*. El Sereno and I had been asked to talk naturally between ourselves, as if we were two old friends meeting up for a chat in the country.

'Fancy meeting you here,' said El Sereno, as I swivelled awkwardly with my feet dangling over the precipice. 'Isn't this a nice spot?'

We continued in this vein for a good ten minutes, until John started putting some questions to us, mainly about Sara Montiel and her films.

'Mike,' he said, 'can you tell us something about the relationship between sex and death in *El último cuplé*?'

Fainting now from hunger, on the verge of sunstroke, and feeling dizzy whenever I looked below, I was worried that my possible last recorded words were going to be some philosophical nonsense about a film I had yet to see.

The hunger passed, to be replaced by dehydration and a burning face the colour of a lobster. We were entering our fourth hour on the arch, and John and his team had left us there stranded on our own while they went to the other side of the gorge to film us from a panoramic distance. I wondered what other man of El Sereno's age would have willingly put up with such an ordeal.

I had begun by now to have serious worries about what I had set up for the following day. This was going to be a day in which John was going to tackle the theme of miracles and faith healing in the Sierra Sur. I had grasped this as my opportunity to have recorded for posterity the soul-reaching voice of the elderly Luis Machuca, who would sing and recite his poems dedicated to his friend the Santo Custodio. But how, I now wondered, would this gentle man with the bad heart cope with the aggression of the film world?

The saintly Luis turned up at El Sereno's house immediately after breakfast the next day. He said he had put his whole morning at our disposal, but that his family would begin to worry if he were late for lunch. I told him that we would be setting off as soon as possible to the shrine of the Santo Luisico at Cerezo Gordo, and that we would be back in Frailes by mid-day. He would be delighted to sing for us, Luis assured me, and did not in the slightest mind all the waiting around I had warned him about. I wanted to embrace him. Instead I left him sitting on a bench outside the town hall while I went inside to sort out some paperwork that Sonsoles said was necessary for Wednesday's event to go ahead. I needed the mayor's signature to confirm that the showing of the film was going to be a purely private function; but no one knew where the mayor had got to. I looked at my watch, certain that John would be getting impatient. El Sereno, meanwhile, who had taken Fiona under his wing, had disappeared with her to go cherry-picking, and had still not returned. My phone rang. 'Where the hell are you, Michael?' shouted Ella.

Before the arrival of the film crew at Frailes, time had ceased to have the same importance for me as it did in London. At Frailes, to be an hour or so late did not really matter, let alone twenty minutes; but time was now money, and I had to obey a different clock to the permanently stopped one of the town hall. When the Suzuki eventually made its leisurely appearance, I told El Sereno with as much calm as I could muster that the film crew had been ready to leave for some time. I was anxious that none of the mounting tension would be sensed by Luis, whose heart I believed capable of stopping on the slightest emotional exertion.

The Suzuki led the way to the hamlet of Cerezo Gordo, but before leaving Frailes we had to stop at Luis's house, where he wanted to pick up a file of his handwritten transcriptions of all the popular songs and poems ever composed about the Sierra's saints. 'What's the deal now, Mike?' John frantically asked as I waited outside the Suzuki for Luis to come back with what he described as his 'book of miracles'.

Driving up afterwards into the Sierra on this beautiful Monday morning had an initially calming effect; but the laying out of all the electric cables inside the shrine of the Santo Luisico, the need to mend a fault in the sound equipment, and endless further delays, again created a mood out of harmony with the surroundings. I thought of the television crew who two years before had failed to film the miraculous image of the faith healer; and I wondered if John and his team of unbelievers would suffer a similar fate.

I preferred to fix my attention on Luis Machuca, who, like some enlightened mystic to whom all the cares of this world no longer mattered, sat reading and singing from his file on the lives and miracles of the Santos Luisico and Custodio, mindless of the shouts around him. For him the cult of these faith healers was not the semi-secretive phenomenon people had always told me about. It was something to be shared as widely as possible, which was why the appearance of a film crew at Frailes was not a vulgar intrusion but a God-given sign that the deeds and sayings of these miracle-workers of the Sierra Sur were deserving of international attention.

'I want everyone to know about the Santo Custodio,' he said, 'otherwise his wisdom will be forgotten.'

I took the opportunity to put to him the question I had been meaning to ask for ages. What was Custodio like as a person?

'He was the most wonderful person imaginable,' came the immediate reply. 'There was a calm and peace about him that were transmitted to all those who were in his presence.' And with that he returned to his recital, his arm held by a loving Fiona, now more receptive than ever to the message of serenity that Luis wished to impart.

'Get him to stop talking, Mike,' commanded John, anxious that the man's voice would be worn out before the recording had begun. The radiance on Luis's face, and his obvious love of all the attention he was getting, made me less worried about him than I had been at the start of the day. Two hours later, however, after countless re-takes, re-arrangement of the equipment, and other technical interruptions, I was sure we would totally exhaust him. When John finally insisted that 'we're going to have to keep the dude for the afternoon', I reacted sharply saying that his family would be sick with anxiety. 'You're being over-protective, man,' John said.

Perhaps he was right. Luis was now so enjoying himself, and so convinced of the importance of what he was doing, that he would certainly have been disappointed if we had taken him home. When we moved on to La Hoya he smiled contentedly as we sat him down for lunch at the end of our long table. And when the crew prepared for some tracking shots within the sanctuary of the Virgin of La Cabeza, he quietly walked over to the bar and provided me with my most lasting image of that day. To the background of John's shouts, the arguing voices of Ella and Sonsoles, and the general bilingual confusion, Luis stood with his file laid out on the counter, reciting the miracles of the Santo Custodio to a rapt audience of shepherds and their young children.

John was berating two of the crew for not having properly checked the equipment before coming; Ella was trying to have some replacement parts sent from Granada; and Sonsoles was informing us all about the time of Sara Montiel's arrival the next day. 'She's not fucking coming until eight in the evening?' exploded John. 'You must be joking, man. That wasn't part of the deal.' Luis continued his reading, while Ella, Sonsoles and I went back into the dining room to reach an agreement about how we were going to look after Sara during her two-night stay in the area. Sonsoles, who had just been on the phone to the diva's agent, told me that Sara, to my relief, apparently had no objections to staying at Puerta Alta, nor had she any special dietary requirements. All she needed was a completely new set of sheets and pillows, and a hairdresser on standby in case of a coiffure emergency.

Luis, having been filmed singing outside the places sacred to the Santos Luisico and Custodio, stayed resolutely with us once we were back in Frailes. He was worried that he had not done full justice to the Santo Custodio, and I suggested he come with us to the village cemetery, where he could perform again in front of the candles and floral offerings placed before the tomb of a mentally retarded son of Custodio who had died young.

After filming at the cemetery, we went down the hill, and started again in the Cueva, where we were immediately drawn into the emotional storm gathering over Frailes. A frantic Ferminillo entered the bar to complain about being neglected, and to ask when the copy of *El último cuplé* was going to arrive. 'I need it now, now!' he shouted. 'I need to run it through the projector, I can't just leave everything to the last moment.'

I assured Ferminillo it was on its way from Seville, and rushed into the street to wave down the car of Miguel Montes the cook. Would he come over tomorrow night to Puerta Alta to prepare supper for Sara Montiel and the film crew? 'I can't, Maiquel, it's too short notice.'

'There's a call for you,' said Villi when I re-entered the Cueva. The village's best hairdresser was on the phone, telling me she had appointments from faithful clients she was unable to cancel. A desperate Sonsoles came up to me. She had failed to get hold of the owner of Puerta Alta to confirm Sara's arrival. Could I help? A call on one of my mobiles came through; and then a call on the other. People had started believing that Sara really was coming.

The interest of the press was becoming frenetic, and so too was the demand for invitations. The requests came mainly from 'important' local personages, who were now offering to make available funds to help me with the cinema's restoration. I turned down their offers, referring their requests to El Sereno, who had begun explaining to the card-players of the Cueva why it was impossible to invite everyone. Trying to escape from the souring atmosphere, we left the bar and, getting into the Suzuki, headed with Fiona to the Bar Lady Diana, but were stopped every few metres by villagers begging to be invited.

A few hours of respite were provided by the night. But by nine o'clock on the Tuesday morning, my two mobiles were ringing again as I walked towards the cinema, where John and Ella were waiting for me at the door.

'Get a fucking move on, Mike!' screamed John, impatiently stomping around with a look of intense fury as I tried to terminate an interview with the *Radio COPE*. 'I'm going to have a fucking heart attack,' he continued fuming, as Ferminillo harangued us again about when the film was going to arrive, and said something about having to go later in the day to Granada to get a replacement lens for the projector.

'Don't worry,' said Ella. 'The film's on its way from Seville, everything's going to be fine.'

While Ferminillo stood on the stage ready for his interview, I walked up to the top of the cinema, where I found Miguel Montes about to switch on the projector. I had never seen it before work successfully at close quarters, and I gaped like an overawed child at a fireworks' display when a blinding flash of light shot out of the machine, to be followed immediately by a cloud of smoke. The potential danger of the whole cinema going up in flames became suddenly apparent.

The mood that day at lunch time seemed suspiciously easygoing. Then I noticed that John and Ella were missing from the table. John's mother-in-law told me that 'there had been some problems in getting the film'. I left the room to go and look for them, and passed Ella on her way in. Her frayed nerves had made her drop by now all attempts to be sweet and charming. 'Everything's fine,' she said impatiently, 'everything's fine.' Then I saw John in the street, with his head in his hands, and hoped he would tell me the truth. 'It's that fucking Antonio Pérez dude,' he said in a tone of surprising resignation, as if there was no more point in being angry. 'I knew he was a shifty bastard the moment I saw him.'

Antonio Pérez, a highly reputable Sevillian producer who had claimed he would be able to get a copy of *El último cuplé*, had come up against the same bureaucratic hurdles that we ourselves had faced, and with the same result. Our only remaining hope was a copy of the film in a private collection in Almería; but we would not know about this until tomorrow morning.

'I can't believe I'm saying this,' groaned John, 'but I'm coming round to accept that we're going to have to make do with a video version.' Until we knew absolutely for certain that we would not get the film, he added, it would be better not to say anything to Ferminillo or to anyone else. I said I sincerely hoped I was not expected to be the eventual bearer of the news. 'It's going to kill him.'

However, I was still fired by hope. Miracles had got us this far; and miracles would save us at the last minute, just as they would come to the aid of Merce, whose every plea to remain in Frailes had been rejected, and who already had received her marching orders for the following week. My impassioned state gave an edge to my performance later that afternoon in the cinema, when John filmed me standing in violent chiaroscuro behind the screen, with reverse images of acrobats somersaulting above my waving arms. I must have appeared demented.

The afternoon drew quickly to a close; and the time was fast approaching when the unbelievable was due to happen. Sara Montiel was travelling by high speed train from Madrid, together with a niece of hers who was directing the forthcoming stage show about her life. At Cordóva they would be collected by the main Spanish producer of John's documentary, and by a family friend of Sara's who was the son of the late Juanita Reina, Ferminillo's favourite singer of the 1950s. The train was expected at 6.30; and the journey by car from Cordóva to Frailes was estimated to take no more than an hour and a half. As we did not want Sara to be seen in the village before the next day's press conference, we would meet her at the outlying petrol station, and from there go directly to Puerta Alta. Paco, the producer, would ring Sonsoles once they had passed Alcalá; and she in turn would ring me. It was almost nine o'clock and I had heard from no one. Then the call came. The vehicle carrying the legendary actress would be arriving in less than ten minutes.

I embarked with El Sereno on our new adventure. The Suzuki had become for me like Don Quixote's emaciated old mare Rocinante; but, as we set off on our quest to rescue the great princess, I could not decide whether I was the deluded knight and El Sereno my Sancho Panza, or vice versa. More importantly, the car would not start. Our faithful Suzuki, which had always served us so well, had chosen this vital moment to show signs of fatal exhaustion. Don Quixote's Dulcinea, in the form of Ella, was sitting at the back, mobile in hand, and getting frantic. We all got out to give the car a push; and it spluttered finally into life, determined despite age and infirmity to undertake possibly its last and certainly its most glorious mission.

A limpid evening sky of purples, reds and distant orange clouds gave an ethereal beauty even to the surroundings of the petrol station. Advancing towards us across the darkening olive fields came a white stallion disguised as a Toyota. A glow that was not quite of this world flickered from a back window, as if from a votive image perceived in a state of mystical ecstasy. 'Look how beautiful she is,' said El Sereno, the man who had once claimed disappointment at seeing Sara in real life. She might have timed her arrival so that the rays of the setting sun would be turned like a spotlight on her face, igniting her features into a blaze of tawny gold. Flames of loose, orange-tinted hair, and jewellery in silver and precious stones, so heavy that they seemed like the adornments framing an Iberian deity, shimmered above a white flowing dress which absorbed the colours of the sky.

Most ordinary mortals would have bowed low before so blinding an apparition; but my friend, who was my Sancho Panza and Don Quixote all in one, approached the car without temerity, put his head through the driver's window, and extended his hand to the princess who had inspired a million dreams.

'You're as beautiful as I'd always imagined,' he declared. Then he told the driver to follow our car closely as we headed deeper into the land of miracles.

The transcendental moment of the meeting had lifted me into a sphere higher than that of practical problems and petty irritations. My two mobiles rang a few times, and then the signal was lost, leaving me suspended in the middle of a call from some radio programme. I drifted into reverie, safe in the knowledge that no one could reach us any more. We had abducted the princess, and were taking her to a place we held sacred. I was no longer listening properly to the orders and criticisms issuing from the back from an ever more exasperated Ella, who had failed in her role as Dulcinea, and had now turned into the harsh taskmaster of reality. 'When we get to Puerta Alta El Sereno will have to drive back immediately to Frailes to collect the others . . . It's essential that the crew and Sara have time to get to know each other before filming tomorrow . . . The whole purpose of the event is to make a documentary . . . If it wasn't for John and I none of this would have happened . . .' Her words vanished into the reddening landscape, into that infinity of space which the remote, blood-orange snows of the Sierra Nevada so mystically conveyed.

El Sereno and I welcomed Sara and her friends to Puerta Alta, whose absent owner had instructed us to treat the place as if it were our own home. We helped Sara towards the studded wooden portals of our humble mansion, clearing the ground before us of dogs, geese and a peacock, whose jerky, hesitant stride resembled that of our illustrious guest as she negotiated the stony ground in heels over four inches high. We showed her everything that our house had to offer, from its souvenirs of the bullfighter Jesulín de Ubrique to the hunting trophies from our African safaris. Her face was too heavy from cosmetic improvements to register more emotion than a smile as slight and enigmatic as that of the Mona Lisa. But there was at least one hint that behind those stiff plastered features, with their suggestion of a lifetime of glamour, high living, and torrid affairs, there still remained something of the simple girl from the small Manchegan town of Campo de Criptana. 'Come here, auntie,' shouted her niece. 'You're going to love this, there's a jacuzzi in your room.'

If there was anyone who was going to bring out the human being that lay behind the diva's mask, it was El Sereno. When I saw how Sara was charmed by his courteous yet naively direct manner, with its complete absence of sycophancy, I sensed already her pleasure in renewing contact with a world from which she had been separated by years of urban sophistication. But the diva in her resurfaced with the appearance of the film crew. She sat in the courtyard, extending a frigid hand to the new arrivals, while I talked to Juanita Reina's son, Federico, a plump, effeminate man with a fastidiously trimmed beard and moustache.

With everyone crammed together around the dining room's giant oak table, supper was an occasion lacking in the grace, etiquette and fast-flowing Sevillian wit that Federico was no doubt used to. Juan Matías from the Rey de Copas had been inveigled to do the cooking, and was struggling with the kitchen's limited facilities; his brother, José Luis, totally out of his depth, was serving the film crew long before getting around to the guest of honour, whom he almost covered in red wine. El Sereno and I, as befitting the lords of the mansion, flanked Sara at the head of the table.

The conversation was as awkward as the service and it was only when John began asking Sara about Hollywood that she showed any sort of interest in talking. She then revealed a remarkably good command of English and soon had the attention of half the table, enunciating in an unstoppable flow seemingly rehearsed lines on her favourite subject, herself. She talked about her enormous popularity in America, and about how her life might be turned into a film starring Jennifer López. She went on interminably about her recent memoirs, which had been infinitely more successful than those of any other actresses of her calibre. She could even quote the exact sales figures. Then John got up for a discussion of next day's shooting, and Sara withdrew again into bored, sporadic utterances. I was the only person left trying to speak to her, and the strain was showing.

Then I remembered the note left in my room by the English visitor to Frailes a week before, stressing Sara's interest in the inexplicable; I told her about the Santo Custodio. Her huge eyes, with their broad ring of mascara, and their false lashes as large as a tarantula's legs, focused on me with a witch-like intensity. She wanted to know everything. I mentioned my chance encounter with the Australian couple in Slovakia; and I confided, as I had to no one else before, my feelings of having come to Frailes in fulfilment of a destiny ordained by some protective spirit lurking in the Sierra Sur. Sara nodded, and confessed that her life too had been controlled by forces such as these; her mother, a psychic, had predicted all that would happen to her. She was not religious, but she believed in a guardian figure who had made sure that the sorrows and frustrations of her private life had been balanced by the joys of her career. She wished to find out more about the Santo Custodio, and about whether his powers had been inherited. I said that he had received them from the Santo Luisico, and that he had handed them on to the Santo Manuel, and that no one knew who had them now. And her eyes, which had ensnared so many hearts, were fixed on me more frighteningly than ever. 'It is you,' she announced, without a trace of mockery. 'It is you who have the powers.'

The next morning I was wandering with swollen eyes towards the bar where the crew had breakfast. Slates retrieved from the deeper recesses of the cinema had been hung at strategic points in the village, and were chalked with the words: '*Gala Reopening of the Cinema España. This Evening at Nine o'clock. El último cuplé, Starring Sara Montiel.*' It had been over thirty years since Ferminillo had gone round Frailes in the middle of the night to set out the coming day's attraction. The handful of passers-by who paused to read the notices were confronted with the final proof of the unimaginable: the cinema that had long been given up for dead was coming back to life.

Only there was no film to show. A glum Ella and Sonsoles were waiting in the bar to tell me the worst. The time for miracles was over. A technician would be arriving later in the day from Seville to set up a video projector in the Circle. Needless to say I was the one who had been chosen to tell Ferminillo that the projector he had so lovingly coaxed back into life was not going to be used. I rebelled. The man famously incapable of saying no came out now with a 'No!' so resounding that Ella and Sonsoles were left for a few moments hesitant and sheepish. Nerves, lack of sleep, and my pounding heart incited me into a near frenzy as I shouted that I did not want to be present when Ferminillo realized that he had been strung along all this while by phoney assurances.

I had not yet begun to prepare my welcoming speech for Sara Montiel in the cinema, and the time left for thinking seriously about it was rapidly running out. I had anticipated some spare time during these last hours before the event, when John and his team would all be in Puerta Alta, filming an 'exclusive' interview with Sara Montiel. But the calls on my mobiles became more relentless than ever, and soon I was running around the village like a headless chicken, talking to journalists, escaping from people whom I saw approaching, and trying to carry out the endless remaining small tasks that El Sereno and I had been landed with: searching for a carpenter to make some last repairs to the cinema's benches; retrieving from the town hall a special chair on which Sara could sit on that evening; buying sweets, drinks and *pipas* to be sold in the *Ambigú* and by ushers in the aisles; working out the final details about how we would receive Sara Montiel; keeping the poet Antonio Carvajal happy.

This last task was proving the most stressful of all, and the one that almost tipped the balance between sanity and nervous breakdown. I had invited him not just as an original member of the Frailes Group but as someone who could write a poem that would serve as the prologue to John's documentary. He agreed to do the poem, but said he would be unable to come to Frailes on June 13, as this was his saint's day, and he had organized in Granada a party with a large group of his friends. However, without my being told, he had come all the same, and was waiting with his friends in the Cueva, upset that a welcoming committee had not been there to receive the world's greatest poet. If Sara Montiel was a diva showing signs of being a human being, Carvajal was a rational human being who had inexplicably turned into a diva. In between my numerous missions and interviews, I had to rush to and from the Cueva to gauge the state of his impatience. But all was to no avail, for he and his admirers would eventually storm out of the village, vowing never to return. He took his poem with him, which was perhaps all for the best. It was reputedly a hymn of praise to Sara's breasts; and he had intended reading it out to her on the cinema's stage.

Ferminillo, informed in the end by his niece Mari Tere of the non-arrival of the film, reacted fortunately with an unexpected stoicism. This calmed me briefly as I endured a day that became more hectic and anguished as it progressed. There was no time to attend to friends from afar; no time to have lunch; no time to finish all my allotted tasks; no time to give a moment's thought to what I was going to say that night when I stood in the cinema attempting to make a dual homage to Sara and to Frailes. In a state beyond exhaustion, with my nerves on edge, and my head heavy and in pain, I made my way to the press conference. It was six o'clock. The mayor, after accepting at the very last moment that Sara would really be coming to Frailes, had offered the press the use of the still to be inaugurated *Casa de Cultura*. For the past twenty-four hours a team of decorators and electricians had been struggling to bring to completion this modern cultural centre, the construction of which had necessitated the demolition of the old town hall. The building, with its curious façade of yellow neo-Baroque pilasters, stood at the top of a flight of steps leading to the small square dominated by the majestic House of the Armandos, and now crammed with people.

For the first time in the Frailes's history a large group of reporters, press photographers and television cameramen had gathered in the village. They were packed closely together at the top of the steps, where they jostled for space with a welcoming committee made up of the mayor and his eight councillors. My arrival, and that of El Sereno shortly afterwards, were assumed to herald the appearance of the woman popularly known as the Saritísima. But the minutes passed, and nothing happened; and we would still all be waiting half an hour later, by which time the novelty and incongruity of the press invasion of Frailes were beginning to wear off.

Then the white Toyota finally came, preceded not by the hooting motorcycles that John had hoped for, but by an old van, whose driver had offered to help out when he had come across a car whose occupants had looked obviously lost. I would later hear from Sara herself that they had taken a wrong turning on the way from Puerta Alta, and then had been guided in the completely opposite direction by the *Guardia Civil*.

Such was El Sereno's determination to escort the Saritísima up the steps to the *Casa de Cultura* that even the journalists moved aside to let him pass. This was his duty as her host and I had no other choice but to help him. The jealous Federico, Juanita Reina's son, was hoping for his moment in the spotlight, and seemed distinctly peeved when he found his role usurped by an Englishman and his elderly village friend. The two of us, meanwhile, supported the Saritísima on either arm as she advanced towards the *Casa de Cultura*, dressed in a torrent of purple and gold. The murmurs of astonishment that greeted her as she emerged from the car were followed by exclamations of admiration, and by a chorus of '*Guapa! Guapa! Guapa!*' ('Beautiful! Beautiful! Beautiful!') – a cry normally heard only in religious processions featuring such venerated devotional images of the Virgin as Seville's Macarena.

We proceeded into the cultural centre's main hall, where Sara, faced with questions about *El último cuplé* and her reasons for coming to Frailes ('I received a letter which touched my heart') soon came into her element. She was one of those actresses who shone in real life only when the cameras were upon her. She was funny, she sang, she was completely outrageous. I would have liked to have known what was going through the heads of the elderly village women in black (widows for the most part, or else as virginal as El Sereno's sisters) as they listened to Sara expounding on the importance of having sex at least three times a day.

We were more than an hour behind schedule when the conference ended. There was no time for Sara to go back to Puerta Alta, so she went instead to El Sereno's house, where I locked the garden gates behind her to prevent journalists and admirers from getting in. Later, as I took a shower, I heard noises and commotion, as well as a cry from Ernesto imploring El Sereno 'not to do it, you're no longer a young man!' I preferred not to think what new mischief my friend was up to, and tried, unsuccessfully, to concentrate on my imminent speech.

The bells of the church struck nine, and I hurried out of El Sereno's house with my shirt half undone. I had not realized it was quite so late. The daylight had almost gone, and John would be going mad. I ran towards the cinema. The crepuscular streets were frighteningly empty. I could hear only a distant din that was getting louder. I turned a corner, and saw the way ahead blocked by a crowd as numerous and excited as I had seen at any Spanish festival. When it parted miraculously before me, I realized that I this time was the focus of its attention. There were cheers and shouts of 'Maiquel!' I was being kissed and embraced on all sides.

I was seeing faces I recognized from all over Andalucía. I was being swept along by a crowd far greater than the whole of Frailes's population. And I realized we had coincided with the St Anthony's Day procession, and that all its candle-bearing participants had come over to us. Drunk with tiredness and emotion, I was oblivious to danger or to rational thought. I had put all my trust in the Santo Custodio.

Darkness had set in, and the faces of the expectant crowd glowed under the yellow light of candles and street lamps. Nothing had happened yet, but there were signs that the great moment was almost upon us. El Sereno, whom I had lost sight of for the past half hour, reappeared. He was battling his way fast in my direction. The sounds of a car could be heard, then a mounting roar. Headlights cast their beams like giant torches on the street below us. Cries and shouts echoed in the night. The car door opened. The Saritísima lifted her hands to greet the faithful. El Sereno and I, as we had done before, positioned ourselves on either side of the living legend. We were like proud bearers waiting to pick up a processional float.

'Hold it Mike, don't move yet, I'll give you the signal.' John was screaming instructions. His whole crew was lining up in front of us. The intensifying chorus of '*Guapa! Guapa! Guapa!*' almost drowned his voice. The crowds were pushing in. The full range of cameras was now in place. Every possible microphone had been taken out. We could hardly keep still a moment longer. John's eye was pressed against his video's viewfinder. He raised a hand into the air: 'Go! Go! Go!' The crew began a solemn march backwards up the hill, swaying with the surge of the crowds. Women were trying to touch Sara's dress. We advanced without stopping. Imaginary drums were beating in my ears. Adrenalin was making me more light-headed than ever. 'Keep it easy, Mike,' 'You're going too fast,' 'You're blocking the camera.' '*Guapa! Guapa! Guapa!*' We held on more tightly to our precious Virgin. The crush of the crowds was getting tighter. The cinema's doors were now only a few metres away. 'Hold it Mike!' '*Guapa! Guapa! Guapa!*' 'Get out of the fucking way!' *Apocalypse Now* and the Seville Holy Week had rolled into one.

We were going in. Ferminillo and his family were waiting inside. Ferminillo threw himself on the ground and kissed her hand, while his sister Carmela grabbed me by the arm and would not let go. 'If only our father had been here!' Merce, her sister Isa, and two other women were standing in a row beside the bar. They were dressed as I had asked in traditional village costume, and carried the same wicker baskets that Merce had brought me the day I had first known her.

'We want to offer you,' she said in that voice which had once helped win me over to Frailes, 'the best of our village's products . . .'

The pressure of people attempting to come in behind us cut short her talk, and we moved into the auditorium, which was already almost filled to capacity. I secured for Sara the mayor's pompously carved wooden chair. As she sat in it, flanked by the crumbling maroon walls, her eyes staring madly towards the screen, the shadowy forms of people streaming in unceasingly behind her, she looked less like the Virgin than the Queen of Darkness summoning her witches to an orgiastic coven. Now her powers appeared unlimited. There was no end to the Goya-like grotesques who were laughing, shouting, grabbing seats, turning the cinema into an infernal cave glowing with lanterns and swarming with bats. Had all control been lost? I fought against the flow of the crowd to try and reach the *Ambigú*, where I found the mayor all on his own, attempting to push away the countless people still desperate to get in. Between us we succeeded in bolting the front doors. The groaning, creaking floorboards overhead seemed to be mocking our efforts.

Still not sure as to what I would say, I climbed up on to the stage to address a huge audience. Straining my vocal chords to a degree I thought might break them completely, I began:

'Strange things have been happening in Frailes. That an Englishman should be standing on the stage of an abandoned village cinema introducing to you all one of the greatest stars of the Spanish screen seems far too implausible even for fiction. But Frailes is no ordinary village. For me it is a place of miracles and hidden surprises, one of which is the cinema you are now in . . .'

Now I had to announce that tonight's miracle was complete save in one important respect: 'I feel like the mayor in *Welcome Mister Marshall* who has to tell the whole village that Mister Marshall won't be coming after all. For tonight we have secured the celebrity, but not the film we had promised, at least not in the version that can be shown on this cinema's miraculously maintained projector.'

Despite this disappointment, I was keen to make the audience understand why a woman as famous as Sara Montiel could interrupt a busy international schedule to come to a village such as Frailes. A true village homage to Sara, I said, rendered without falsity, pretensions, or the empty words employed by politicians, was a far more appropriate way for Spain to celebrate the national heroine from Campo de Criptana than some lavish city gala underpinned by commercial or personal interests. 'We are in a cinema called the Cinema España,' I cried, as the emotion in my voice rose to compensate for my growing hoarseness, 'and during these wonderful hours we are going to spend here tonight, Frailes, with her sane and welcoming people, will be turned into the heart and soul of Spain itself.'

I was glad that I had never seen *El último cuplé* before. The film whose showing here in Frailes had expended so much of my energy, was not in itself a masterpiece worth struggling over. It had many of the clichés of romantic Spain, together with those of a rags-to-riches story in which a simple girl is exposed to a world of wealth and corruption. No semen, as far as I was aware, flowed again down the aisles of the Cinema España, though there was a man who went below the stage to use toilets that had not been functioning since the 1970s. My drunken friends on whom I had been counting to animate the scene had been excluded from the cinema by the mayor. The audience, after its initial hysteria, settled down into a disappointingly respectful silence. The film, for all its period charm, no longer had the power to excite.

The beautiful heroine, after a series of disappointing affairs, finds true love with a handsome bullfighter. The bullfighter dies in the ring. His widowed paramour develops a serious heart condition, and is advised never to sing again. She moves to Paris, but comes back to Madrid to give a final performance in the theatre where she had once been so happy. Curiously, the theatre in question had a proscenium arch that seemed like a grand, pretentious version of the one in which the film was now being projected. Life and art became momentarily confused. The young and beautiful Sara Montiel expired on the screen before us only to reappear a few minutes later as an ageing woman standing on a dirty and decrepit stage. The mayor gracelessly presented her with a ceramic plaque featuring Frailes's bogus coat of arms, whose entwined pair of keys had always incensed heraldic pedants from the one-key Alcalá. Merce, still in rustic attire, curtsied as she gave Sara a bunch of flowers prepared by the local youth unemployment scheme. Then El Sereno led Sara off to her car.

That night at El Rey de Copas, towards the end of an interminable supper, when we reached what I had christened '*El último soufflé*', I heard from Sara herself a story that for me justified alone her whole visit to Frailes.

'Did you hear what happened to me in El Sereno's bathroom?' she asked. I had wondered what the afternoon's commotion had been all about, but the whole issue had escaped my harassed mind. She had, she now told me, got stuck in her bathroom after part of the latch had fallen off. She had cried out for help, and the chivalrous El Sereno devised a daring scheme of rescue. He placed a ladder against the outside wall and prepared to climb into the bathroom to repair the latch. But the ladder was not long enough, and there was a gap of at least one metre between its last rung and the window. Undaunted, and to the horror of those watching from below, he hurled himself onto the window ledge, shouting as he did so, 'Cover yourself Sara, I'm coming in.' The actress stretched out her hands to help, and pulled him into her famous heaving bosom. From now on, she said, she would call him 'my Romeo'.

When, late next morning, I went to see Sara's Romeo, I found he had been up for several hours collecting large boxes of cherries for her. He was in his Suzuki, returning from his fields on the cemetery hill, and I had never known him looking so rushed. Gesturing to me frantically to get into the car, he sped off even before I was able to close the door.

'Sara's about to leave,' he explained, 'and we've got to get to Puerta Alta in time to say goodbye.' The Suzuki, as rejuvenated as he himself seemed to be, kicked up clouds of dust as it swerved around hairpin bends. I pleaded with its driver to slow down, but he was not listening. 'We've got to get there,' he mumbled, 'we've got to get there.'

There was no sign of the Toyota when we arrived. The profound look of disappointment on El Sereno's face almost brought tears to my eyes. But then the caretaker at Puerta Alta, Juan Pedro, assured me that Sara and her group had not left, and that their car was just hidden behind the building. El Sereno scuttled off to the Suzuki to take out the goods that he had brought for her. On the dining room's massive oak table, I helped him lay out four whole boxes of cherries, a crate of Matahermosa wine, two huge rounds of cheese, and a specially inscribed litre bottle of *Serenolivo*. 'But she's taking the train at Cordóva,' I protested. 'She can't carry all this.' But El Sereno was not listening to me.

Sara, dressed this time in casual travelling clothes, and looking almost like a human being, walked down the stairs into the room, and put on an expression of amused surprise as she surveyed the bounties that her Romeo had brought for her. He laid his arm around her waist as I photographed them together. 'My Manolillo,' she murmured affectionately.

The night after Sara left, John set up his cameras and I was interviewed at three in the morning standing up to my neck inside the Santo Custodio's Cave. Fearful all the time that the sinister man in white would come to chase us away with a stick, I gave a confused answer to John's impossible question about the relationship between the Santo Custodio and the Cinema España. But at least I was able to bring in a curious fact that I had learnt earlier that night from Ferminillo. On the day of the faith healer's death, 15 August 1960, *Bridge over the River Kwai* was showing at the cinema. The news of the death spread quickly through the darkened building; and, when the film was over, three-quarters of the audience made their way to La Hoya to help carry the body on its final journey, to the village cemetery of Noalejo.

On the last day of shooting John had Pancanto kill a goat in front of the cameras. John needed a death for his documentary; and bringing his whole crew to a bullfight would have been too costly and impractical. They had virtually run out of money, and there was not even anything left in their budget for a final meal. El Sereno and I proposed paying for the goat, and getting Pancanto to prepare it for a celebratory last supper under the walnut tree. Rafael and other friends from the village came along, and we all were able to joke about the stress of the last few days, while waiting for John and his crew to make their appearance. They turned up late and sullen. John, as angry as I had ever seen him, strode towards me.

'Why the fuck did you do it, Mike?' he screamed. 'We had the fucking exclusive, man!' I said I did not know what he meant, and then realized he was referring to my tiny part in Canal Sur's extended news feature on the Cinema España, which had been broadcast earlier that evening. I had not received a penny from anyone, nor had the cinema's owner; but I did not want to argue the technical meaning of the term 'exclusive'. The values of 'archaic hospitality' had been confronted by those of a modern world that seemed impure. My village friends sang songs and played music to try and cheer me up. But I felt as if the germ of an alien mentality had been introduced to Frailes's virgin soil.

'The village is now famous the world over,' said El Sereno, keen as always only to see the positive aspects of a situation. To a certain extent he was right. The publicity Frailes had received was, in his words, 'something that not even millions of pesetas invested for this purpose could have paid for'. The fairy tale story of Sara's visit to a forgotten Jaén village made it to the front pages of the Spanish press, and was an item on all the main news programmes. Three days after the event there was a huge round of applause in the Cueva when Sara appeared on television to say that the homage paid to her in Frailes was the most moving of her life, and that El Sereno's olive oil had helped revitalize her skin. Fraileros from all over Spain, and even beyond, amazed that their village had become a national talking-point, experienced an enormous surge of pride.

Myths continued to be propagated. The idea, for instance, that the Cinema España had been shut down by Franco's police after the showing of *El último cuplé* had been repeated by Sara herself at the press conference, and was now enshrined in the history of the Spanish cinema.

Many people got in touch with me to find out what my intentions were regarding the newly 'reopened' Cinema España. I had received proposals for plays, musicals, flamenco recitals, and even for an annual festival of old Spanish films. But to all these suggestions I had to say that the cinema was not mine, and that Ferminillo was unlikely ever again to open its doors except for a purely commercial proposition. Only Merce truly understood that the event on June 13 was just a spectacular one-off with no follow-up in mind. It had been a romantic gesture in the true sense of the term – a gesture undertaken in response to an overwhelming emotional urge, but in the knowledge of its ultimate futility.

Sometimes I worried that all the recent excitement had turned El Sereno's mind. My Sancho Panza had become more quixotic than ever, and certainly more like a child. One week he descended by rope into a narrow cave over fifty metres deep; the next week he became obsessed by the idea of being photographed next to Spain's teenage pop idol Alejandro Sanz. He stayed in regular touch with Sara Montiel, but the love I hoped would blossom between these two emblems of the Spanish psyche came to nothing. Sara, after a life time of professing interest in older men, became engaged to a thirty-two-year-old Cuban. El Sereno, meanwhile, returned to the pursuit of younger women.

No miracle occurred to save Merce from being sent to a village in the opposite corner of Jaén. The unchanging rhythms of the seasons reasserted themselves, and reality returned, at the very moment when a breakthrough in Frailes's fortunes had once again seemed imminent. Politicians and the Church, relegated to a secondary position during the Sara Montiel event, were now fully back in control. The official opening of the *Casa de Cultura*, barely two weeks after Sara's entertaining press conference, was a dull affair presided over by an Alcalaíno politician and by a parish priest whose contribution so far to the village's culture had been less than useful.

Summer was soon in full swing, and with it came the usual round of festivals to divert people's minds from anything too problematic or profound. Frailes's population swelled with the annual return of its emigrants, and everything was put on hold until the end of the four-day August *Feria*, which opened, as it always had done, with a bicycle race, and closed, in no less statutory fashion, with a post-midnight handout of melon and *migas*.

When the village's seasonal visitors started going home, I lazed around in a hammock in Merce's and Caño's garden, thinking of ways to delay my return to Britain. Merce was in a similar state of mind. As she sunbathed on the lawn besides me, counting the days she still had left before going off to her distant new place of work, she dreamt of salvation both for herself and for Frailes by becoming the village's next mayor. Then one afternoon, in the middle of a long discussion about our respective futures, she suddenly recalled a person whom she had been wanting to introduce me to for ages.

'Maiquel,' she announced excitedly, 'you can't leave Frailes until you've met Esperta.' She said she would take me immediately to see her.

Esperta, a woman in her mid-nineties, was one of the village's personalities most involved in the world of the esoteric. During the funeral Mass of the Santo Custodio, she had created a scene of collective hysteria by pointing in the air to the resurrected figure of the saintly faith healer. Most people in Frailes thought she was mad.

Esperta lived on her own in a large, rambling house next to Merce's parents. Outside was a small, jewel-like garden with flower beds, privet hedges, and a central fountain; inside were rooms with darkly tiled walls, gilded neo-Rococo furnishings, and a mass of curios and religious prints. Merce went inside first, and then told me to follow her. Esperta was sitting on a rocking chair in front of a large modern television set. She was not entirely unlike Sara Montiel, and had an unruly mob of dyed black hair, coatings of make-up, and witch-like eyes.

'This is the English writer that people have been talking about,' said Merce, holding her arm. 'Do you know about him?'

Esperta had a dazed look, like that of someone in an advanced state of Alzheimer's. Merce, who had not seen her for some time, had heard rumours that her mind, which had always verged between great lucidity and half-sane ramblings, had gone completely of late. Staring at me for a moment, Esperta shook her head, and went back to looking at her garden through the window. But Merce did not give up. She began explaining to Esperta that I had come to Frailes after hearing of the Santo Custodio while I was in Slovakia.

Esperta suddenly turned round to speak. She knew all about Merce's *oposiciones*, and thought it terrible that Merce had been forced to leave her job in the village. 'Your place is here,' she said emphatically, 'with us.' Something in her had been ignited, and from being an apparent vegetable she soon became a person able to deliver an incessant, stream-of-consciousness monologue in which she sporadically revealed a considerable understanding of what was happening in the village, and a remarkable, up-to-date grasp of world politics. In between references to Bush, Blair and Sharon ('All politicians are the same, whether they are socialists or not'), she returned repeatedly to the subject of the parish priest, who for her was a phoney, dishonest and money-grabbing man. She had donated to the church a statue of the Sacred Heart of Jesus, but her request to have it covered in a mantle had been ignored. She would never enter the building again.

Esperta was a fervent Christian, but above all a devotee of the Santo Custodio, who in turn had appreciated her own talents and personality. 'The Santo Custodio, may he rest in peace, told me that I had been given by God gifts that few people have.' She picked up from a side table a yellow notebook in which she had written down all the numerous visions she had had in the course of her life. 'I have seen the Virgin as clearly as I see you,' she said, addressing Merce, 'and I have seen God the Father, and he has a white beard just like the man you have brought to see me.'

Merce, suffering from what she said was a metaphorical headache brought on by all her recent problems, was anxious for Esperta to give her the 'blessing'. Esperta rose to her feet to touch Merce on the forehead, and then firmly rub her hands all over her front. She told her to turn round so that she could do the same to her back. Then she looked towards me, and asked Merce to tell her again where I was from. 'From England?' she said, surprised. 'Is he a believer? Well, it doesn't matter if he isn't. I'll give him the blessing all the same.'

I stood upright, waiting for the hands of the faith healer to revive my spirit. 'You'll feel at first a cold sensation,' she warned, 'but then a great warmth will come over you and a feeling of complete serenity.'

Esperta had also the gift of telling the future. She had seen a table turn the colour of blood just before the outbreak of the civil war. And she had predicted the death of her husband, who had been one of the many Nationalist soldiers killed while guarding the sanctuary of the Virgin of La Cabeza at Andújar, Jaén's most sacred shrine.

But what she saw now was worse, far worse. The Santo Custodio had warned her that terrible things were going to happen, because the 'modern world had become so bad'. Seeing my preoccupied look, she assured me that Frailes itself would be out of danger. 'And nowhere else?' asked Merce. 'Perhaps Valdepeñas de Jaén,' she replied, before prophesying the destruction of whole communities, countries left in ruins, a vast international conflagration in which 'the West will be in mortal combat with the East', and 'giant skyscrapers will fall into the dust'. But Frailes would be saved, for the village was protected by the mantle of the Virgin and the spirit of the Santo Custodio.

It was the beginning of September in the year 2001.

Epilogue

The Last of the Romantics

'Every season of the year has its beauty,' said El Sereno, 'just like every stage of life.' The leaves were falling abundantly from the trees, giving the street cleaner Bubi more work than ever. He carried out his task with philosophical resignation, stopping briefly to welcome me back to Frailes before I walked with El Sereno into the garden I thought I would never see again. I wondered this time if I would be here for good.

The morning of September 11 had seen me in London, writing one of the chapters of this book. Later that day I had a call from Merce saying that she, Caño, and Juan Matías would be flying out the following day to come and stay with me. She agreed it was not the best moment to be travelling, but they wanted to see, before it was too late, the strange and dangerous world where I lived. Their visit seemed also to be undertaken in the same spirit with which they had once regularly phoned me whenever they had worried about my safety or state of mind. They saw it as a rescue mission. 'What is Frailes?' one of my English friends asked when I told him this. 'Is it a village, or is it a sect?'

I was no longer quite sure. The lure of the place was now so great that the mission to London of the Fraileros succeeded in persuading me to buy a return ticket to Spain at the soonest possible opportunity, before airports were shut down, and the world had sunk into chaos. I held out in England for ten days more after they had left, but was back in Frailes for my saint's day, September 29. Sitting again in El Sereno's garden hut, safe once more in the village's embrace, I could let out at last a sigh of relief. Andalucía was reputedly the European centre of the al-Qaida terrorist network; and the caves around Frailes could have been an excellent hiding place for Bin Laden. However, the calm, apparently unchanging nature of village life, and the sense of peace that the surroundings induced, allowed me to look more dispassionately at the events of the outside world.

Yet even here I had occasional intimations of a coming apocalypse. When the bombs started dropping on Afghanistan, reawakening in the elder villagers memories of the civil war, the most terrible storm in years broke out over Frailes. I was sitting late at night in the garden hut when the entire horizon towards Córdova and Granada was streaked with continual flashes of lightening. As I dashed back to the *Mesón* before the rain started, I passed villagers in their dressing gowns standing in their doorways with expressions of fear and amazement. Within minutes hailstones as large as bullets were pounding down like machine-gun fire, covering the ground and destroying crops. Close on the heels of this catastrophe came another. Great tongues of flame soared one night into the sky, dramatically illuminating the walls of the village's largest abandoned mansion. It was past midnight, and I was walking home. I went closer to see what was happening, and was almost immediately knocked to the ground by an explosion that woke up all the neighbours. An arsonist, seemingly, had set fire to a fork-lift truck, though no one in Frailes believed such a crime was possible.

As the war in Afghanistan progressed, and Frailes was beset by cold autumn winds, the peace of the countryside was disturbed by the constant sounds of gunshots. The hunting season was in full swing, and almost every man in the village, apart from El Sereno, was an addict of the sport. What had been a necessary means of survival for people of the generation of Merce's father was now principally an enjoyable way of killing time. I joined Merce's brothers and Caño on several of their hunting expeditions, but did so largely as an excuse for long walks through virgin countryside. They tried to convince me that if I really wanted to appreciate the beauty and mystery of hunting I should come with them in January, when the partridge season began. This was the time when the male partridge began singing to attract the female. A caged male was placed a few metres away from the bush where the hunters remained silent and hidden. When the singing began, females on heat started approaching, followed by jealous males determined to protect their territory. The killing that subsequently ensued sounded to me like a cruel and cowardly massacre; but to hunting enthusiasts was an allegory of sex and death of the kind that might have interested John.

I preferred the hunt for mushrooms, in which entire families took part. The first edible mushrooms of the autumn were those that grew around the rotting barks of elms; but the more prized ones were to be found in flat, exposed areas covered in thistles. Merce had a particular skill in uncovering mushrooms. One Sunday early in October, when walking across a high and remote rocky plateau, she responded with ecstatic, childlike joy on coming across a solitary 'thistle mushroom', the season's first. She skipped away laughing and singing into the distance, and then suddenly stopped, as if she had remembered something. When I caught up with her, she pointed to the mountain range in front of us, on the top of which a huge, metallic pole now glared in the sunlight. The politicians had tricked us. They had always talked about their commitment to the environment, and about the possibility of turning this area into a national park. But we now had proof that they had rushed ahead with a project to line the highest ranges of the Sierra Sur with long rows of electricity-generating windmills. We felt as if our virgin paradise had been violated. 'Let's make the most of this day,' said Merce. 'Next week we might find this wilderness bristling with modern technology.'

Sure enough, by the end of October, tall windmills like giant ventilating fans could clearly be seen even from El Sereno's garden. Their appearance on the horizon, though of considerable fascination to El Sereno himself, reinforced my ever more acute sensation of the passing of time. Enclosed for ever longer hours in my writing hut, and now rarely leaving the confines of the garden, I became increasingly conscious of the ageing process, not just in myself, but in El Sereno's whole household. His elder sister Mercedes was becoming progressively deafer, while the younger one Carmelita was rapidly losing her memory, and focusing her mind largely on her dogs. Rasputin was found dead one morning from eating rat poison; but Curra had given birth to two puppies, who now accompanied their mother on her nocturnal visits to my hut. Carmelita spent her days looking for them all, and her pathetic cries of 'Curra! Curra!' came to sound to me like the wails of a mourner at a funeral.

El Sereno, deprived for any length of time of visitors, became worryingly quiet, sad and old. Happily, the publicity generated by his mill and the Sara Montiel event seemed never-ending, with particular interest now being shown by television channels. Rarely a week passed without some television reporter coming to film either El

Sereno or me, or, preferably, the two of us together. We had become a double act, like Laurel and Hardy, and were obliged to repeat on film walks we had done together and other notable joint exploits. El Sereno, loving all the acting, was able without difficulty to come out with such comments as, 'Maiquel, today I'm going to take you to an estate I think you'll love. It's called Puerta Alta.' For me, in my autumnal mood, this staged repetition of past moments came to seem morbid and regressive.

The possibility that the curious two-person team we had formed would be broken up if I did not settle permanently in Frailes encouraged El Sereno in his efforts to find me a house to buy there. One day he announced that he had at last found the ideal place. It was the highest house in the village, and came with half a hillside. It was old, in quite good condition, and stood proudly on its own, behind a luxuriant walnut tree. I set my heart on the place; and he said he was sure I would be able to secure it for around £7,000. My only worry was that I would be tempted afterwards to contribute to the very British and generally tedious tradition of writing books about the restoration of idyllic Mediterranean properties. This worry increased when I realized there was material enough for such a volume merely in the description of the manner in which I had set about trying to buy the place.

The owner, known as 'El Señorico', was a remarkably fit seventy-year-old goatherd who by now was one of Paqui's two or three remaining regulars at the Discoteca Oh!. I got on very well with him, and we often had drinks together; but, as El Sereno said, 'There are no friends when it comes to business.' I was advised not only not to tell anyone else about my interest in the house, but also to feign in front of El Señorico a complete indifference. However, as the price of the property kept on rising, more direct methods became necessary. I ended up making sure I always had £7,000 in cash in my pocket whenever I entered Paqui's disco. I was hoping to get him drunk, and place the money straight into his hands in front of a witness. But even this tactic failed. Part of the problem was that all his actions were supervised by a no less wily goatherd called Kuki, whose family history came eventually to interest me almost as much as the house itself. Kuki was none other than the great-nephew of the man who had famously progressed from selling goat's milk to becoming rector of Seville's University. Kuki's childless great-uncle had even acquired, through marriage, the title of Marquis de Campoameno; but the true beauty of the story was that his descendants, as I now learnt, had all gone back to dealing with goats. I thought this symptomatic of Frailes's whole history.

The slowness with which all transactions were conducted in the village was intrinsic to the place's charm; but, as time passed, and nothing was achieved, I knew that the only way of getting the house was to disregard El Sereno's advice and to seek instead that of Merce. This seemed almost like disobeying one's father so as to plead with some intermediary between the earthly and spiritual realms. Merce, now suffering the first symptoms of a mysterious illness, and encountering hindrance at every corner in her attempts to become mayor, may have failed to solve her own problems. But she had retained her remarkable gift for sorting out those of others. Within less than a day of telling her about the house high on the hill, an agreement with the owner had been reached.

At last, after more than thirty-five years of coming to Spain, I had a possession that tied me more firmly to this country. It was suitable as yet only for goats, fleas and El Señorico's decrepit donkey, though there was at least a Star of Bethlehem, assembled in light bulbs on the rocks above, to serve as a frivolous reminder of the property's symbolic importance. The journey to get there had been a long one. The satisfaction of having finally arrived, however, was balanced by the occasional worry that I would end my days like the drunken Cabildo, all alone in a house falling into ruins. Thoughts about mortality, which had come to me so often while first settling in to village life, returned more strongly as All Souls Day approached, and Frailes prepared to honour its dead.

For several days beforehand there was an unending succession of people and cars climbing up to the cemetery with flowers, brooms, mops, and even paintbrushes. El Sereno's sisters, who so rarely left the house, themselves devoted many hours to cleaning and giving a fresh coat of whitewash to the modest family mausoleum. Their brother stayed behind, but I could not but notice, on the morning of All Souls Day, November 2, how much time he was spending staring at the cemetery from his garden. Then I saw that he had a postcard in his hand. I went over to talk to him, and discovered that this card was from a friend of ours who was on holiday in Switzerland.

'Maiquel,' he asked, with genuine interest, 'how much do you think this would cost?' He had placed his finger on a cable car in the photograph. He was seriously thinking of installing such an attraction in Frailes, so as to make the journey from his house to the cemetery quicker and more enjoyable. To think up such schemes in old age seemed in itself a defiance of death.

Another television crew turned up that day in Frailes. They were making a film about esoteric Andalucía, and had been told that El Sereno was the best possible guide to anything connected with the Sierra Sur. Their specific interest in this area was in the Santo Custodio, whose tomb in the village of Noalejo was the object of particular devotion on All Souls Day. Merce, now back in Frailes on sick leave, decided to come with us. Leading the way in the Suzuki, we guided the crew over the rough mountain road that led from Frailes to Noalejo by way of the hamlet of Cerezo Gordo, where the Santo Luisico had lived. A large group of Fraileros, who had set off at three in the morning, were undertaking on foot this arduous, twenty-kilometre journey; many others were walking from La Hoya del Salobral, and even from Valdepeñas. By the time we arrived at Noalejo's cemetery, the numerous groups of pilgrims from different parts of the Sierra Sur were all congregating around the Santo Custodio's tomb. Covered in corrugated iron, and decorated with a riot of plastic flowers, this was one of the most hideous and depressing objects of pilgrimage I had ever seen.

The sight of all the pilgrims pressing themselves against this gloomy and to me unspiritual shrine strengthened further my recent change in attitude towards the Santo Custodio. Over the past few weeks I had had long conversations about him with Merce and with the anthropologist who had written *The Route of Miracles*, Manuel Amezcua. All of us were agreed that the Catholic Church, in trying to usurp his cult, had both vulgarized it and damaged its whole basis. I had been with Amezcua at La Hoya, where he had been showing round an elderly and impressionable American couple not unlike the two Australians I had known in Slovakia. When the man in white, whom Merce so loathed, had taken the couple away to feel the energy emanating from some stones near the saint's cave, Amezcua commented on how completely alien to the spirit of the Santo Custodio this whole place had become. The Catholic love of relics, images and mass worship, in combination with such pseudo-mystical concepts as energy-giving stones, were extraneous banalities that had nothing to do with the essentially simple and highly personal cult that had once existed around the faith healer. I had had some idea of what he meant when I had been invited in the summer to the saint's-day pilgrimage connected with the Santo Luisico. It was the most unusual and basic 'festive pilgrimage' I had ever been to. There was no commercialization and not a drop of alcohol. All it consisted of was a hushed get-together of about fifty people, who stayed up all night, shifting silently like spirits around the isolated shrine.

For Merce, even the cult of personality was an irrelevance. The Santo Custodio was merely a spiritual force whose physical features were only of anecdotal significance; the Santo Custodio could have been anyone. He was a force who resided in a world that had remained simple and unspoiled; he was someone whose presence could still be sensed in the house at La Hoya where his physical embodiment had lived.

We left the television crew filming the scenes of hysterical devotion at Noalejo. Merce proposed going to La Hoya to see if we would be allowed into the Santo Custodio's curious and, for her, magical house, which was now the home of Santo Custodio's son Enrique. I had only managed once before to visit this place, a good year and a half after my first attempt to do so. I had been on that occasion with El Sereno and one of his 'girl friends', and the experience had been totally disillusioning. Enrique, a bachelor in his seventies who lived on his own, was thought by many to be the person who now had 'the powers'. He had always rigorously denied this; but this had not stopped daily devotees from wanting to come and see him and touch his hands and clothes. When he had opened the door to us on that occasion he had done so partly to get rid of one such group of admirers.

Enrique had the appearance of someone whose whole life had been poisoned and worn out simply through having had his father's powers attributed to him. I had never seen anyone, not even a dying person, who had such a look of death about him. His features were difficult to describe. He had a cloth cap, old and shabby grey clothes, and a bluish grey pallor that sent a chill through my body. El Sereno had made the great mistake of introducing me as a writer. Enrique had refused to shake my hands. 'All writers are liars,' he said. He hated all the commercialization around his father's cave. He hated all forms of publicity.

In Merce's eyes this gave him a great purity. If it had not been for her I doubt if I would ever have attempted to see Enrique again. At first he was as distant towards us as he had been before. El Sereno, respecting the local custom of bringing him gifts, offered him a litre bottle of *Serenolivo*. But he turned it down as if it were poison. 'I don't want it, I have my own oil,' he repeated, deaf to El Sereno's explanations that this was a special olive oil made 'ecologically' from hand-picked olives. He did not want us to go beyond the narrow entrance vestibule, which he said was where his father received visitors. He looked – if this were possible – more like death than he had done the last time I had seen him. A drop of condensation hung from his nose; but he was as indifferent to this as if he had been a funereal carving exposed to the elements.

Then Merce began talking, and I noticed a slight softening in his behaviour. We were welcomed into the back room of his house, which was where he spent most of his days. There was a plain wooden chair and a fire, but nowhere comfortable to sit. The fire was of a kind that El Sereno remembered from his childhood, but which no one used any more in the Sierra Sur. It comprised a slowly burning, densely packed mound of hay, which was topped up daily. The hay came from Enrique's own fields, and was harvested by volunteers. As the atmosphere relaxed, and the conversation turned to the ancient traditions of the area, Enrique gave Merce and myself some keys, and told us to take a look around the rest of the house. He himself remained talking with El Sereno.

Nothing, absolutely nothing had been changed in the house since the Santo Custodio's day. There was no running water; the floor was made of pebbles; the furnishings were of the most basic kind; the only decoration on the faded plaster walls was some old family photographs and some foxed prints of the Christ of the Cloth and other religious subjects. Recalling the first time I had stepped into the Cinema España, I thought that this place too had the atmosphere of a mausoleum, except it was not someone's youth that was buried here but a living person.

'Enrique owns a lot of land. People shower him with gifts. They do all his work for him. He could easily live in a comfortable modern house, but he has chosen this.' Merce continued telling me about Enrique as we walked upstairs, where a jungle of dusty flowers was laid out in baroque abandon within the morbidly dark bedroom that had been the Santo Custodio's.

It was Merce's belief that Enrique, despite his protestations, was the true successor to his father. Whereas Esperta's visions had a strong admixture of images and ideas derived from watching television all day, Enrique had the gift for making sparse enigmatic comments that were as open to interpretation as the prophecies of Nostradamus. Nothing he said, according to her, was without its meaning, as she had discovered several years before, when she had been to see him with her youngest son Alejandro, then suffering from a throat tumour. He told them to go away quickly, as he had to block up some mouse holes so that 'nothing could get in or out', a phrase used the next day by the doctor who had had to carry out an emergency operation on the child.

When we went back to the room with the fire, Enrique said something that revealed, if nothing else, that he had a good ironic sense of humour. I was trying to work out what a strange dark object was that sat on a side table, when I realized it was an ancient television set with a screen shrouded in filthy green plastic cling film. It seemed a total incongruity in this house that was virtually without electrical fixtures. Enrique said he did not know how to use it, and El Sereno offered to turn it on for him. There was crackling and some flickering of lights at the back, but no image. El Sereno shook his head and confessed it was not working. 'What do you mean?' said Enrique, staring fixedly at the screen, 'I can see perfectly.' We all laughed, and it was not until later that Merce read into this statement a profound commentary on life and its apparent mysteries, and our inability to perceive what was in fact crystal clear.

The rest of the day was spent largely with the dead. The whole of Frailes, and Fraileros from far afield, chatted together within the flower-congested cemetery as if attending a rather formal party. Memories of the recent dead, and anecdotes about villagers of the past, were sparked off by the tombs and the oval-framed photographs attached to them. Paqui, with a daughter on either hand, visited the grave of her young father, and then that of an even younger cousin who had hung himself from a walnut tree. The kindly Luis Machuca held on tightly to his skipping granddaughter as she led him off to see his late wife. The mayor paced up and down, and a drunken, red-faced Bubi assumed a respectful stiffness before the tomb of his mother. As the light faded, vignettes such as these became like snatches from a dream, and the wandering bodies came to seem as phantasmal as souls.

In the afternoon I went to the cemetery with Merce, and at night, when the place was a mass of burning candles, with El Sereno. His sisters, respectful always of traditions, had prepared for us beforehand the prerequisite All Souls Day supper – a gnocchi-like dish called *gachos*, followed by a dessert of sweet potatoes served with oil and sugar. 'See you in the morning,' I said to them afterwards, to which they replied as always, 'If God wills.' In these moments of morbid reflection, I was struck with the thought that sooner or later God would not be willing, and that my Frailes companions one by one would be turned into anecdotes to be shared around on the day the dead were celebrated.

I was coming to think of death in terms of Paqui's disco at closing time, when the the music was switched off, the mirror ball stopped whirling, and a cold shudder came with the return of the house lights and the opening of the main door. It was long past midnight, and I was at the entrance of the cemetery, looking with El Sereno at the simple stone slab where his body would eventually lie.

'Maiquel,' he said, stirring me from my dreamy state, 'if you like, I could add a codicil to my will allowing you to be buried here beside me.'

My vision of the Discoteca Oh! was now succeeded by the fantasy that El Sereno and I were the protagonists of a sentimental feature film that was drawing to an end. The camera was panning away as the two of us, the last of the romantics, stood contemplating the extinction of our race.

'I specially chose to have the mausoleum right at the cemetery's entrance,' continued El Sereno, trying to persuade me of the locational advantages of my future resting place. 'I thought it best just in case I got bored with the company of the dead.'

And as he said this my mind was off again, flying by cable car over Frailes, and then into the yellow Suzuki, which had already challenged death so many times. We had embarked on our posthumous exploits, and were driving high into the mountains to do battle with the windmills, to chase away the evil politicians, and to ensure for future generations the purity of the Sierra Sur.

Acknowledgements

ORIGINALLY I HAD planned to name here every inhabitant of
Frailes who had helped in some way with this book. However,
these good intentions were soon lost in a confusion of Custodios,
Manolos, Antonios and Mercedes, and I realized that full acknowledgements would have to include almost the entire village population.

I would like at least to express my enormous gratitude to the Town
Hall of Frailes, not least for allowing me such open access to all its
facilities, from photocopiers to the Internet. There is also a small
group of village friends who have made a particularly important contribution to the narrative. Among these is Fermín Murcia, owner of
the Cinema España, and Ernesto del Moral Campos, a regular companion at breakfast and on my long walks through the mountains.
José Chica, José Garrido García (Bubi), Antonio López Gúzman ('el
praticante'), Fermín Mudarra and Carmen Serrano López have considerably enlivened my Frailes nights, while Miguel Montes and
Rafael Fríos Arenas will always have a special place in my affections
for being among the first Fraileros to welcome me into their midst.
Santiago Campos, as librarian, historian, chronicler of my Frailes
existence and future next-door neighbour, has been a friend of inestimable value.

But my thanks are due above all to those Fraileros who have virtually adopted me as a member of their families. One of my four
'family homes' here is the idiosyncratic *Mesón*, whose owner Paqui
Machuca has wonderfully looked after me, as have her mother
Inmaculada, her daughters Inmaculada and Marta, her sister
Mercedes and her cousins Carmen, Luis and Antonio. At the Rey de
Copas I have been continually spoilt not just by the chef Juan Matías,

but also by his parents Antonio and Matilde, his brother José Luis, and his sisters Matilde and María Ángeles. As for Manuel Ruíz López ('El Sereno'), Merce García Castillo and Manolo Caño, I can only say that I know of few better people into whose hands a writer could fall. The extent of my debt to them and to their families is greater than anything that could succinctly be put into words, as readers of this book will understand.

Outside Frailes, I must thank all the many local historians who have greatly extended my love and knowledge of the Sierra Sur, notably Manuel Amezcua, Juan Infante, Francisco Martín, José Luis Pantoja, José María Suárez and Manuel Urbano Pérez. The numerous visitors I have had from all over Spain, Europe and America also deserve an especial mention, in particular those who, anonymously or otherwise, became unwitting participants in the story I have told, such as Enrique Andrés, Antonio Carvajal, Juan Antonio Díaz, Francisco Fernández, Sarah Fitzgerald, Lola Flores, Elizabeth Hebdige, Carmen María Garrido, Ian Gibson, Robert Goodwin, Ignacio Henares, Nicolai Iul, Sara Montiel, Paco Millán, Cees and Simone Nooteboom, Ella von Schreitter, John Shahnazarian, Carmen Suárez and Magdalena Torres Hidalgo.

Alexander Fyjis-Walker read through an early draft of this work and made useful suggestions. My thanks also to James Hughes for his brilliant job in shortening and copy-editing the manuscript, to Jackie Rae for her habitual and unfailing support, to my mother Mariagrazia Jacobs, to my agent David Godwin, and to the staff at John Murray, especially my patient and enthusiastic editor Caroline Knox, without whom I might never have turned my experiences in Frailes into a book.